CREATING A MODERN HOMESTEAD

ALSO AVAILABLE IN THE HOMESTEADER'S GUIDE SERIES

*The Backyard Gardener: Simple, Easy, and Beautiful Gardening
with Vegetables, Herbs, and Flowers*

Family Table: Farm Cooking from the Elliott Homestead

*The Farm Girl's Guide to Preserving the Harvest: How to Can,
Freeze, Dehydrate, and Ferment Your Garden's Goodness*

*The Homesteader's Herbal Companion:
The Ultimate Guide to Growing, Preserving, and Using Herbs*

*The Homesteader's Natural Chicken Keeping Handbook:
Raising a Healthy Flock from Start to Finish*

Seasons at the Farm: Year-Round Celebrations at the Elliott Homestead

Welcome to the Farm: How-to Wisdom from the Elliott Homestead

CREATING A MODERN HOMESTEAD

TRADITIONAL SKILLS FOR REAL, EVERYDAY LIFE

VICTORIA PRUETT
OF *A MODERN HOMESTEAD*

FOREWORD BY AMY K. FEWELL

LYONS PRESS

ESSEX, CONNECTICUT

An imprint of The Globe Pequot Publishing Group, Inc.
64 South Main Street
Essex, CT 06426
www.globepequot.com

Distributed by NATIONAL BOOK NETWORK

Text and photos copyright © 2025 by Victoria Pruett
Foreword © 2025 by Amy K. Fewell
Unless otherwise noted, all photos by the author.

All rights reserved. No part of this book may be reproduced in any form or by any electronic or mechanical means, including information storage and retrieval systems, without written permission from the publisher, except by a reviewer who may quote passages in a review.

British Library Cataloguing in Publication Information available

Library of Congress Cataloging-in-Publication Data

Names: Pruett, Victoria, author.
Title: Creating a modern homestead : traditional skills for real, everyday life / Victoria Pruett.
Description: Essex, CT : Lyons Press, 2025. | Includes index.
Identifiers: LCCN 2024060419 (print) | LCCN 2024060420 (ebook) | ISBN 9781493090495 (paperback) | ISBN 9781493090501 (ebook)
Subjects: LCSH: Self-reliant living. | Home economics. | Urban homesteading.
Classification: LCC GF78 .P78 2025 (print) | LCC GF78 (ebook) | DDC 641.3—dc23/eng/20250225
LC record available at https://lccn.loc.gov/2024060419
LC ebook record available at https://lccn.loc.gov/2024060420

♾️™ The paper used in this publication meets the minimum requirements of American National Standard for Information Sciences—Permanence of Paper for Printed Library Materials, ANSI/NISO Z39.48-1992.

CONTENTS

Foreword by Amy K. Fewell vii
Introduction 1

CHAPTER 1: From Scratch Cooking 11

CHAPTER 2: Keeping a Deep Pantry .101

CHAPTER 3: Food Preservation, Part I: Canning and Freezing 123

CHAPTER 4: Food Preservation, Part II: Dehydrating and
Freeze-Drying 165

CHAPTER 5: Growing Your Own Food 185

CHAPTER 6: Keeping Backyard Chickens. 233

CHAPTER 7: Baking with Sourdough 259

Final Thoughts 275
Index. 279

FOREWORD

My family began our homesteading journey in 2009, before the COVID-19 pandemic, when there was little to no online information about homesteading. Thankfully, I grew up with a grandmother who cooked from scratch and kept a garden and with a grandfather who had a beef cattle farm. My dad kept a large garden each year, too, but there wasn't much canning happening in our home. It's not uncommon for a young person living in a modern world to take little interest in habitually learning at the elbow of her elders, even though the teaching is there. It wasn't until I had a home and children of my own that I really began to think, "Isn't there a better way to live than the modern way I've been living?" I was preaching a life of intelligent design by the intelligent Creator, yet I was living a life that didn't reflect this commitment in our food and land stewardship choices.

When our first son was diagnosed with childhood asthma at the age of one, the decision was final: I needed to figure out how to tend to my family more naturally, and biblically. It all started with food—we began in a garden, and so to the garden I would return. We got a few chickens, took on a raw milk herdshare, built our first garden, and began diving headfirst into natural remedies, all on a half-acre plot in a subdivision. Our neighbors thought it was the best thing in the world, and it inspired them, too.

As I scoured the Internet for information on the basics and how to make my life easier, there was nothing easily at my fingertips. I had to learn the hard way how to make biscuits from scratch. (I assure you, it's more about method than ingredients.) I had to figure out my yearly tomato debacle in the garden all on my own. I had to learn how to make a sourdough starter without the thousands of e-books that now exist. A friend of my mother's reached out to me through snail mail to send me a dehydrated starter she had held in her family for over a hundred years. It was like Christmas morning when I opened the envelope. But the joy soon ended when I had to hold a funeral after I killed that beautiful starter. The woes of learning how to homestead were real, especially when it came to making real food with little direction from a generation that was dying, holding the skills I needed.

VII

Try, try again—that was the motto. There is something special about having to do things all on your own. I couldn't help but think how much easier it would be with grandma by my side, though. You appreciate the outcome more when you have to try harder, but it's still difficult. God created us to be workers and thinkers, but there were so many times that I wished I had a guide or manual to just tell me what to do. If I could have had a book that said, "These are the basic things you eat and here's how to make them at home more naturally," it would have jump-started my homesteading journey even more. Thankfully, there is now a book just like that—the one you're holding in your hand.

I remember the first time I met Victoria online. We were in a bloggers group together long before homesteading was the norm. She has carefully taken years of her own experiences—many of the same experiences I've had—and turned them into one of the most comprehensive handbooks I have ever seen in the homesteading world. This is the book I wish I'd had as a young homesteader, wife, and mother just getting started from scratch.

Maybe you're reading this book because you just want more inspiration. Or maybe, like Victoria and me, you've been in the trenches and you really need something that makes your life easier. I assure you, this is that book. And one day, you'll be the one teaching others to do the things you have learned within these pages.

I am ecstatic to see our generation now guiding the next wave of homesteaders who are coming into the fold. Just as our grandparents taught us (even if we weren't paying attention), we now get to teach the generations to come. Millions across the world have become the new generation of homesteaders, and they homestead out of conviction and necessity, not just because it's trendy. Our health depends on it. Our children depend on it. And for many, with rising inflation and wavering economic times, our budgets and bank accounts depend on it. Why not take the leap and dive all in? Why not live more sustainably, naturally, and beautifully?

As you continue along your homesteading journey, remember this: It's not just about you; it's about creating a community and world that is better than it was. It is the way God intended for us to live. Your learning today will impact the generations to come. We are not the dying generation withholding secrets from the late 1800s and early 1900s. We are now a generation that says, "I don't want a life of convenience food; I want a life of real food." In the world of technology, the coming generations can never say, "We didn't know any better." And friend, I promise you, it will change the world, starting one family at a time.

—*Amy K. Fewell*
TheFewellHomestead.com

INTRODUCTION

Twelve years ago, I was living with my husband in our first home (after nine years of apartment living) in the fastest-growing county in Texas, on a tiny, postage stamp–size subdivision lot. Going from a tiny apartment to a house had been a dream for a long time, but once we got there, I found myself still dreaming of more: of my grandparents' homestead, of wide-open spaces, and of fresh produce. My grandparents had lived in deep West Texas for most of my childhood, and we made the nine-hour drive to see them a few times a year. Their property was about eight acres of near-desert land, but my grandfather had the greenest thumb anyone could ever have. He

My grandfather used to pull us in a rusty red wagon behind his riding lawn mower for hours at a time. We begged him for rides, and those times are some of my fondest farm memories!

transformed that desert soil into an oasis that allowed him to grow a beautiful vineyard, a kitchen garden, and cultivate his own private pine forest.

I remember my brother and I eating all the fresh grapes we could, then canning the rest into jelly with my four-foot-eleven grandmother in her tiny kitchen. We made pecan brittle in the fall and picked fresh vegetables from the garden in the summer. Eventually, my grandparents moved to the city to be near us, as my mom was their only child. But they never forgot their roots. With every house they lived in after their West Texas property, my grandfather always kept a garden. Sometimes it was just a few beds, and other times he kept a full two-acre garden (mind you, he was in his mid-eighties at the time!). Even up until his death at ninety-four years old, he loved puttering around in the garden, weeding and watching things grow.

His death came only a few weeks after the birth of our son, his namesake, James. And as I sat with our baby in my home on that tiny subdivision lot my husband and I had purchased, I realized that I wanted so much more for myself and for my family. I didn't want to rely on the grocery store system for my food supply, or to be so busy with the demands of modern life that we weren't able to slow down every once in a while. After a long talk, my husband, Jason, and I decided that we wanted to change our lives. We knew we wanted a higher quality of food for our family and to take more of a hand in our food supply and self-sufficiency, while also enjoying a slower pace of life. We didn't want to continue trading our time for money so that we could buy what we needed; instead, we wanted to spend our time directly cultivating the food or products that we longed to consume.

Since we didn't have land on which we could garden or keep chickens, we needed to find a way to create a modern homestead in the city. For us, that looked like learning to truly cook high-quality food from scratch, finding local producers to partner with, and keeping a deep pantry through bulk dry-goods purchases and food preservation. In less than a year, we had completely removed ourselves from the modern food supply and had created a version of homesteading that we could accomplish in the city. This idea of modern homesteading led me to start my website, A Modern Homestead, to help others learn how to embrace the idea of homesteading no matter where they live.

In 2016, we made the move onto a piece of family land and expanded our homesteading practices to include gardening and animal husbandry. We even had a dairy cow for a while (I'll tell you more about her shortly). Ultimately, we have spent a decade learning which parts of homesteading fit our desired lifestyle and which parts don't, to create the modern homestead of our dreams.

Maybe you are looking around at your life and wanting more as well. Maybe you are realizing that you long for a slower pace of life, or a lifestyle that allows you to be more self-sufficient in a world that seems more and more unstable. Creating your own modern homestead is an exciting endeavor, but also one that can seem overwhelming. My goal for this book is to help you see that you can incorporate many traditional skills into modern life, without having to pick up and move to the country or completely change your life.

This is the very average subdivision home where we started our homesteading journey. You can start anywhere!

CRAFTING YOUR HOMESTEAD

Embarking on your own homesteading journey is a deeply personal experience, and it's important to remember that there's no one "right" way to do it. As you move through this book, you might find certain ideas and practices that resonate with you immediately, while others don't quite fit. That's okay! The beauty of modern homesteading lies in its flexibility—the freedom to adapt traditional skills to suit your life and your needs.

Since we are fortunate enough to live in a time that doesn't require us to homestead fully in order to survive, it's completely reasonable to cater your activities and goals to what makes you feel the most fulfilled, rather than focusing on the tasks needed to make it through the winter. One of the most empowering aspects of

Our son, James, was thrilled when he picked our first home-grown strawberries!

James watching his daddy unload our first batch of mulch when we first moved to the homestead.

homesteading is the ability to pick and choose the practices that best align with your personal values, lifestyle, and goals. Unlike many other pursuits, modern homesteading isn't about rigid adherence to a prescribed set of activities. Instead, it's about crafting a lifestyle that brings you joy, sustains your family, and connects you with the land in a way that feels authentic. This journey is yours to shape, and part of the process is learning to listen to your own instincts and make choices that align with your desired lifestyle.

You might find that gardening is your true passion, so you dedicate most of your time to growing a variety of vegetables, herbs, and fruits. Or maybe animal husbandry speaks to you, and you enjoy the routine of caring for chickens, goats, or bees. Some homesteaders dive deep into food preservation, finding satisfaction in the process of canning, fermenting, and drying the food that they harvest or purchase. Others might focus on crafting, building, or self-sufficiency projects that align with their creative or practical interests.

What's crucial to understand is that your modern homestead should reflect your priorities and passions, not simply be a re-creation of what someone else thinks you should be doing. There's no shame in deciding that certain practices aren't for you. Perhaps you try beekeeping but find it too labor intensive, or you experiment with making soap only to realize that it doesn't spark the joy you hoped it would. These observations are part of the journey—discovering what enhances your life and what doesn't. There is no shame in discovering what doesn't fit!

In the end, the goal is to create a homestead that feels like home—a place where you're free to explore, experiment, and embrace the practices that truly resonate with you. Freedom of choice is what makes homesteading so fulfilling, and it's important to keep that concept in mind as you build your own path.

QUESTIONS TO ASK WHEN STARTING OUT

You may already be in the middle of crafting your homestead, or you may be at the onset and just starting to make plans. Either way, reflecting on your motivations and goals will help provide clarity as you move forward. Unfortunately, we failed to give them thought in the beginning, and I wish we had! Now, we counsel all new homesteaders to take a beat before diving in, to first ask some questions and set some goals with a clear head.

Grab a notebook and write down all the things you want to do on your homestead and why. The *why* is very important! Often, when we see someone else homesteading we decide *their* practices are the only valid way to homestead, without any real reason or practicality behind our thought process, which then all too frequently leads to hardships and frustration when we try to fit our own lives into that same mold.

1. Why is this task important to me?
2. If I bought the product of this task, such as honey from my beekeeping efforts, what would it cost me each month or year?
3. Can I buy the same quality locally that I can produce myself?
4. Am I willing to forsake other tasks to prioritize this one?
5. What does each season of the year look like for this task?

You might start out with a picture-perfect idea of homesteading but find that as you incorporate that idea into your own life, it doesn't actually serve you the way you thought it would. It's okay to let go of one idea in favor of finding another that works for you and your family!

Hopefully, you are able to see how vital these questions can be to the process. They aren't meant to keep you from doing any given task, but rather to help you understand the why and how of getting that task done, enabling you to prioritize what is most important to you.

You may discover through this practice that you can purchase the same quality eggs at a local farmer's market for less money than it would cost you to raise and keep chickens yourself. This would allow you to save the effort and time of keeping chickens for another task, while also supporting other local producers. Or you may find that you cannot purchase the same quality, so you move keeping chickens higher on your priority list. Or perhaps you *can* purchase eggs for the same price or less, but keeping chickens is truly fulfilling to your soul, so you raise them anyway. There is no wrong answer—but asking the question before you start can often help you avoid future issues.

THE TRIAL-AND-ERROR PROCESS

Homesteading is, at its core, a process of trial and error. And while something may look great on paper, even after careful consideration you will inevitably find that some things work well for you while others don't. This is a normal part of the journey. It's important to approach the process with an open mind and a willingness to experiment, and to not get discouraged if something doesn't work out immediately or just doesn't feel right after a solid effort.

When you first start out, it can be tempting to try everything at once—keeping chickens, baking sourdough bread, tending a large garden, making soap, preserving food, and more. I don't recommend this because it can lead to overwhelm that isn't actually associated with the tasks in front of you but rather comes from the fact that you've introduced too many things at once.

But no matter how many skills you choose to try, you may find that certain activities don't fit as seamlessly into your life as you'd imagined. For example, you might discover that sourdough baking, with its precise timing and care, feels like more of a chore than a pleasure. Or perhaps you realize that keeping chickens, while rewarding, requires more daily attention than you can comfortably give.

The key is to view these experiences not as failures but as valuable learning opportunities. Every time you try something new, you're gaining insight into what works for you and what doesn't. It's perfectly okay to decide that a particular practice isn't for you and to move on to something else. What matters is that you're exploring, learning, and finding what truly enhances your life.

When something doesn't work out, also don't be afraid to reassess and adjust your approach. Maybe you find that gardening in raised beds is more manageable than maintaining a large plot, or that buying sourdough from a local baker gives you the same joy without the stress of maintaining a starter. The point is to keep experimenting and refining your practices until you find the right balance for you.

WHEN A DREAM TURNS INTO A HARDSHIP

For as long as I can remember, I dreamed of having a dairy cow. The idea of fresh milk every morning, straight from our own cow, was something I romanticized for years. Eventually, that dream became a reality. We brought home a beautiful A2-certified dairy cow, and for three years she was a cherished part of our family.

At first, it was everything I had hoped for. There's something magical about the connection you feel when you milk your own cow, knowing that the milk on your breakfast table was produced just a few hours earlier. But over time, we began to realize that the demands of caring for a dairy cow didn't align with the way we wanted to live. The daily milking schedule, the commitment to her care, and the sheer amount of milk we had to process became overwhelming. It wasn't just a matter of work; it was the

Our beautiful Red Devon mama, Buttermilk, with her calf, Serenity.

realization that the rhythm of our lives was out of sync due to the responsibilities of dairy farming.

After much consideration, and with heavy hearts, we made the difficult decision to sell our sweet cow back to the rancher we had purchased her from. It wasn't easy to say goodbye—we had invested so much time and energy into making that dream a reality, and letting it go felt like a failure at first—but once she was gone, we felt an unexpected sense of relief. Suddenly, our days felt more balanced and our homestead more manageable. The decision to let go of something I had dreamed of for so long wasn't easy, but it was the right choice for our family. As time passed, I realized that letting go of our dairy cow had created space for other things that brought me joy. I had more time to spend with my family, more energy to devote to the garden, and more peace in my daily routine.

This experience taught me an important lesson: not every dream fits into the reality of your life, and that's okay. It's essential to recognize when something isn't working and to have the courage to make changes, even if it means letting go of something you once thought was essential.

REEVALUATING AND ADJUSTING OVER TIME

While some tasks or projects may become glaring in terms of their strain on your life, it's important to regularly reevaluate all your homesteading practices to ensure they're still working for you. As your life and needs change, you may find yourself having to adjust or end tasks that you do still truly enjoy and benefit from. These changes may be for a season, or they may be permanent. This is why regular evaluations are so important.

External factors such as weather patterns, financial changes, a family crisis, or other unexpected events can also impact your homesteading plans. Being able to adjust and adapt to these changes is key to maintaining a successful homestead. For instance, if a particularly harsh winter makes it difficult to maintain a large garden, you might instead decide to focus on indoor projects or explore new skills such as crafting or fermenting.

While constant evaluation goes on naturally on a regular basis, real evaluation to consider big changes should happen much less frequently. You don't want to make permanent decisions based on a bad day; instead, you ideally want to have a full year of experience with a task before you decide its fate. Why wait a full year? Well, keeping chickens in the fall is a breeze, but it's less enjoyable in the heat of the summer. Likewise, gardening in the spring may be the best thing you've ever done, while cleaning out the garden in the winter turns out to be a chore you never want to see again! Understanding exactly what any given task looks like in reality during all seasons will allow you to make the best decision for your situation.

Remember that removing something from your homestead doesn't have to be permanent and it doesn't mean the experience was a failure. Not at all! We learn very valuable lessons from everything we try—lessons that can be used in the future to make our next efforts even more comfortable and successful. Yes, making the decision to stop a homesteading practice can be an emotional process, but it's also a necessary one. Sometimes the greatest joy comes from letting go of one task to make room for another.

EMBRACING YOUR UNIQUE HOMESTEADING JOURNEY

As you move forward on your homesteading journey, remember to stay open to change, be willing to let go of what isn't working, and celebrate the practices that bring you joy. Your homestead is a living, evolving entity, and finding your flow is about creating a rhythm that feels right for you.

So, embrace the freedom to create the modern homestead of your dreams, and don't be afraid to make adjustments along the way. In the end, the goal is to create a homestead that enhances your life, not one that burdens you.

CHAPTER 1

FROM SCRATCH COOKING

Cooking from scratch is an important skill to have when you are developing your homestead and establishing food security for your family. Many people are transitioning away from processed foods as more information comes out about how those highly processed foods impact our mental and physical health. Ten years ago, my family started our own journey by switching from being a "food household" to an "ingredients household"—meaning, of course, that our food is made from whole ingredients, and isn't sitting in the pantry or freezer ready to eat. That's not to say that I don't make a few extra pizzas and freeze them! But it is to say that the pizza we eat has only six ingredients, all of which are whole food items and none of which are chemicals or stabilizers.

If you decide to make this switch too, either you will be purchasing ingredients in bulk from online sources or from local farmers, or you will be growing whole foods yourself. Regardless of how you choose to gather your supplies, knowing how to turn those ingredients into delicious meals that your family will love is crucial to fully benefiting from your food supply. This chapter will help you make the switch into whole foods, while still enabling you to enjoy many of the same tastes and favorite dishes that you and your family are used to.

A NOTE ABOUT INGREDIENTS

Before we dive into the actual recipes, I want to discuss my recommendations for ingredient *quality*. While all flour may be considered equal, we are continually learning more about how the quality of each ingredient truly impacts our life, and that all flour is *not* in fact equal when it comes to nutrient quality. The same idea goes for many other ingredients as well. Here are a few of the varieties and qualities of ingredients that I recommend using, if possible.

Einkorn Flour

Celiac and gluten sensitivities are so common today, and modification of wheat along with pesticide treatment of crops are credited for a big part of that fact. Einkorn flour comes in as a miracle wheat for everyone, but especially for those with gluten sensitivities or Celiac disease. Heralded as the original wheat, einkorn has never been hybridized or modified in any way. It is the wheat our bodies know how to process. In fact, einkorn doesn't contain the same gluten protein as any other wheat, so the gluten response is not triggered at all. As a result, it's been my experience that even those with Celiac disease can easily tolerate and process einkorn flour! Over the last twelve years, we have been blessed to help more than sixteen million people with Celiac disease or gluten sensitivity learn how to bake with einkorn flour, including three diagnosed Celiacs in our own family. While I have only ever heard from people with Celiac disease that they were able to enjoy einkorn without consequences, it is possible that some with the disease may not be able to tolerate it fully. However, I have watched customers hold an EpiPen, due to their past severe reactions to wheat, while taking a bite of an einkorn pastry and they had no reaction to einkorn! I use einkorn flour for the recipes I'm sharing in this book, but there is information on page 23 for using other wheat varieties.

Dairy

While many people are allergic or sensitive to the pasteurized milk products found in most grocery stores, some people are finding out they can still consume and enjoy the health benefits of grass-fed, A2/A2, raw dairy. If your state allows raw milk and you decide to try it (note that the CDC and FDA warn against consuming unpasteurized dairy), look for grass-fed, grain-free, raw milk from A2/A2 cows for the best experience. My family was unable to consume dairy for almost ten years before discovering raw milk. It's been more than fifteen years since then, and we enjoy it now daily, without issues! You can make your own butter, yogurt, and even cheese from raw milk, or look for options in your state to purchase raw milk–based products instead.

Note that any type of milk, animal or plant based, can be used in our recipes unless otherwise stated.

A1 and A2 refer to different types of protein found in milk. In the United States, most cows produce A1 milk, while in Europe most of the cows produce A2 milk. As more information is discovered about how the human body reacts to the different protein types, we are learning that our bodies can tolerate and benefit from A2 milk but cannot properly process A1 milk. Look for A2/A2 milk-producing dairies if you are dealing with a dairy allergy. Milk labeled A2/A1 means that both proteins are present and may still cause digestion issues.

Butter

Grass-fed butter contains high levels of vitamin A, K2, and beta-carotene, among many other things. Not only is it delicious, but it's also great for the health of your teeth and bones. Avoid margarine or vegetable oil–based butters if possible, and instead opt for whole, grass-fed butter. If you cannot tolerate dairy, look for coconut oil, palm shortening, or tallow as a replacement. Which one you choose to use in place of real butter will depend on the recipe. Coconut oil and palm shortening can be used in any dish, whereas tallow will alter the flavor of sweet dishes and should be used for savory items only. Note that we use salted butter in all of our recipes, but you can use unsalted if you prefer.

Oils/Fats

Seed oils such as sunflower, soybean, and vegetable often cause inflammation when used in cooking, especially when stored for too long. Instead, opt for cold-pressed olive oil, avocado oil, or coconut oil when possible. For frying, we like to use tallow or coconut oil, with tallow reserved for savory items and coconut oil used for anything.

FROM SCRATCH COOKING 13

Sweeteners

Highly processed sugar is difficult for the body to process and can actually leach nutrients from the body as a result. Instead, try to find whole, unbleached cane sugar, such as panela, or use coconut sugar or maple syrup. Note that when "sugar" is called for in my recipes, any type of granulated sugar will work without recipe modifications. If you choose to use a liquid sweetener (like honey or maple syrup), and more than a few tablespoons are called for in the recipe, you may need to add additional flour to reach the proper batter or dough texture.

Pastured Meat

Animals raised on pasture have fewer health issues and require fewer, if any, medical interventions during their life. Those benefits are passed on to us as we consume grass-fed meat. Look for both grass-*fed* and grass-*finished* meat; farmers can still claim their meat is grass fed even if their animals were fattened with grain for the last several months of their lives. Additionally, look for the country of origin and choose a producer that raises animals in the country where you live, if possible.

Organic Fruits and Vegetables

It's an unfortunate fact that due to poor soil management over the last few centuries, our produce has far fewer nutrients than it did even a hundred years ago. The best way to ensure your produce is nutrient dense is to grow it yourself in high-quality soil. Short of that, purchasing organic produce, when possible, will give you more nutrients than conventionally grown produce. Organic produce also has the benefit of little to no pesticides used during its growth. This means there are fewer pesticides for your body to deal with and detox, so you receive more of the nutrients from the food you eat.

EQUIPMENT

Though there are many kitchen tools referenced throughout this chapter, most are optional. I'm going to discuss a few of them here, but I want to reassure you that in most cases you can still make these recipes without spending money on additional equipment!

Digital Kitchen Scale

One piece of equipment that I would highly recommend purchasing is a digital kitchen scale. They are small enough to tuck away in a drawer, only cost about $10 online, and can make or break a recipe. Weighing your ingredients helps to ensure consistent results every single time. For example, a packed cup of flour or cheese could easily be double the weight called for in the recipe, which could completely alter the results.

Blender or Food Processor

A high-speed blender is useful when grinding fresh flour, as it helps you achieve a finer texture after milling without having to sift the flour and thus lose the nutrition in the bran. It can also be helpful for pureeing sauce ingredients—though a food processor or immersion blender would also work well for the latter cases.

Stand Mixer

Whether it's KitchenAid or another brand, having an electric stand mixer that allows for a bread hook attachment can result in finer yeast dough textures. If you do not have a stand mixer, you don't need to rush out and buy one! Just knead your dough by hand until you are ready to invest and know that the process of making bread will be even easier once you do.

Grain Mill

If you want to use freshly ground flour, a grain mill is required. The only exceptions being if you want to grind your flour by hand in a mortar and pestle, or if you have a high-speed blender specifically capable of grinding wheat. Even then, grinding large quantities becomes difficult without a mill. Until you are ready to invest in a grain mill, simply skip the recipes that call for freshly ground flour.

Tortilla Press

A tortilla press is very useful when making corn tortillas, as the dough is too sticky to roll with a rolling pin. Flour tortillas, however, are best when rolled by hand!

Pasta Roller

A simple hand-crank pasta roller helps make thin, uniform sheets of pasta for turning into cut strips in the width of your preference. However, the pasta sheets can also be rolled by hand with a little patience.

CONDIMENTS

It's so easy to grab a bottle of ranch dressing or barbecue sauce at the store that many people never consider making their own from scratch. The truth is that many bottled dressings and sauces not only have unwanted ingredients but also have a huge markup. For example, you can save 90 percent off the cost of ranch dressing by simply making it yourself! You will also be able to control the ingredients, which is so important when seeking to eat for health and wellness.

Please note that there are additional recipes for condiments such as marinara sauce and salsa in the water bath canning section, beginning on page 129, so I have not repeated them here.

Mayonnaise

Most mayonnaise is made with a seed oil, which many people try to avoid. This mayo recipe is easy to make and gives you the option to remove seed oils from the process. We prefer using avocado oil or a mild olive oil; however, use whatever liquid-at-room-temperature oil works for your family. Yields 2 cups.

Ingredients

- 2 large eggs
- 1 teaspoon yellow mustard
- 2 tablespoons fresh lemon juice (this is needed to allow the mayo to stay fresh in the fridge)
- ½ teaspoon salt
- 1½ cups oil

Note: There are several ways to bring these ingredients together: either in a food processor, blender, or immersion blender, or with a whisk, as is traditional. I'm including the process for both options, and you can choose which best works for you.

Instructions

1. **Food Processor or Blender:** Place all ingredients, except oil, into a food processor (or blender) and mix until combined. With the processor running, slowly drizzle oil into the mix. It should take about 1 minute to pour all the oil into the egg mixture. Once oil has been added, check the mayo for consistency. If it is too thin for your liking, add more oil (with machine on) 1 tablespoon at a time until desired consistency is reached.

2. **Whisk:** Add all ingredients, except oil, to a medium-sized bowl and whisk until combined. While whisking, slowly drizzle oil into the mixture. It should take about 1 minute to see emulsification. Once you see the mixture starting to lighten, you can add the oil more quickly. Once the oil has been added, check the mayo for consistency. If it is too thin for your liking, add more oil 1 tablespoon at a time and whisk until desired consistency is reached.

3. This mayo can be stored in a glass container in the fridge for up to three months.

Ranch Dressing

This is a classic tangy ranch dressing that is perfect on salads or for use as a dipping sauce. Use the homemade mayo recipe from page 17 for the best results. This recipe yields the equivalent of a large bottle of store-bought ranch dressing. Yields 2 cups.

Ingredients

1 cup mayonnaise

½ cup milk

1 tablespoon lemon juice

1 tablespoon dried parsley

1 teaspoon garlic powder

1 tablespoon + 1 teaspoon dried dill

½ teaspoon pepper

½ teaspoon salt

Instructions

Add mayo to a medium bowl and then add the milk and lemon juice. Whisk until smooth and let sit for about 5 minutes so the lemon juice can turn the milk into buttermilk. Add the parsley, garlic powder, dill, pepper, and salt and stir until well combined. Taste the dressing and add more of the seasonings as desired. Pour into a mason jar and chill overnight for best results. This dressing will keep for up to 4 months in the fridge. If the dressing separates slightly, stir to recombine.

Chocolate Syrup

Chocolate syrup is a staple in many households, whether children are present or not! My husband has always loved chocolate milk, and this recipe for homemade chocolate syrup has served us well for more than twenty years. Now our son enjoys it as well, so we always have a batch in the fridge ready to pour. Yields about 3 cups.

Ingredients

- 2 cups sugar
- 1 cup water
- ⅓ cup cacao powder or cocoa
- 1 tablespoon vanilla extract

Instructions

1. Combine sugar and water in a medium saucepan. Over medium heat, stir until the sugar is completely dissolved. The sauce will bubble, so your pan must be larger than quantity would normally dictate.
2. Once the sugar is dissolved, add the cacao powder. Stir until thoroughly combined.
3. Bring mixture to a steady boil, stirring constantly for 3 minutes.
4. Remove from heat and add vanilla extract.
5. Allow to cool and then transfer the syrup into the container of your choice.

Note about sugar substitutes: This recipe can be made with white sugar, panela, or maple syrup in equal measure. Maple syrup is our preferred ingredient, but all three options are delicious. If you are using liquid sweetener, reduce the water to ½ cup.

Barbecue Sauce

Sweet and tangy, this barbecue sauce is so easy to make! Use this in place of any barbecue sauce called for in any recipe. You can adjust the spices as desired, but the given recipe makes a classic tomato-based barbecue sauce. Yields 2 cups.

Ingredients

⅓ cup ketchup

¾ cup brown sugar

¼ cup molasses

2 tablespoons apple cider vinegar

1 tablespoon yellow mustard

1 teaspoon garlic powder

1 teaspoon salt

½ teaspoon black pepper

¼ teaspoon cloves (optional)

Instructions

Combine all ingredients in a medium saucepan and simmer over low heat. Do not adjust the seasonings until after the barbecue sauce has come to a simmer because they will change quite a bit during the cooking process. Adjust spices as desired and simmer for 5 minutes. Allow the barbecue sauce to cool slightly before transferring to a glass jar. Store in the fridge for up to 12 months.

Ketchup

This is a classic ketchup recipe that your kids will love, without any added oils or flavorings beyond what you already have in your kitchen. Whether you pair it with a pile of french fries or use it to top your homemade meatloaf, this ketchup is great to keep on hand. Yields about 3 cups.

Ingredients

16 ounces tomato paste

4 tablespoons white vinegar

2 tablespoons sugar

8 ounces water

1½ teaspoons salt

½ teaspoon onion power

¼ teaspoon garlic powder

Instructions

Combine all ingredients in a medium saucepan and whisk until smooth. Heat over medium heat, stirring constantly. Bring to a boil and reduce the heat to low. Simmer for 20 minutes, stirring often. Remove from heat and cool slightly before transferring the finished ketchup into a glass container. Store in an airtight container in the fridge for up to 6 months.

Classic White Gravy

Whether you are using this gravy to smother the chicken fried steak on page 68 or dipping homemade biscuits into it for breakfast, this recipe will serve you well for all your gravy needs. Yields 4–6 servings.

Ingredients

4 tablespoons grease, such as bacon grease

4 tablespoons any wheat flour

½ cup heavy whipping cream

2–3 cups whole milk

Salt and pepper to taste

Instructions

1. If you are making this with the chicken fried steak from page 68, pour the remaining grease left over after frying into a heat-safe bowl or glass measuring cup. No need to scrape the skillet clean; the debris from the frying process will add amazing flavor to the gravy. Otherwise, simply use your favorite grease instead. We love using bacon grease for this recipe.

2. Heat the skillet over medium-low heat and add 4 tablespoons of the grease to the hot skillet.

3. Add flour to the grease and whisk for 2 to 3 minutes, or until a smooth roux forms.

4. Combine the cream and 2 cups of the milk, and slowly drizzle into the skillet, whisking constantly.

5. Continue whisking, bringing the gravy to a simmer. Cook until the gravy is smooth and creamy, about 5 to 7 minutes. If the gravy gets too thick, add a little more milk. Season with salt and pepper to taste.

BREAD AND PANTRY STAPLES

Switching to homemade bread products and pantry staples was the first change I made when seeking to embrace the homesteading lifestyle and mindset. We were living in a tiny house, on a tiny lot, in an overpopulated part of Texas. I couldn't grow any food in my backyard or keep chickens, but I could bake bread and make homemade tortillas—and you can too!

Baking with Einkorn Flour (or Not!)

As I mentioned earlier, einkorn is my wheat of choice, so all the recipes in this book are tailored to that flour—specifically unbleached, all-purpose einkorn—and its liquid absorption rate. However, if einkorn flour doesn't work for your family, for whatever reason, you can use any other modern or ancient wheat you prefer. If you are using another wheat, be sure to use all-purpose flour to achieve similar results.

If you make the various bread recipes from this book without using einkorn flour, you may notice that the dough is dry. If that's the case add more warm water a few tablespoons at a time until you achieve a soft, smooth dough. For cakes, cookies, muffins, or other non-yeast recipes, all-purpose einkorn flour and any other all-purpose wheat flour can be used 1:1 without any modifications to the liquid in the recipe.

Using Freshly Milled Flour

Whether you are using einkorn or another wheat, you may prefer to grind it from berries. I do too! However, since the majority of people just starting out do not yet own an at-home mill, I have formulated these recipes to use all-purpose flour. Thankfully, the process for converting an all-purpose flour recipe to freshly milled is simple!

- When using fresh einkorn flour, use 25 percent more flour by weight than the all-purpose flour called for. For example, if a recipe calls for 400 grams of all-purpose, you will use 500 grams of freshly milled. Be sure to measure einkorn flour in grams, not cups, for consistent results!

- Be sure that your flour is ground very fine, as coarse ground flour will not produce the same results. I like to grind my flour and run 4 cups at a time through a high-speed blender for 1 to 3 minutes to achieve a finer texture without sifting.

- In the case of non-yeast items (cakes, cookies, breads), allow the batter to sit for at least 15 minutes, if possible, to allow the liquid to be absorbed properly.

- In the case of yeast dough, if the dough is too dry, add more liquid a few tablespoons at a time, kneading until the dough is soft and smooth.

FROM SCRATCH COOKING 23

Sandwich Bread

Whether you are building a BLT or making French toast, this classic white bread made with simple ingredients is soft and sturdy enough to hold up to any filling. If using an electric mixer with a bread attachment, you can triple this recipe to yield three loaves at a time and cut down on your kitchen efforts. Yields 1 loaf.

Ingredients

4¼ cups (500g) all-purpose flour

1 teaspoon salt

¼ teaspoon powdered ginger (recommended if using einkorn flour)

2¼ teaspoons (9g) dry active yeast

1½ cups warm water

1 tablespoon maple syrup (optional)

Instructions

1. Add flour, salt, ginger (if using), and yeast to the bowl of an electric mixer and attach a bread hook, if available. If not using a mixer, add ingredients to a large bowl.

2. Heat water to between 100–115°F. Don't go hotter than that or it will kill the yeast. Mix maple syrup (if using) into the water.

3. Slowly add the water/syrup mixture and mix for 10 minutes (YES, 10 minutes) using a bread hook attachment (if possible). If kneading by hand, knead until the dough is smooth and shiny.

4. Once the dough is thoroughly mixed, remove bread hook from bowl, scrape down the sides, and cover dough with plastic wrap.

5. Allow bread to rise in a warm area for 25 minutes.

6. Butter an 8" × 4" bread pan and place dough into the pan.

7. Cover with a buttered piece of plastic wrap and allow to rise for another 20 minutes.

8. Preheat the oven to 350°F and bake for 30 minutes, or until golden brown.

9. Allow to cool for about 5 minutes before turning bread out of the pan and onto a cooling rack.

10. Cool completely before slicing. Store bagged at room temperature for up to 4 days, in the fridge for 2 weeks, or in the freezer for up to 6 months.

To Thaw: Simply place your frozen bread on the counter the night before you'd like to use it. It will thaw perfectly and be ready to enjoy when you wake up.

Biscuits

Soft, tender, and flaky, these biscuits require no buttermilk and can be frozen before baking for easy biscuits at any time. Yields 12–16 biscuits, depending on thickness.

Ingredients

2¾ cups (330g) all-purpose flour

1 tablespoon baking powder

1 tablespoon maple syrup or sugar

½ teaspoon salt

5 tablespoons cold butter, sliced

1 cup milk or buttermilk (you may not need all of it)

Instructions

1. Preheat oven to 400°F.

2. Combine dry ingredients, either in a mixer or by hand.

3. Add butter slices to dry mixture and cut in until mix resembles a coarse crumble. If using maple syrup, also add it at this stage. Mix briefly with a paddle attachment (if using a mixer). Be careful not to overmix.

4. Add less than the full cup of milk to start. You may not need all of it, depending on the type of flour you are using, so add less than the full amount and then add more as needed.

5. Mix until a shaggy dough forms. You should still see pieces of butter streaked throughout the dough, and some parts of the dough will be wetter than others. You do *not* want a smooth and cohesive dough.

6. Scrape the dough onto a well-floured surface. Flour dough and form into a ball. Keep all sides of the dough floured while working.

7. Press or roll the dough into a 1-inch-high disc. Fold the dough in half lengthwise, then in half sideways, so that it is folded in quarters.

8. Roll dough into a 1-inch-high disc and cut with a glass or 2"–3" biscuit cutter.

9. Place on a parchment-lined tray and bake for 12–14 minutes, or until golden brown.

To Freeze: Follow the recipe up to the point of cutting out the biscuits, then freeze the unbaked rounds on a parchment-lined baking sheet. Once the biscuits are fully frozen, remove them from the tray and store them in a freezer-safe container. Bake from frozen for 14 minutes, or until golden brown.

Tortillas

While it may seem intimidating, making homemade flour tortillas is easier than you think! This recipe makes 16 thin and soft tortillas, for the perfect addition to your next meal! You can eat them fresh or freeze them for later.

Ingredients

- 3⅓ cups (405g) all-purpose flour
- ½ teaspoon baking powder
- 1 teaspoon salt
- ⅓ cup lard or tallow, room temperature
- 1 cup hot water (almost boiling)

Instructions

1. Combine dry ingredients in a bowl. Add the lard or tallow and mix well into dry ingredients.
2. Form a flour "mountain" and create a hole in the middle. Add hot water slowly. The hot water will help melt and evenly distribute the fat for the best and most flexible tortillas.
3. Mix until well combined. Turn out onto the counter and knead until smooth. Return dough to bowl, cover, and let rest for 15 minutes.
4. Heat a large pan, skillet, or griddle to medium heat. Cook the tortillas on a dry surface, but do *not* add any grease.
5. Section out 16 golf ball–size portions, round them off, and place them on a floured surface. *Keep the finished portions covered with a slightly damp towel until ready to roll out into tortillas.* Roll each portion of dough on a floured surface until they are as thin as you can make them without tearing.
6. Keep the rolled-out tortillas under a dry towel until ready to cook.
7. Cook one side until bubbles form (about 45 seconds), then flip. Cook for an additional 30–45 seconds on the other side.
8. Once cooked, wrap the finished tortillas in a dish towel to keep them soft and warm.

To Freeze: Freeze in batches of 6–12 by placing parchment paper pieces between each tortilla and stacking them in the desired number. Then place them in a freezer bag and seal well. Thaw overnight on the counter and reheat on a dry, hot skillet for best results.

Use a soft flour sack towel to keep the tortillas warm after cooking. This also increases their flexibility for wrapping into fajitas or burritos.

Corn Tortillas

With just two simple ingredients and a bit of hot water, you can make your own homemade corn tortillas. Note that masa harina is a specific type of corn flour, where the grain has been soaked in an alkaline solution (typically lime water) before being dried and ground. The process of making masa harina not only makes the corn much easier to digest but also causes the corn to become a complete protein that contains all nine amino acids. This recipe calls for a tortilla press and yields 12 tortillas.

Ingredients

- 2 cups masa harina
- 1 teaspoon sea salt
- 1½–2 cups boiling water

Instructions

1. Add masa harina and salt to a mixing bowl. Slowly pour in the boiling water.
2. Work the dough with a wooden spoon until it's smooth and homogenous. The dough should feel smooth, not sticky or dry. If it crumbles, add a touch more water. If it sticks to your hands, sprinkle in a bit more masa harina.
3. Cover the bowl with a damp cloth and let the dough rest for about 30 minutes.
4. Divide the ball into 3 even portions, and then each portion into 4 more portions for 12 even-sized tortillas. Then roll each portion to form a smooth ball. Keep these portions on a plate under a damp towel/paper towel until ready to press.
5. Preheat your cast-iron skillet over medium-high heat. The surface should be hot enough that when drops of water hit it, they sizzle immediately.
6. Lay a sheet of plastic wrap on the bottom plate of your tortilla press. This prevents the masa from sticking to the press. Place the ball of dough in the center of the press. Cover with another sheet of plastic wrap and close the press with firm, even pressure.
7. Peel the tortilla from the plastic wrap and place it on the hot cooking surface. Let it cook for about 30 seconds, or until the edges start to lift slightly off the surface. Flip the tortilla and cook for another minute, then flip again and cook for another 30 seconds or until it puffs up slightly.
8. As you work through the batch, stack your cooked tortillas under a kitchen towel to retain their warmth and moisture.

To Freeze: Freeze in batches of 6–12 by placing parchment paper between each tortilla and stacking them in the desired number. Then place them in a freezer bag and seal well. Thaw overnight on the counter and reheat on a dry, hot skillet for best results.

Butter Crackers

This is a classic cracker recipe that goes with chili or soup, pairs well with cream cheese and jelly, and is sturdy enough to hold a thick slice of cheese. Make these in bulk for an easy snack without the need to buy them at the store. Yields about 85 1½-inch round crackers.

Ingredients

- 2¼ cups (270g) flour
- 1 teaspoon baking powder
- 1 tablespoon maple syrup or sugar
- ½ teaspoon salt, plus some for dusting the top of finished crackers
- ½ cup butter, cold plus 2 tablespoons melted for top of finished crackers
- ⅔ cup milk

Instructions

1. Preheat the oven to 400°F.

2. Add dry ingredients to a food processor and pulse until well combined.

3. Add cold butter in small cubes and pulse until crumbly.

4. Add maple syrup, or sugar, and milk, then pulse until a ball forms.

5. If the dough is still very sticky, add a bit more flour and pulse again.

6. Remove dough from food processor and divide into two balls to roll out separately.

7. Cut a piece of parchment paper to fit your baking sheet, then roll the dough directly on the sheet for best results.

8. Roll out the dough until it's as thin as possible: ⅛" or less is ideal. Cut the dough into whatever shape you desire. You can use a biscuit cutter for round crackers or a pizza cutter to easily cut the dough into club cracker–style portions. You can also find dedicated cracker cutters in many shapes in the shop on my website, A Modern Homestead.

9. Poke holes into each cracker with a fork. I like to do 3–4 rows of holes to make them look like the store-bought version.

10. Remove excess dough (if any) after the cuts have been made and transfer the sheet of crackers to a baking tray. Bake for 10 minutes, or until golden brown.

11. Remove from oven and immediately brush crackers with melted butter. Sprinkle with salt to taste.

12. Allow to cool completely before storing in an airtight container.

Bulk Tip: You can make these crackers in bulk and store them in a large mason jar or similar airtight container for up to 6 months.

Easy No-Egg Pasta

Homemade pasta doesn't have to be complicated. With just a little water and flour, you can create an epic homemade pasta meal in less than an hour! Since this recipe doesn't contain eggs, it's also great for drying to store at room temperature. Yields 4–6 servings.

Ingredients

2¼ cups (300g) flour

¾–1 cup warm water

Instructions

1. Place flour on a clean work surface and make a well. Add ¼ cup of warm water at a time.

2. With your fingertips or a spoon, stir the mixture. Knead in more water as needed until a soft, flexible dough with bounce is formed. You may not need all the water. If you add too much water, add in more flour until the correct consistency is reached.

3. Create the shape of pasta you want to make. You can use a pasta roller to make sheets to fold and cut into strips, or you can use shape attachments as desired. Hand-formed shapes, such as cavatelli, can also be made without any additional equipment.

4. Store the finished shapes on a wax paper–lined tray or a well-floured surface while you finish working with all the dough. Be sure to allow enough time for shaping.

5. Bring 2 quarts of salted water to a boil and drop in the fresh pasta. Boil for 3–5 minutes, or until it reaches the desired texture.

6. Serve the pasta right away with a red sauce or butter and herbs.

Bulk Tips: To freeze, shape the dough and then place in a freezer bag and freeze immediately. Thaw overnight in the fridge before cooking. This pasta can also be air-dried and stored for up to 6 months since it doesn't contain any eggs.

Dark Rye Bread

This dark rye bread, sweetened with molasses, has a strong flavor and an extremely soft yet sturdy texture. A delicious brown bread recipe, it's perfect for Rueben sandwiches, veggie sandwiches, and more! Yields 1 loaf.

Ingredients

- 2¼ cups (270g) all-purpose flour
- ⅔ cup medium rye flour
- ¼ cup cocoa powder
- 1 teaspoon sugar
- 1 teaspoon salt
- 2¼ teaspoons (9g) dry active yeast
- 1 cup brewed coffee + 1 tablespoon (cooled to warm)
- 1 tablespoon butter, softened
- 1 tablespoon dark molasses

Instructions

1. Set aside 1 cup of all-purpose flour and all of the rye flour. Combine remaining ingredients in a mixing bowl or bowl of an electric mixer. With a paddle attachment or beaters, beat for 4 minutes on medium speed.
2. Add rye flour and mix for 1 minute. Add additional flour from the flour reserved in step 1, about ¼ cup at a time and mix again. Texture should be like a very thick gingerbread mix! If it is not, add more flour until you reach the correct texture.
3. Switch mixer to a dough hook and mix for an additional 5–7 minutes or until dough is smooth and elastic. If you are kneading by hand, this may take up to 10–15 minutes.
4. Place dough back into the mixing bowl; cover with plastic wrap and a towel. Let rise for 45 minutes.
5. Prep a baking sheet with parchment paper. With oiled hands (I use a little butter), scrape the dough from the bowl and gently shape into a ball. Place on a parchment-lined tray.
6. Let rise uncovered for 25 minutes.
7. Preheat oven to 400°F.
8. Slash the top in any desired pattern at least ¼" deep with a sharp knife. Bake for 30 minutes and let rest for at least another 30 minutes before slicing.

Note: The bread crust will seem VERY hard when you remove it from the oven. It will soften perfectly as it cools. Do not remove it from the oven early, as the middle will not yet be cooked.

New York–Style Bagels

Bagels are an amazingly versatile item to have on hand, and homemade bagels are the best of the best. Unlike other bagel recipes, this one comes together in less than 20 minutes and is ready to eat in about 2 hours total! These New York–style bagels are chewy on the outside and soft in the middle—perfection. Yields 8 bagels.

Ingredients

3⅔ cups (440g) all-purpose flour

2 tablespoons maple syrup

1½ teaspoons salt

¼ teaspoon ginger powder (if using einkorn flour)

1½ teaspoons (6g) instant yeast

1 cup warm water (115°F max temp)

Instructions

1. Add all ingredients except the warm water to the mixer and attach a dough hook. Start mixer on low and add warm water slowly.

2. Mix for 10 minutes on low. If you don't have a mixer, knead by hand for about 15 minutes, or until the dough is smooth and shiny.

3. Let rise in a greased, covered bowl for 25 minutes. If the dough is too sticky when the rise is over, knead in 1–3 tablespoons of extra flour.

4. On a well-floured surface, divide the dough into 8 pieces and form each into a smooth ball. You may need to flour your hands, the dough, and the surface throughout to keep it from sticking.

5. Once the balls are shaped, poke your finger through the middle of each ball and pull gently with both hands to create the center hole of the bagel.

6. Rest the shaped dough for 10 minutes while you bring a pot of water to boil. Boil each side of the bagels for 1–2 minutes. The longer you boil them, the chewier the exterior texture will be.

7. Place the boiled bagels onto a parchment-lined tray and preheat your oven to 425°F.

8. Bake for 20–25 minutes, or until golden brown. Cool, slice, and enjoy!

Bulk Tip: You can double or triple this recipe and freeze the bagels for later. Simply allow the cooked bagels to cool completely before placing them in a freezer-safe bag and storing. You can slice before freezing or not; that's up to you. These will last in the freezer for up to 8 months. Thaw overnight in a bag on the counter for best results.

Fresh-Milled Sandwich Bread

If you mill your own flour, this recipe makes a wonderful and sturdy sandwich bread for everyday use. Be sure to mill your flour very finely, but no sifting is required. If your mill does not grind very fine flour, you can run 4 cups of ground flour at a time through a high-speed blender for 1 to 3 minutes to achieve a finer texture without sifting. Yields 1 loaf.

Ingredients

- 4 cups (500g) wheat berries, ground
- 1 teaspoon salt
- 1 tablespoon apple cider vinegar (optional, but recommended)
- 1 tablespoon maple syrup (optional)
- 2¼ teaspoons (9g) instant yeast
- 1⅓ cups warm water (115°F)

Instructions

1. Add flour, salt, vinegar, syrup, and yeast to the bowl of an electric mixer and attach a bread hook, if available.
2. Heat water to between 100°F and 115°F. Don't go hotter than that or it will kill the yeast.
3. Into the flour mixture, slowly add the water and mix for 10 minutes (YES, 10 minutes) using a bread hook attachment (if possible). If kneading by hand, knead until dough is soft and smooth.
4. Once the dough is thoroughly kneaded, remove the hook from the bowl, scrape down the sides, and cover the bowl. Allow bread to rise in a warm area for 25 minutes.
5. Preheat the oven to 350°F. Butter an 8" × 4" bread pan and grease your hands before shaping the dough into a log. Place the dough in the pan and allow to rise, uncovered, in a warm place for 20 minutes.
6. Bake for 30 minutes or until golden brown.
7. Allow to cool for a few minutes before turning bread out of the pan and onto a cooling rack. Cool completely before slicing for the best crumb; otherwise, the bread may be dry and crumbly.

Chocolate Oat Granola

This granola is as delicious as it is versatile. You can use it as a cereal on its own, as a yogurt topping, or skip the crumbling step and cut into easy homemade granola bars. Feel free to experiment with whatever mix-ins you like! Yields about 6 cups.

Ingredients

- 4 cups old fashioned oats
- ¼ cup (30g) flour
- ½ cup chopped almonds
- ⅓ cup brown sugar
- 1 cup dark chocolate chips
- ½ teaspoon sea salt
- ½ cup butter, melted
- ½ cup maple syrup
- 1 teaspoon vanilla extract

Instructions

1. Preheat the oven to 350°F. Mix all your ingredients in a large bowl. Work the mixture well until the sugar and butter are fully incorporated and your oats are completely coated.
2. Line a half-sheet baking tray with parchment paper and spread your granola into an even layer. This will keep the granola from overbaking in some areas while underbaking in others.
3. To get those delicious clumps of granola, be sure to press your granola down a bit with the back of a spatula.
4. Bake for 25–35 minutes, or until your granola is golden brown.
5. Be sure to let your granola cool completely before you attempt to break it up. Crumble into whatever size chunks you prefer. Or cut into bars and wrap in parchment paper if desired.
6. Keep your homemade granola in an airtight container for 6–12 months. Enjoy!

Bulk Tip: While you can easily double this batch, make sure that you only bake one batch per half-sheet baking tray. Otherwise, the granola will burn on the top but not bake all the way through.

Potato Chips

There's nothing like a crisp potato chip, and these homemade chips are the best you'll ever have. Made without seed oil, you can make plain salted potato chips or mix up the barbecue seasoning to create your own delicious flavored chips. Yields 48 servings.

Ingredients

3 pounds russet potatoes

Coconut oil (or oil of choice)

Barbecue Seasoning

1 cup packed brown sugar

½ cup sugar

3 tablespoons garlic powder

2½ tablespoons paprika

1½ tablespoons onion powder

1 teaspoon chili powder

1 teaspoon salt

Instructions

1. Wash potatoes, removing any green skin or black spots from flesh.
2. Thinly slice the potatoes and heat coconut oil in a large, heavy-bottom pan to 275°F.
3. Carefully, rapidly drop the potato slices into the oil one at a time, only cooking 1 cup at a time.
4. Allow to fry for a few minutes without stirring, then gently stir every few minutes until they are evenly browned (this time will vary depending on thickness).
5. Remove the fried chips from the oil and place them on draining towels. Season with salt or barbecue seasoning to taste. For a heavy barbecue seasoning coat, add warm chips to a plastic bag along with about ¼ cup of seasoning and shake well for 15–20 seconds.
6. Repeat all steps until potatoes are all cooked and coated as desired.
7. Store them in zip-top mylar bags with a silica pack for up to 1 year.

Tortilla Chips

Using the homemade corn tortillas from page 29, you can easily make your own tortilla chips. They store well and last up to a year when stored properly. Yields 4–6 servings.

Ingredients

16 corn tortillas

4 cups coconut oil (or oil of choice)

Sea salt to taste

Instructions

1. Grab your corn tortillas and, using a sharp knife or a handy pizza cutter, slice them into fourths or sixths, ensuring a consistent chip size. I like to cut them into fourths, but depending on the size of your tortillas, sixths might be better.

2. Heat the oil over medium-high heat until a tortilla sizzles upon contact, signaling the perfect temperature to start frying. This is usually around 350°F –375°F.

3. Work in manageable batches, adding the tortilla wedges to the hot oil without overcrowding. Fry them until they are a nice golden color. This process takes about a minute or two in total. Use tongs to transfer the chips onto a plate lined with paper towels, allowing any excess oil to drain away.

4. While they are still warm, season your chips! Sprinkle sea salt for classic simplicity, or venture into more adventurous territory with a dash of chili powder or a hint of lime zest.

5. Give your finished chips a moment to cool before serving. Pair them with your favorite dip or enjoy them on their own!

Bulk Tip: Make this recipe in bulk and store them for up to a year in zip-top mylar bags with a silica packet for best results. *Note:* If fried in tallow, the shelf life of these chips is six months.

Hoagie Rolls

Perfect for sandwiches or just to enjoy on their own, these hoagie rolls can also be adapted for use as hot dog buns or hamburger buns. Simply adjust the size and bake until golden brown. Due to the size of this recipe, it works best when made in an electric mixer with a bread hook attachment. Yields 6 hoagie rolls, 8 hamburger buns, or 12 hot dog buns.

Ingredients

- 1¼ cups orange juice, heated to 105°F–115°F
- 2¼ teaspoons (9g) instant yeast
- 1 tablespoon maple syrup
- 5⅔ cups (675g) all-purpose flour
- 5 tablespoons butter, room temperature
- 1 teaspoon salt
- ¼ teaspoon powdered ginger (if using einkorn flour)
- ¼ cup butter, melted (reserved for brushing tops before baking)

Instructions

1. Heat the orange juice to 105°F–115°F while you prep the dry ingredients. If using dry active yeast, place it in the warm orange juice (off the heat) along with the maple syrup and mix well. Allow to sit for 5 minutes before adding to the dry mix.

2. Add the remaining ingredients (except the butter needed to brush on the tops before baking) to the mixing bowl of an electric mixer and add the dough hook.

3. Pour in the orange juice and mix with the dough hook on low speed for 5–10 minutes. The dough should be smooth and slightly sticky. However, it should not stick to your hands when pinched. If it's too sticky, add 2 more tablespoons of flour and mix again briefly.

4. Remove the dough hook and cover the bowl tightly. Let the dough rise in the bowl in a warm place for 30 minutes.

5. Divide dough into 6 equal pieces and shape into logs about 8 inches long. Place each piece on a parchment-lined baking tray. Repeat until all rolls are shaped. Score each 3 times evenly along the top diagonally.

6. Let the dough rise again for 60 minutes in a warm place. The dough will not double in size, but it should rise some.

7. Preheat the oven to 350°F. Brush the tops of the rolls with melted butter and bake for 35 minutes, or until the tops are golden brown and the internal temperature of the rolls is 185°F.

8. Allow the rolls to cool for at least 1 hour before slicing. This will prevent very crumbly rolls!

To Freeze: Simply allow your hoagie rolls to cool completely and then place them UNCUT in a freezer-safe bag. Freeze for up to 6 months. Thaw at room temperature for a few hours when ready to eat.

Fresh-Milled Honey Wheat Bread

Soft and slightly sweet, this is a wonderful loaf for fresh-milled grain. We love this bread with a healthy spread of butter and a bowl of the harvest vegetable soup from page 64. Yields 1 loaf.

Ingredients

- 5 cups (640g) wheat berries, ground
- 1½ teaspoons (6g) instant yeast
- 1 teaspoon salt
- ¼ teaspoon powdered ginger (if using einkorn)
- ⅓ cup oil (we use olive or avocado oil)
- ⅓ cup maple syrup (less if desired)
- 1½ cups warm water

Instructions

1. Grind the wheat berries on the finest setting your flour mill allows. Set the flour aside and gather remaining ingredients. If the flour is not very fine, you can process it in a blender for 1–3 minutes after grinding.

2. Add to the bowl of an electric mixer instant yeast, salt, powdered ginger, and your fresh ground flour. Add oil and maple syrup.

3. Heat water to 115°F and start the mixer with the dough hook attached. Slowly pour the water over the flour mixture and mix for 10 minutes on low. If the dough is very dry as it mixes, add more water, about a tablespoon at a time, until the dough is smooth and sticky.

4. Transfer the dough into a greased bowl and cover with cling wrap or a lid. Rise in a warm place for 30 minutes.

5. Turn dough into a greased 8" × 4" loaf pan and leave uncovered. Let rise for 60 minutes someplace warm. *Note:* This dough is STICKY. You will likely not be able to shape it, so just scoop the dough into the pan and gently smooth the top with wet hands.

6. Preheat oven to 325°F. Bake for 40–45 minutes, or until you get a clean toothpick test from the center of the bread. Immediately remove bread from pan after taking out of the oven and coat the top of the loaf with butter to soften the crust.

7. Cool for 30–60 minutes before slicing.

Sweet Cornbread

Not all cornbread is sweet, some are savory, but this recipe is a sweet cornbread that pairs wonderfully with the cowboy beans on page 69. Bake in a skillet, pie pan, baking dish, or even as muffins. Yields 6–9 servings.

Ingredients

2 cups yellow cornmeal

1 cup + 2 tablespoons all-purpose flour (135g)

2 teaspoons baking soda

Dash of salt

2 eggs

½ cup butter, melted

½ cup maple syrup

1½ cups milk (or buttermilk)

Instructions

1. Preheat oven to 375°F and grease an 8" × 8" baking dish.
2. In a large mixing bowl, combine all ingredients and beat well until fully combined and no lumps are present.
3. Pour mixture into baking dish and bake for 40–50 minutes, or until a clean toothpick test is achieved. If the cornbread rises too much for a toothpick to reach all the way through, use a butter knife instead.
4. If baking as muffins, bake for 22–25 minutes or until a clean toothpick test is achieved.
5. Serve with butter and honey or plain.

Note: You can use white sugar in place of the maple syrup, but you may need an extra ¼ cup of milk to get the right texture.

BREAKFAST CLASSICS

While some breakfast items such as biscuits and bagels have already been covered in the Bread and Pantry Staples section, there are a few additional classics that I want to share with you. Some are meant to be occasional treats, like cinnamon rolls (page 47), and others can be enjoyed more regularly, like the loaded cheesy eggs (page 51) or the blueberry muffins (page 46).

Thick and Creamy Yogurt

A staple breakfast item that is packed with protein and can be dressed up or down as desired, yogurt is high on the list of recipes everyone should be able to make. Use an animal milk for this recipe, as non-animal dairy requires a different process. Yields 18 cups.

Ingredients

1 gallon milk

2 cups plain yogurt

Instructions

1. Pour milk into a large saucepan and gently heat over medium heat until the milk reaches 140°F. Stir often to avoid scorching the bottom of the saucepan. Stir before testing the temperature to ensure you are getting an accurate reading.

2. Once the milk reaches the desired temperature, remove it from the heat and allow it to cool on the counter to 120°F. Stir before testing the temperature to ensure a proper reading.

3. Once your milk is between 115°F –120°F, gently add your yogurt. You do NOT want to mix this until well combined. Leaving some large chunks in the mix will allow the yogurt to really take hold and culture the milk into more yogurt.

4. Place a lid on the pan and use one of the warming methods mentioned below to maintain the temperature between 110°F –115°F for at least 8 hours, or up to 16 hours.

5. After the fermentation period, ladle your finished yogurt into jars or containers of your choice. Store in the fridge. *Note:* The yogurt will thicken as it cools.

6. This is optional, but if you want to make Greek yogurt, you can strain your yogurt with cheesecloth, coffee filters, or a dedicated yogurt strainer.

7. Once chilled, you can portion out the desired amount of yogurt and add your mix-ins such as fresh fruit, homemade granola like the one I share on page 37, and a touch of maple syrup!

WAYS TO KEEP YOGURT WARM DURING FERMENTATION

- **Yogurt maker:** You can invest in a yogurt maker with precise temperature control to maintain the ideal incubation conditions. They're usually small and don't allow for large amounts of yogurt, so keep that in mind.

- **Dehydrator:** A dehydrator will not only help you keep yogurt at a precise temperature, but it is also a tool that you can use for more than just making yogurt, such as beef jerky, dried fruits, and fruit leather. This is how we make our yogurt, and I love using my dehydrator in this way!

- **Warm towels:** Wrap your yogurt container in warm towels or blankets to insulate it and keep the temperature stable. The temperature will usually maintain for about 4–6 hours, so for a longer ferment time, this is not ideal.

- **Crockpot/Water bath method:** Fill a larger container with hot water, place your yogurt container inside, and use your crockpot as a water bath to regulate the temperature. This will limit the amount of yogurt you can make at a time, so check the capacity that your crockpot can accommodate.

FROM SCRATCH COOKING 45

Blueberry Muffins

This bakery-style blueberry muffin recipe is perfect for enjoying them fresh, or for making them in bulk to freeze. With high tops and fluffy insides, they are delicious with or without the optional crumble topping. Yields 18 muffins.

For Blueberry Muffins

- 2¾ cups (330g) all-purpose flour
- ½ tablespoon baking soda
- ½ teaspoon salt
- ½ cup butter, room temperature
- 1 cup sugar
- 2 large eggs
- 1 cup milk
- 1 tablespoon vanilla extract
- 1½ cups blueberries, fresh or frozen

Optional Crumble Topping

- ¼ cup sugar
- 1 tablespoon all-purpose flour
- 2 teaspoons butter, melted
- ⅛ teaspoon ground cinnamon

Instructions

1. Preheat oven to 425°F and add liners to a 12-cup muffin baking pan.
2. In a large bowl, combine the flour, baking soda, and salt.
3. Add the butter, sugar, and eggs, and mix until well combined. Add the milk and vanilla and whisk again until smooth.
4. Fold in the blueberries until just incorporated. Be careful not to overmix!

46   CREATING A MODERN HOMESTEAD

5. Optional: Prepare the crumble topping by mixing all the ingredients in a small bowl. Use a fork or your fingers to fully incorporate the butter into the dry ingredients.

6. Divide the batter into the 12 muffin liners, top with crumble if desired, and bake for 5 minutes at 425°F.

7. With muffins still in the oven, reduce the heat to 375°F and bake for another 15 minutes, or until golden brown and a toothpick inserted into the center of the muffin comes out clean.

To freeze: Place cooled muffins in gallon bags and freeze for up to 8 months. To reheat, place in a cold oven and set the temperature to 350°F. Heat for 20–25 minutes until the center is warm. Or you can thaw them at room temperature overnight.

Cinnamon Rolls

A classic breakfast treat, these cinnamon rolls are soft and fluffy and covered in cream cheese icing. You can make these for any special occasion or freeze them for later. Yields 15 large cinnamon rolls. The recipe can be cut in half, if desired.

Dough

9⅓ cups (1,120g) all-purpose flour

4½ teaspoons (18g) instant yeast

2 cups milk or orange juice at 115°F (we prefer orange juice)

5 tablespoons butter, room temperature

¾ cup sugar

1½ teaspoons salt

1 tablespoon vanilla extract

Filling

¾ cup butter, room temperature

1⅔ cups sugar

1 tablespoon molasses

4 tablespoons cinnamon

Icing

2½ cups powdered sugar

6 ounces cream cheese

2–4 tablespoons milk

2 teaspoons vanilla extract

Instructions

1. In a saucepan, heat the desired liquid to 115°F.

2. Add the remaining ingredients for the dough to the bowl of an electric mixer. You can knead the dough by hand if needed, but the process will be easier in an electric mixer.

FROM SCRATCH COOKING 47

3. Add the heated liquid to the mixture and knead with a dough hook on low for 10 minutes. The dough should be smooth, bounce back when pressed, and not stick to your fingers.

4. Remove the dough hook and cover the bowl with a plate or cling wrap. Allow to rise in a warm place for 25 minutes.

5. After rising, form the dough into a ball and roll it out into a long rectangle. Try to keep the dough between ¼ and ½ inch thick.

6. Combine the filling ingredients into a bowl and mix until well combined. Spread over the dough in an even layer. You can use a spatula for this step, but the back of a large spoon also works well!

7. Roll the dough from its long side if you want smaller rolls, or by its short side if you want fewer, larger rolls. Try to keep the roll as tight as you can.

8. Slice the roll into 1½-inch sections and place them into a greased 9" × 13" pan. Let rise for 90 minutes.

9. Add a little milk or cream to the pan, in all the spaces between the rolls, just enough to coat the bottom of the pan and not much more.

10. Bake at 350°F for 30–40 minutes or until golden brown with an internal temperature of 185°F. Once baked, allow to cool slightly (if you can wait!).

11. Mix powdered sugar, cream cheese, milk, and vanilla together until smooth. Drizzle over rolls and serve warm.

To freeze: You can double or triple this recipe and freeze the unbaked extras in one of two ways: first, by placing them in metal baking tins so that you can bake a whole pan directly from the freezer or, second, by placing the cut rolls on a wax paper–lined baking tray to freeze. Once frozen, you can transfer them into a freezer bag to take out and bake one at a time later. To bake from frozen, remove the desired number of rolls from the freezer and allow them to sit at room temperature for at least 30 minutes. Preheat the oven to 350°F and bake as normal.

Yeast Donuts

Skip the bakery and make your own donuts at home. Not only are homemade donuts easier than you may think but making them yourself allows you to control the type of oil and sweetener used in the recipe. Yields 12–15 donuts, depending on thickness.

Donut Ingredients

1 egg

3½ cups (415g) all-purpose flour

2 tablespoons maple syrup

1 teaspoon salt

2¼ teaspoons (9g) rapid rise yeast

2 tablespoons butter

1 cup milk

Oil for frying (we use coconut oil)

Chocolate Glaze

½ cup powdered sugar

2 tablespoons cocoa or cacao powder

1 teaspoon vanilla extract

2 tablespoons milk

Plain Glaze

½ cup powdered sugar

1 teaspoon vanilla extract

1 tablespoon milk

Instructions

1. Combine all dough ingredients except the milk and butter into the bowl of an electric mixer.

2. In a small saucepan, melt the butter and remove from heat. Stir in the milk and pour into the mixing bowl.

3. Mix with a bread hook until dough is smooth and shiny. If dough is still sticky, add an additional ¼ cup of flour at a time until it is pliable but doesn't stick to your fingers when pressed.

4. Remove the dough hook and cover the mixing bowl with cling wrap and a towel. Let rise for 20 minutes for einkorn, or until dough is doubled if using non-einkorn flour.

5. Turn out the risen dough on a well-floured surface and roll to about ¾-inch thick. Use a donut cutter to form the donuts.

6. Place cut donuts and holes on a wax paper–lined baking tray.

7. Continue to reroll and cut dough until all is used.

8. Heat oil in a large skillet to 350°F or over medium heat. The oil should be about ½-inch deep.

FROM SCRATCH COOKING 49

9. Test the heat with an initial donut hole. If it starts to cook right away, the oil is ready; if there is a delay, leave the donut hole until the oil starts to bubble on the surface of the dough, then add additional donuts.

10. Cook on one side until it starts to brown, then flip and cook another 1–2 minutes, or until brown.

11. Remove from oil and drain on a paper towel–lined baking tray.

12. Repeat until all donuts are fried. Mix glazes individually and whisk until smooth. Double individual glaze recipe if only using one flavor.

13. Dip the tops of hot donuts into desired glaze and place on a platter. Serve warm.

Loaded Cheesy Eggs

This is one of my favorite breakfast recipes and we make it multiple times a week since we have so many fresh eggs coming in from our hens. Loaded with bacon and cheese, this dish is sure to be a favorite in your family too. Yields 4–6 servings.

Ingredients

1 tablespoon butter

8 eggs

4 ounces shredded cheddar cheese

8 strips bacon, cooked and chopped

Salt and pepper to taste

Instructions

1. Add butter to skillet and melt over medium heat.

2. Crack eggs into a large mixing bowl and whisk. Pour eggs into the hot pan.

3. Add bacon, cheese, and salt and pepper to the top of the eggs and let sit for 2–3 minutes before folding the eggs in half on themselves, like an omelet.

4. Let cook for another 2–3 minutes, then stir and break up with a spoon or spatula.

5. Continue cooking until eggs are at desired consistency. Serve immediately on their own or inside a flour tortilla.

Bulk tip: Make a batch of flour tortillas from page 28 and a batch of these eggs to create 16 breakfast burritos. Wrap in foil and place in a freezer bag for up to 6 months. To reheat, place in the fridge the night before and then heat in a 450°F oven for 20 minutes, or until the center is warm.

Crispy Breakfast Potatoes

These perfectly seasoned breakfast potatoes pair well with the loaded cheesy eggs on page 51 and make an excellent addition to any breakfast or brunch. Be prepared for these to disappear as fast as you can make them! Yields 4–6 servings.

Ingredients

1½ pounds russet potatoes, peeled and quartered

2 tablespoons butter

2 tablespoons olive oil

Salt and pepper to taste

Pinch of cayenne pepper

½ teaspoon garlic powder

½ teaspoon onion powder

¼ teaspoon smoked paprika

Fresh rosemary, thyme, 1 garlic clove (all optional)

Instructions

1. Bring a pot of salted water to a boil, then add the potatoes. Cook for about 10 minutes or until they are just tender but still firm. Drain the potatoes and cool to room temperature. Once cooled, dice them into ½-inch pieces.

2. In a large skillet (12 inches or larger), over medium-high heat, add the butter and olive oil. If you're using fresh herbs, add the rosemary, thyme, and one smashed garlic clove. Let them sizzle for a minute to infuse the oil, then remove and discard the herbs and garlic.

3. Add the diced potatoes in a single layer to the skillet. Season them generously with salt, pepper, cayenne, garlic powder, onion powder, and smoked paprika. Toss to coat the potatoes evenly with the seasoning.

4. Cook the potatoes for 8–10 minutes, flipping and tossing them every 2–3 minutes so they brown evenly on all sides. Adjust the seasoning to taste.

5. Once the potatoes are golden and crispy, remove them from the skillet and serve immediately.

Waffles and Pancakes

This batter can be used for both fluffy and slightly sweet waffles and pancakes, with only a bit more milk used for waffles. It can be made in bulk and frozen, or just enjoyed fresh! Yields 6–8 waffles/pancakes, depending on the size.

Ingredients

- 1¼ cups (150g) flour
- 1 cup milk (¾ cup for pancakes)
- 1 egg
- 2 tablespoons butter
- 2 tablespoons sugar
- 1 teaspoon baking soda
- Pinch of salt
- 1 teaspoon vanilla extract

Instructions

1. While prepping the batter, start heating your waffle iron or skillet over medium heat.

2. In a medium-sized bowl or mixer, combine all ingredients and mix until the batter is smooth and lump-free.

3. **For waffles:** Use a measuring cup to fill your hot waffle iron according to its instructions and bake until it indicates that they're done. Remove the baked waffle from the waffle iron. Repeat until all the batter is used.

4. **For pancakes:** Melt butter in the skillet and when it's sizzling, use a ⅓ measuring cup to portion 2–3 pancakes at a time. Cook until large bubbles appear on top of the pancakes and then flip them. Cook for another 1–2 minutes before removing from the pan. Repeat until all the batter is used.

5. Eat right away with your toppings of choice.

To freeze: Stack finished waffles/pancakes in piles of 6 and allow them to cool completely before storing. Place them into your freezer (trying not to squish them!) and let them fully freeze. To reheat, place the desired number directly on the rack in a cold oven. Turn the oven to 375°F AFTER adding pancakes/waffles and allow the oven to reach temperature. Once the preheat is complete, remove the goodies and enjoy! *Note:* Heat times can vary by oven, so you may have to remove them early or leave them in longer.

Easy Quiche Base

Use this recipe to create a classic quiche and customize it to your liking with optional mix-ins. You can also use this recipe for mini quiches instead. Either way, this recipe is delicious, fresh or frozen! Yields 8 servings.

Ingredients

1 unbaked pie crust (see the flaky pie crust recipe on page 80)

4 large eggs

½ cup whole milk

½ cup heavy cream or heavy whipping cream

¼ teaspoon each salt and pepper

1 cup shredded or crumbled cheese

Up to 2 cups additional mix-ins, such as bacon, chives, spinach, ham, or cooked potatoes

Instructions

1. Prepare pie crust: If you are making your pie crust fresh, make that first and roll it into the desired size (standard pie dish or mini pies), fill your pans, and place them in the

54 CREATING A MODERN HOMESTEAD

freezer for about 15 minutes. If using a premade pie crust, follow the instructions on the box to prebake.

2. Preheat the oven to 375°F. For full-size pies, place parchment paper over the bottom of the crust and fill with pie weights, then bake for 15 minutes. Mini pie crusts can be baked without weights for 10–15 minutes.

3. Carefully remove the weights and parchment (if applicable) and, with a fork, prick the bottom of the pie.

4. Bake for another 7–10 minutes, or until the bottom starts to brown.

5. Reduce the oven temperature to 350°F and begin preparing the filling.

6. By hand or with an electric mixer, mix all filling ingredients, except any additional mix-ins, until well combined.

7. Fold in the optional mix-ins and pour the filling into the pie shell(s). Cover full-size crust edges with foil or a pie shield to prevent burning. Mini pies can be baked without a shield, since their baking time is not as long.

8. Bake until the center is set, about 45–55 minutes for full-size quiches and about 25–30 minutes for mini quiches.

9. Allow to cool for at least 15 minutes or serve fully cooled. Top with any desired garnishes and enjoy!

Bulk tip: No matter the size of the quiches, this recipe can be made in bulk and frozen for future enjoyment. After baking and cooling the quiches, place them in a single layer on a baking sheet and freeze until firm. Then transfer them to a freezer-safe container or bag. They can be stored in the freezer for up to 6 months. To reheat, simply bake them in a preheated oven at 350°F until heated through, about 20 minutes for mini quiches and 30–35 minutes for full-size quiches. The heating time required may vary depending on how many are being heated at a time. Aim for an internal temperature of 165°F.

I like to make mini quiches in bulk and freeze them for a quick and protein-packed breakfast option.

FROM SCRATCH COOKING 55

CLASSIC SIDES

From simple roasted vegetables to homemade baked beans and everything in between, these are classic side dishes your whole family will love. I've tried to focus on recipes with vegetables that you might be growing in your garden or buying from your local farmer's market so that you can easily enjoy seasonal bounties.

Roasted Vegetables

Oven roasting is such an easy and delicious way to enjoy your vegetables. No matter what vegetables you have on hand, the process is the same and will yield crispy edges and perfectly seasoned bites every time. Yields 6–8 servings.

Ingredients

- 2–3 pounds fresh vegetables
- 3 tablespoons butter, melted
- 1 teaspoon salt
- ½ teaspoon garlic powder
- ½ teaspoon black pepper

Instructions

1. Preheat the oven to 400°F and grease a half-sheet metal baking pan.
2. Chop the vegetables into bite-sized chunks, as needed. Vegetables like broccoli florets and asparagus can be left whole.
3. Mix butter and spices in a small bowl and set aside.
4. Into a large bowl, add the vegetables and then pour the seasoned butter over the top. Mix well to coat.
5. Evenly spread the seasoned vegetables over the prepared baking tray and bake for 15 minutes. Toss the vegetables on the tray and rotate the tray a half turn.
6. Bake for another 20 minutes, or until the vegetables turn brown and crispy at their edges and are tender inside (the final cooking time may vary based on your oven).
7. Serve immediately and enjoy!

Carrot Raisin Salad

This is one of my all-time favorite side dishes; I could eat it every day. Growing up, I always felt so guilty eating it because I thought it was full of sugar and mayo. But the reality is just the opposite. Now I have no guilt about enjoying our fresh carrots this way as often as I can! Yields 8–10 servings.

Ingredients

1 pound (4 cups) carrots, peeled and shredded

½ cup raisins

½ cup pineapple chunks (optional)

¼ cup mayo (use homemade, if possible)

1 tablespoon lemon juice

1 tablespoon maple syrup

Dash of salt

Instructions

Note: You can use a box grater or a food processor with a grating attachment for quick and consistent results when shredding the carrots.

1. In a mixing bowl, whisk together mayonnaise, maple syrup, lemon juice, and salt until you have a smooth, creamy dressing.

2. Add the grated carrots and raisins to the dressing. Gently mix them in until they are well coated.

3. Cover the salad bowl and chill in the refrigerator for at least an hour. This resting time allows the flavors to meld and the salad to achieve its full potential.

4. When you're ready to serve, give the salad a final toss and enjoy!

Note: If you can make this salad at least a day in advance, the flavors will have time to combine more, creating an even better salad.

Fried Okra

A classic Southern dish, this recipe is perfect for making fresh or for prepping in bulk to freeze for frying later. It's best when served with mashed potatoes; you can find my recipe on page 59. Yields 4 servings.

Ingredients

2 pounds fresh okra

1 egg, beaten

2 cups (120g) flour (cornmeal can also be used)

Salt and pepper to taste

4 cups oil for frying (we use coconut oil)

Instructions

1. Cut the okra into rounds and discard the tops. Place okra in a medium bowl.
2. Pour egg over the okra. Mix well, until all pieces are coated in egg.
3. Add flour to a medium bowl and place 2 handfuls of coated okra at a time into the flour. Mix well to coat each piece completely in flour.
4. Heat oil in a heavy bottom pan to 350°F. Remove okra from flour bowl and carefully drop one piece at a time into hot oil, frying about 1 cup total of battered okra per batch. Fry until golden brown.
5. Remove the fried okra with a slotted spoon and place on a paper towel–lined plate or tray. Season with salt and pepper to taste.

To freeze: After breading and before frying, place the okra on a wax paper–lined baking sheet. Place the tray in the freezer for at least 4 hours. Once the okra is frozen, you may need to break up large clumps before transferring it to gallon freezer bags. Freeze until ready to fry. Place frozen okra directly into hot oil and fry until golden brown. Season to taste and enjoy!

Mashed Potatoes

This mashed potato recipe uses the whole potato, including the skin. Since the skin contains many nutrients, we opt to leave it in our mashed potatoes. However, you can peel the potatoes completely before boiling, if you prefer. Yields 6–8 servings.

Ingredients

- 3 pounds potatoes
- ½ cup butter
- 1¼ cups whole milk
- Salt and pepper to taste

Instructions

1. Wash and peel the potatoes (optional) and boil until soft.
2. While still hot, place potatoes into the mixing bowl of an electric mixer with a paddle attachment in place. You can also mash by hand or with a handheld mixer, as needed.
3. Run mixer on low for 30 seconds to break up the potatoes; there will still be many chunks.
4. Slice the butter into chunks and add it to the mixer bowl. Resume mixing on low.
5. Slowly add the milk and continue mixing until the desired texture is reached. Add salt and pepper to taste and mix well to combine.
6. Serve right away and enjoy!

While mashed potatoes can be made by hand, using an electric mixer allows bulk batches to be mixed with ease.

Coleslaw

Just like the carrot raisin salad I share on page 57, coleslaw is often regarded as an "unhealthy" side dish. In reality, it can be a delicious way to enjoy a few fall and winter vegetables! Use the recipe on page 17 to make your own mayo to really increase the quality of this dish. Yields 8–10 servings.

Ingredients

3 cups finely shredded green cabbage

2 cups finely shredded purple cabbage

1 cup finely shredded carrots

Dressing

½ cup mayonnaise

1 tablespoon white vinegar

2 teaspoons sugar

½ teaspoon celery seed

Salt and pepper to taste

Instructions

Combine all dressing ingredients in a large bowl. Toss with cabbage and carrots. Refrigerate for at least 1 hour before serving to allow flavors to blend.

Macaroni and Cheese

This recipe for creamy macaroni and cheese sneaks in two eggs for some extra protein and does not require baking. You can use any shape pasta you want. Your family will ask for this over and over again! Yields 6–8 servings.

Ingredients

- 12 ounces elbow macaroni (or pasta shape of your choice), dry
- Salt for pasta cooking water, a pinch
- ¾ cup milk
- 2 large eggs
- 6 ounces cheddar cheese, grated
- 6 ounces Colby-Jack cheese, grated
- ¾ teaspoon sea salt, or to taste
- ⅓ cup sour cream (optional)

Instructions

1. Bring a large pot of water to a rolling boil. Add salt once the water is boiling, then add the pasta and cook until it's al dente (time may vary based on shape). Reserve ¾ cup of the pasta cooking water, then drain remaining water and set pasta aside in the pot.

2. In a medium saucepan, combine milk, eggs, cheeses and ¾ teaspoon salt. Place saucepan over medium-low heat and cook 6–8 minutes, whisking constantly until completely smooth and thickened. As soon as the sauce starts to thicken, remove it from the heat. Do not overcook or boil, or it may curdle!

3. Off the heat, whisk in sour cream then stir in drained pasta. Season with salt to taste. If the sauce gets too thick, you can thin it out with some of your reserved pasta water.

Maple Baked Beans

Every year on Independence Day, my dad makes his famous maple baked beans. They are so delicious that the batch disappears in minutes and then we start the countdown until we get to enjoy them again. You can use canned beans or cook dry beans the day before making this recipe. Either way, this recipe is a must-have for us every year! Yields 6–8 servings.

Ingredients

- 6 cups navy beans, cooked and drained
- 1 red bell pepper, deseeded and diced
- 1 yellow onion, diced
- ½ cup salt pork or bacon, diced
- 1 cup brown sugar
- 1 cup maple syrup
- ½ tablespoon Worcestershire sauce
- 2 tablespoons yellow mustard
- ½ cup ketchup

Instructions

Add all ingredients to a medium saucepan and stir well. Over medium heat, cook the beans until the sauce reduces and thickens. Add more sugar or mustard to taste. Remove from heat and allow to set for at least 15 minutes before serving.

Maple baked beans ingredients ready to be mixed and heated.

French Fries

While you can (and I often do) just cut potatoes into fry strips and cook them in hot oil, this recipe makes the best golden-brown and crispy french fries you've ever had! You can also freeze them after resting and before the second frying for easy homemade freezer fries. Yields 4 servings.

Ingredients

2 pounds starchy potatoes, such as russet, goldrush, or long white varieties

2 tablespoons white vinegar

Tallow (or oil of your choosing)

Salt to taste

Instructions

1. Peel and cut potatoes into ¼-inch-thick fries, making sure they're evenly sized for consistent cooking. Place the cut fries into a bowl of water while you cut the rest.

2. Rinse the fries in cold water for about 15–20 seconds to remove excess starch.

3. In a pot, bring water to a simmer and add vinegar. Add the fries to the water and simmer for 10 minutes, then drain them by lifting with a slotted spoon. (Dumping them into a colander will break the potatoes.)

4. Allow the fries to rest on clean tea towels for 5 minutes. The steam will dry them if they are left alone.

5. Heat oil to 400°F and fry the potatoes for 50 seconds in 3 separate batches. Remove them from the oil and let them drain in a single layer on paper towel–lined trays.

6. Allow the fries to cool for about 30 minutes before frying again.

7. Reheat the oil to 400°F and fry the potatoes a second time, again working in 3 batches, until golden and crispy, about 4 minutes per batch.

8. Drain the fries onto a paper towel–lined tray and season with salt or your favorite seasoning.

Bulk tip: After step 6, once the fries have drained from their first dip in the hot oil, lay them in a single layer on a wax paper–lined baking tray and freeze until solid. Once they are fully frozen, remove them from the tray and store them in freezer bags. Fry directly from frozen until golden brown or bake if desired.

SOUPS AND MAIN DISHES

Even if you don't have space for a garden or livestock, you can still nourish your family with wholesome, homemade main courses made from scratch. Whether you're simmering a pot of soup on the stove or creating a satisfying main dish from pantry staples, these simple, delicious recipes will bring warmth and comfort to your table.

Harvest Vegetable Soup

Originally, this recipe was born out of a need to use all the vegetables from our garden, and it's turned into a beloved recipe that we make as often as we are able. We even plan our garden around its ingredients to make sure we have enough on hand to enjoy this soup all fall and winter. Yields 8–10 servings.

Ingredients

3 pounds potatoes (or 1 quart canned potatoes)

2 pounds carrots (or 1 quart canned carrots)

2 pounds green beans (or 1 quart canned green beans)

2 cups canned corn (or more, if desired)

½ head green cabbage

1 cup tomato paste or 2 cups tomato sauce

2 cups water or broth of choice (more as needed)

1 tablespoon salt

1 tablespoon garlic powder

½ teaspoon black pepper

Instructions

1. Wash, peel, and chop all vegetables if fresh produce is used.

2. Pour the tomato sauce or paste into a large pot. If using paste, add 1 cup of water and whisk until smooth.

3. Pour or place all remaining ingredients into the pot. If you're using canned vegetables, pour the liquid into the pot as well, so that all the vegetable nutrients are retained.

4. Once all the vegetables are in the pot, add enough water or broth to cover the vegetables.

5. Over medium heat, cook the soup until the root vegetables are soft. Add more liquid as needed to maintain a soup consistency as the vegetables cook down. Remove from the heat and serve.

Note: If the vegetables are home-canned with added salt, reduce the salt to half and season to taste.

Roasted Chicken

While these are so easy to grab at the grocery store, being able to roast a chicken at home is very simple and will allow you to increase the quality of food your family is consuming. Grab a whole chicken from your local farmer's market or raise them yourself for a delicious comfort meal any time. You can also remove the meat after roasting the whole chicken to use in chicken salad, like the one I share on page 74, or add it to the vegetable soup on page 64 for an even heartier soup. Yields 1–3 pounds of meat.

Ingredients

1 whole chicken (3–5 pounds)

3 tablespoons butter, room temperature

Salt, pepper, and garlic powder

Instructions

Preheat the oven to 500°F. Place the whole chicken, breast side up, onto a skillet or roasting tray. Rub the butter evenly across the top of the chicken and generously season with the spices. Bake for 15 minutes and reduce the oven temperature to 350°F. Continue baking until the internal temperature at the thickest part of the chicken is 165°F. Remove from the oven and baste with the juices if desired. Allow to rest for 5–10 minutes before carving.

Classic Meatloaf

A family favorite, this meatloaf with a delicious ketchup glaze is a comfort meal that is on constant rotation. It's typically served alongside mashed potatoes and a green vegetable but is versatile enough to go with any side you prefer. It's also perfect for making in bulk to freeze for an easy meal any time. Yields 4–6 servings.

Meatloaf Ingredients

2 pounds ground beef

1 cup diced onion

2 large eggs

1½ teaspoons garlic powder

3 tablespoons ketchup

¾ cup breadcrumbs (optional)

1½ teaspoons salt

¼ teaspoon black pepper

½ teaspoon paprika

Glaze Ingredients

¾ cup ketchup

1½ teaspoons white vinegar

2½ tablespoons maple syrup

1 teaspoon garlic powder

¼ teaspoon black pepper

¼ teaspoon salt

Instructions

1. Grease an 8" × 4" or 9" × 5" loaf pan and preheat the oven to 375°F.
2. In a large bowl, add all of the ingredients and mix until well combined.
3. Add the meatloaf mixture to the loaf pan and press down firmly to compress. Even out the top and bake uncovered for 40 minutes.
4. In a small bowl, mix all of the ingredients together for the sauce. Once the meatloaf has baked for 40 minutes, remove it from the oven and spread the sauce evenly over the top.
5. Return the meatloaf to the oven and bake an additional 15–20 minutes. Rest meatloaf 10–15 minutes before slicing.

Bulk tip: Double or triple this recipe and bake it in 9" × 13" pans instead. Cool after glazing and baking, slice the meatloaf into the desired portion sizes, and place on a wax paper–lined baking sheet. Freeze until solid and then transfer into freezer bags. To reheat, place the frozen meatloaf on a baking tray and place in a 375°F preheated oven until the center is warm. Cover with foil prior to reheating, if desired, but this is optional.

Mix-ins such as black beans and shredded carrots can be added to this meatloaf recipe to stretch the meal further. Use no more than 1 cup of mix-ins per pound of ground beef for best results.

Chicken Fried Steak

Another Southern classic, this chicken fried steak recipe is perfect for Sunday dinner, or any special occasion! Serve with the classic white gravy recipe from page 22 and a side of mashed potatoes (page 59) and fried okra (page 58) for the best country meal. Yields 4 servings.

Ingredients

4 cube steaks (about ⅓ pound each)

2 teaspoons ground black pepper, divided

2 teaspoons salt or sea salt, divided

1½ cups buttermilk

2 eggs

2 teaspoons hot sauce (optional)

1½ cups all-purpose flour

½ teaspoon garlic powder

½ teaspoon onion powder

½ teaspoon smoked paprika

½ teaspoon baking soda

½ teaspoon baking powder

1 cup tallow for frying (or oil of your choice)

Instructions

1. Pat the cube steaks dry with paper towels and season with 1 teaspoon each of salt and pepper.

2. In a large bowl, whisk together buttermilk, eggs, and hot sauce (optional). In a second bowl, whisk together flour, remaining salt and pepper, garlic powder, onion powder, paprika, baking soda, and baking powder.

3. Dredge the cube steaks in the flour mixture, shaking off excess, then dredge in the buttermilk-egg mixture, letting excess drip off, and then once again in the flour mixture, shaking off excess. Let the coated steaks rest for 10 minutes to make sure that the breading adheres during the frying process.

4. Add ¼ inch of oil to a cast iron skillet or frying pan and heat over medium-high heat to 320°F–340°F. Preheat oven to 225°F.

5. Once oil is hot and ready, fry each steak for about 3–4 minutes per side, or until golden brown. Fry just two steaks at a time so as not to overcrowd the pan, or the breading will fall off. Drain on paper towels, then place the steaks on parchment-covered baking sheets and put them in the oven while you make the gravy.

Cowboy Beans

Also called border beans, this recipe was a staple in my house growing up. It's simple, filling, and perfect when paired with a big skillet of sweet cornbread! This recipe makes a very large batch, so plan to enjoy it for a few meals, or freeze some of it for later. Yields 8–10 servings.

Ingredients

2 pounds pinto beans, dried

1 pound salt pork or bacon

2 heads garlic, diced finely

4–10 chilis of your choosing

Salt to taste

Instructions

1. Sort beans to remove rocks and broken beans. Rinse twice and drain.

2. Add beans to a large pot and cover with at least 2 inches of water above the level of the beans.

3. Over medium heat, bring to a simmer and reduce to low.

4. Simmer for 1 hour and then add the whole salt pork to the pot.

5. Simmer another hour and add the diced garlic.

6. Simmer for 1 more hour and add the chilis. Add salt to taste at this point as well.

7. Simmer for another 1–6 hours, until the desired texture is reached.

8. Throughout the process, add more water as needed to keep the beans barely covered. If you do add more water, it must be boiling water so as not to disrupt the cooking process. Stir frequently to keep the beans from scorching as the simmering continues.

Sloppy Joe Sandwiches

When it comes to classic comfort food, there's nothing like a good sloppy joe recipe. Instead of using canned sauce, this recipe uses whole foods like ground beef, onions, peppers, brown sugar, ketchup, and mustard! Ready in 30 minutes, this recipe will be a new family favorite. Yields 6–8 servings.

Ingredients

- 1 small onion, finely diced
- ½ small bell pepper, any color, seeded and finely diced
- 1 tablespoon butter
- 1 pound lean ground beef
- ½ teaspoon salt, or to taste
- ¼ teaspoon black pepper, or to taste
- 1 tablespoon garlic powder
- 1½ teaspoons yellow mustard
- 1 tablespoon brown sugar
- 2 cups ketchup
- ⅓ cup water
- 8 hamburger buns

Instructions

1. In a skillet, heat butter over medium-high heat. Add the onions and peppers and cook until soft and tender. Remove them from the skillet. If you have picky eaters, you can blend the sautéed onions and peppers into a smooth sauce by adding them with all the sauce ingredients to a blender while the meat is browning.
2. Add the ground beef to the skillet and break it up into smaller pieces as it cooks. Season with salt, pepper, and garlic powder.
3. Pour in the remaining ingredients and add the onions and peppers back in. Cook over medium-high heat until the sauce comes to a simmer.
4. Reduce the heat to low and simmer for 10 minutes, add more salt and pepper if needed.
5. Spoon the finished sloppy joe mix onto buns and serve right away!

Classic Lasagna

This easy, homemade lasagna recipe is loaded with savory meat, gooey cheese, and bursts of flavor in every mouthful. Better than any restaurant lasagna, and less expensive too. Make this for a crowd or freeze it in portions for a quick and hearty meal any time. Yields 9 servings.

Ingredients

Meat Layer

1 tablespoon olive oil

2 pounds ground beef

1 medium onion, finely diced

2 large garlic cloves, minced (or 1 teaspoon garlic powder)

3 cups marinara sauce

½ teaspoon sea salt

¼ teaspoon black pepper

Pasta

9 lasagna sheets cooked al dente and ready to use (or homemade, fresh lasagna sheets)

Cheese Layer

2 cups ricotta cheese

2 large eggs

2 tablespoons fresh parsley finely chopped, plus more to garnish

¼ teaspoon salt

6 cups mozzarella cheese shredded, divided

Instructions

1. Heat olive oil in a pan and sauté the ground beef and diced onion until beef is no longer pink. Mix in minced garlic and sauté until fragrant.

2. Pour in marinara sauce, season with salt and pepper, and bring to a simmer. Cover and simmer for 5 minutes.

3. In a bowl or blender, combine ricotta cheese, eggs, parsley, and salt until smooth.

4. Preheat the oven to 375°F.

5. Spread ½ cup meat sauce in a deep 9" × 13" casserole dish.

6. Add a layer of lasagna noodles over the sauce. Make sure that the entire pan is covered (about 3 sheets).

7. Spread ⅓ of the remaining meat sauce, sprinkle 2 cups mozzarella, and top with half of the cheese sauce.

8. Repeat the noodle, cheese, and meat layers for three total layer sets. (Your third and final layer will only have the shredded mozzarella on top.)
9. Cover with foil and bake for 45 minutes.
10. Remove foil and bake for another 3–5 minutes until golden.
11. Let the lasagna rest for 30 minutes before slicing.
12. Garnish with parsley and serve this delicious, homemade lasagna!

Bulk tip: If you'd like to freeze some of this lasagna for later, you can do so easily! Once the lasagna is baked and cooled, slice it into portions, wrap each portion tightly in plastic wrap and foil, and store in the freezer for up to 3 months. When ready to enjoy, thaw in the refrigerator overnight and reheat in the oven.

Potato Soup

Thick and creamy, I have been perfecting this loaded baked potato soup for the last twenty-four years and it is perfect on a chilly day. Fresh-cooked or canned potatoes will both work perfectly in this recipe. Yields 10–12 servings.

Ingredients

- 1 cup butter
- 1 cup (120g) all-purpose flour
- 1 gallon milk of your choice
- 3 pounds cooked potatoes (or 2 quarts of canned potatoes)
- ½ pound of cooked, chopped bacon
- 16 ounces grated cheddar cheese
- Salt and black pepper to taste
- ½ cup chopped green onions (optional)
- 1 cup sour cream (optional)

Instructions

1. Over medium-low heat, melt butter in a large soup pot. Reduce heat to low and add flour to make a roux. Whisk roux until smooth.
2. Add milk 2 cups at a time, mixing thoroughly after each addition until the roux is very smooth.
3. Allow to cook over low heat for 15–30 minutes, or until it starts to thicken. Stir occasionally to prevent burning.
4. Add remaining ingredients and cook for an additional 15 minutes, or until thickened to your desired texture. Stir frequently and keep the heat on low to avoid burning.

Note: This soup is even better the next day, as the flavors will have more time to blend. If the soup becomes too thick, simply thin with more milk to restore the desired texture.

FROM SCRATCH COOKING

Chicken Salad

Whether you are using canned, grilled, oven-baked, or even the meat from a roasted whole chicken, this chicken salad turns out perfectly every time. Packed with crunchy, sweet pickles and apples, and balanced with garlic and green onions, it's even better when paired with fresh bread. Yields 8–10 servings.

Ingredients

- 4 cups cooked chicken, shredded (We use grilled chicken breasts seasoned with salt, pepper, and garlic.)
- 1½ cups mayonnaise
- 1 red apple, washed and diced into small pieces
- ½ cup diced sweet gherkin pickles
- ¼ cup chopped green onions
- ½ teaspoon salt
- 1 teaspoon garlic powder
- 1 teaspoon black pepper

Instructions

Shred chicken while warm or use a mixer with paddle attachment to quickly shred the chicken to the desired texture. Combine all ingredients in a large mixing bowl and mix until well combined. Add additional mayo or spices as needed, for your personal tastes. Serve on fresh bread or a bed of lettuce.

Note: This chicken salad is even better the next day, so make it a day in advance, if possible, to allow for the best experience.

Spinach Ravioli

Amazing as a fresh pasta dish, but also wonderful to make in bulk and freeze, this spinach and mozzarella ravioli is on heavy rotation in our home. Serve with butter or plain with a sprinkle of Parmigiano Reggiano cheese. Yields 9–12 servings.

Ingredients

Pasta

3⅓ cups (400g) all-purpose flour

2 cups warm water, 90°F

Filling

12 ounces shredded mozzarella

1 cup frozen chopped spinach, thawed

1 egg

1 teaspoon nutmeg

6 cloves garlic, minced

½ teaspoon ground black pepper

1 teaspoon salt

Instructions

1. Combine pasta ingredients and knead until smooth. Rest under a towel for 20 minutes.

2. While the dough rests, mix the filling ingredients until well combined and set aside.

3. Roll dough by hand or in a pasta press into very thin sheets, making sure to roll out an even number of similar sized sheets. Lay rolled sheets on a well-floured surface.

4. Add filling to a piping bag or use a teaspoon to dollop the filling onto half the rolled sheets, space the dollops about 2" apart.

5. Place the remaining pasta sheets over the sheet with the cheese filling and press between the dollops to seal around the filling. Use a pizza cutter or knife to cut the pieces apart.

6. Bring a large pot of water to a boil. Add ravioli. Reduce heat to a gentle simmer; cook until ravioli float to the top and are tender, about 3 minutes.

7. Serve with browned butter or plain with grated cheese.

Bulk tip: To freeze these for later, place the finished and uncooked ravioli in a single layer on a wax paper–lined baking tray and freeze flat until solid. Remove from tray and place in a freezer bag. Boil from frozen for 1–2 minutes longer than fresh, or until they are tender.

Perfect Pot Roast

There are some recipes that are just soul-satisfying, and a fall-off-the-fork-tender pot roast is one of them. Fresh or home-canned vegetables can be used interchangeably or in combination with wonderful results. Yields 6–8 servings.

Ingredients

2 tablespoons butter

2–5 pounds chuck roast

4 cups broth of choice or water

3 pounds potatoes (~8 cups), peeled and cut into chunks

2 pounds (~4 cups) carrots (or any root vegetables you want), peeled and cut into chunks

2 large yellow onions, cut into chunks

Salt, black pepper, and garlic powder to taste

Instructions

1. In a skillet, melt butter over medium heat. Sear all sides of the roast, seasoning with salt, pepper, and garlic powder generously as you turn the roast. Remove from heat.

2. Add chunked potatoes and carrots to a large roasting pan, along with any other root vegetables you like to add. Place the roast on top so the root vegetables are under and surrounding the roast on top of the root vegetables. This keeps the more delicate vegetables from getting soggy.

3. Add the onions and any non-root vegetables you want to include around the roast. Season with salt, pepper, and garlic powder.

4. Pour broth over the roast and vegetables and cover with a lid or foil.

5. Bake in a 350°F oven for 4 hours.

6. Check meat for tenderness; if it needs more time, cook for an additional 1–2 hours.

Easy Homemade Pizza

Having a few pizzas in the freezer at the ready-to-bake stage has saved us on busy nights quite a few times. Though we often make them to enjoy fresh, we also like to double the batch and freeze the extras. This recipe makes two 14" pizzas that can be topped with whatever toppings you prefer.

Ingredients

1 teaspoon sea salt

1½ teaspoons (6g) yeast

4¼ cups (500g) all-purpose flour

1 cup warm water, 105°F–115°F

Toppings

1 cup pizza sauce

8 ounces shredded cheese

Additional toppings, as desired

Instructions

1. Combine salt, yeast, and flour in the bowl of a mixer. Mix on low with a dough hook, adding warm water slowly until a smooth ball forms. If the dough is too sticky, add more flour a few tablespoons at a time. If it's too dry, add water 1 tablespoon at a time.

2. Cover the mixing bowl and allow the dough to rise for 30 minutes in a warm place.

3. Remove the dough from the bowl and divide into two equal balls.

4. On a lightly floured piece of parchment paper large enough to cover your baking tray, roll the dough with a rolling pin until it is the size of your pizza pan or ¼" thick, whichever comes first.

5. Pull the parchment paper with the rolled dough onto the baking tray and allow to rise for 20 minutes.

6. Preheat the oven to 450°F and assemble your pizza, beginning with the sauce. Use a spoon to spread sauce, then add cheese and other desired toppings.

7. Bake for 16–19 minutes, or until the cheese is starting to brown.

8. Rub crust edges with melted butter (optional).

To freeze: Place the prepared but unbaked pizzas on a large piece of plastic wrap and bring the edges up and over the top of the pizza. Add another piece of plastic wrap if needed to ensure the whole pizza is covered. Repeat the process with foil and freeze in a single layer. Stack pizzas once they are well frozen. To bake from frozen, remove pizza from freezer and remove all wrappings. Place pizza on a pizza tray and bake in a 425°F oven for 18–22 minutes, depending on how crispy you like the crust.

Melt-in-Your-Mouth Meatballs

This recipe for classic meatballs is naturally gluten free and can be made with beef, pork, or Italian sausage. We like to make these in bulk and freeze them to serve with einkorn pasta on cold nights. Yields 16 medium meatballs.

Ingredients

1 pound ground beef or meat of choice

¼ cup diced white onion

1 egg

1 tablespoon Italian seasoning

1 teaspoon salt

1 teaspoon garlic powder

½ teaspoon black pepper

2 tablespoons butter or oil of choice

2 cups pasta sauce

Instructions

1. Gently combine all ingredients, except sauce and butter, in a medium bowl. I like to use my hands for best mixing, but you can use a spoon instead if you want! Just don't overmix.

2. Form the meatballs by rolling sections of the mixture until smooth and round. I like to make 16 medium-sized meatballs with this recipe. However, you can also make 10 or 12 depending on the size you want the finished meatballs to be.

3. In a hot skillet with a little butter or oil of your choice, brown the meatballs on all sides.

4. Remove the meatballs from the skillet and place them in an oven-safe dish. Pour your favorite pasta sauce over the top, cover, and bake at 350°F for about 30 minutes.

5. At this point, your meatballs are ready! You can serve them right away or freeze them for later.

Bulk tip: If you're going to freeze the meatballs, line a baking tray with wax paper and place them in a single layer on the tray. Freeze fully and then place in a freezer bag for later. When you're ready to enjoy these meatballs again, place your desired number in a skillet with some butter or oil and heat until warm. You can also heat them in the microwave for a few minutes, or in the oven in a dish of sauce for about 20–25 minutes. Heating time will vary, so check for an internal temperature of about 165°F.

FROM SCRATCH COOKING

SWEET TREATS

There's nothing like a sweet treat to finish off a delicious meal. These desserts are special enough for a holiday table, but simple enough for everyday enjoyment. Many of these recipes have been in my family for three generations, and I'm so pleased to be able to share them with you.

Flaky Pie Crust

This is a light and tender pie crust recipe that pairs perfectly with sweet or savory dishes. It yields 2 pie crusts! You can freeze this pie crust or use it right away.

Ingredients

- 2¼ cups (270g) all-purpose flour
- 1 cup cold butter, cubed
- ¼ cup water
- Dash of salt

Instructions

1. Add flour and cubed butter to food processor. Pulse until pea-sized balls form in the dough or cut in with a pastry knife.
2. Add salt and water. Pulse just until a solid dough ball forms and you can still see streaks of butter throughout the dough.
3. Divide the dough into 2 equal balls. Roll out one of the balls onto a floured surface until large enough to cover your desired dish. Rotate the dough with each roll of the pin, maintaining a well-floured surface below.
4. Transfer dough into a pie pan. Repeat with second dough ball.
5. Transfer both pans into the freezer for 30 minutes prior to baking.

Note: Use as called for in any given recipe requiring pie crust.

Bulk tip: Make these crusts in bulk and freeze. You can make pie crust rolls by rolling the dough out on wax paper, then rolling the paper up like a rolled map. You can also roll them out and place them in freezer-safe metal or paper pie pans. Freeze in a single layer, then stack and place in freezer bags.

Chocolate Chip Cookies

A warm chocolate chip cookie straight out of the oven is so satisfying, especially when they are made from scratch. This recipe makes 40 average-sized cookies, or 28 extra-large cookies. You can bake them all fresh, or portion and freeze the dough to bake later.

Ingredients

- 2 cups butter, room temperature
- 3 cups sugar
- 1 tablespoon molasses
- 1 tablespoon vanilla extract
- 4 eggs
- 2 teaspoons baking soda
- 1 teaspoon salt
- 5⅔ cups all-purpose flour (675g)
- 1½ cups dark chocolate chips

Instructions

1. Preheat the oven to 350°F.
2. In the bowl of an electric mixer, combine the butter, sugar, molasses, and vanilla. Cream the mixture until it is fluffy.
3. Next, add eggs one at a time. Beat on high for at least 30 seconds after each egg. The mixture should look like buttercream frosting at this point.
4. Add baking soda and salt. Mix briefly.
5. Add flour 1 cup at a time. Start very slowly to avoid kicking flour out of the bowl. Mix for 30 seconds after each cup.

6. Add chocolate chips and mix until thoroughly incorporated.

7. Spoon dough onto cookie sheet with a teaspoon and bake for 12–16 minutes, depending on their size, or until the edges are golden brown.

8. The cookies may appear underdone, but if baked for any longer they will be too crispy. Allow to sit for 5 minutes before serving so the center can solidify slightly.

Note: If you want very thick cookies, as opposed to flatter cookies, portion and freeze the dough for a minimum of 2 hours before baking. Or portion and freeze until solid, then store in a freezer bag until ready to use. To bake from frozen, preheat the oven to 350°F. Once heated, place cookie portions on a baking tray and bake for 12–16 minutes, depending on their size, or until the edges are golden brown. Allow to sit for 5 minutes before serving so the middle can firm up slightly.

Ultimate Chocolate Cake

A midnight chocolate cake straight from the pages of my great-grandmother's handwritten cookbook, this is a chocolate lover's dream. Topped with chocolate buttercream frosting, this recipe can be made as a two-layer 9" round cake or in a 9" × 13" pan.

Ingredients

Cake

1 cup butter, room temperature

1⅔ cups sugar

3 eggs

2 cups (240g) all-purpose flour

⅔ cup black cocoa (Dutch cocoa also works well)

⅓ teaspoon baking powder

1⅓ cups milk

1 teaspoon vanilla extract

½ teaspoon salt

1¼ teaspoons baking soda

Buttercream Frosting

½ cup butter, room temperature

4 cups powdered sugar

1 tablespoon vanilla extract

¼ cup milk

1 cup cacao or cocoa powder

Instructions

1. Preheat the oven to 350°F.

2. In a medium mixing bowl, cream the butter and sugar until smooth. Add the eggs and mix again until smooth.

3. Add half the flour, all the cocoa, baking powder, baking soda, and salt to the bowl and mix well.
4. Add the milk and vanilla to the batter and mix well.
5. Finally, add the remaining flour and mix well. If using a mixer, beat on medium-high for 1–3 minutes, or until the mixture changes color to a lighter shade and the volume has increased.
6. Grease and flour two 9" cake pans or a 9" × 13" pan. Pour batter into prepared pans.
7. Bake the 9" cake pans for 30–35 minutes or the 9" × 13" pan for 35–45 minutes.
8. Allow the cake to cool completely before icing.
9. **For the buttercream frosting:** In a medium-sized mixing bowl, add butter, powdered sugar, vanilla, cacao powder, and 2 tablespoons of milk. Whip until the frosting becomes fluffy and thick. Add more milk as needed if the frosting is too thick.
10. Add frosting between the layers and then coat the top and sides well or scoop it on top of the 9" × 13" pan and even it out with a spatula. If you want a thick layer of frosting on the layer cake, double the recipe.

Classic Vanilla Cake

This classic vanilla cake is wonderful for any special occasion, and we often use it for a traditional birthday cake. A tender cake with rich vanilla buttercream frosting, no matter when you make it, is sure to be a hit. This recipe can be made as a two-layer 9" round cake or in a 9" × 13" pan.

Ingredients

Cake

3 egg whites

1 cup butter, room temperature

4 cups (480g) all-purpose flour

2 cups sugar

4 eggs

2 teaspoons vanilla extract

1 cup milk

2½ teaspoons baking powder

½ teaspoon baking soda

1 teaspoon salt

Buttercream Frosting

1½ cups butter, room temperature

4 cups powdered sugar

¼ cup milk

1 tablespoon vanilla extract

Dash of salt

Instructions

1. Preheat oven to 350°F. Butter two tall, straight-sided cake pans. I use 8" pans, but you could use a 9" or even a square or rectangular pan—just make sure it has high sides.

2. Once the pans are buttered, dust with flour and remove any excess flour.

3. With electric mixer whip the egg whites to stiff peaks and set aside.

4. In a separate bowl cream the butter and sugar until light and fluffy. Add the whole eggs, one at a time, mixing well until each is incorporated. Add the vanilla extract and the milk.

5. Alternating between the dry ingredients and the wet, add to the butter and sugar. Mix until combined after each addition. Beginning and ending with the dry mix works best!

6. Using a spatula, fold in the egg whites. Stop when the egg whites are combined but not completely incorporated.

7. Pour the batter evenly into your pans. Bang the cake firmly on the counter (keep pan flat) to make sure there are no air pockets.

8. Bake for 40 to 45 minutes or until a toothpick comes out clean. Allow the cake to cool completely before frosting.

9. **For the frosting:** Place butter in the mixer and whip until smooth. Slowly add the powdered sugar, about a half cup at a time. Scrape down the sides often. Mix until all is well combined.

10. Slowly add milk.

11. Add vanilla and salt.

12. Frost the top of one cake layer and add the second cake on top. Frost the top and sides evenly, as desired.

Note: You can make this cake in a 9" × 13" pan as well. Just grease it first, no flouring needed. Bake at 350°F for 35–40 minutes, or until it passes the toothpick test. If you are baking in a 9" × 13" pan, cut the frosting recipe by half. Since it will be a single-layer cake, half the icing is plenty!

Fruit Pie

Whether you enjoy apple pie, cherry pie, or even grape pie, this standard recipe for fruit pie will allow you to create a delicious dessert with whatever fruit you have on hand.

Ingredients

2 pie crusts (the recipe on page 80 makes 2 crusts)

5 cups fresh fruit, washed, drained, and chopped

¾ cup sugar

3 tablespoons all-purpose flour or cornstarch

1 teaspoon ground cinnamon (optional)

1 teaspoon vanilla extract

1 tablespoon lemon juice

1 tablespoon butter, cold

Instructions

1. In a large bowl, stir fruit, sugar, flour, cinnamon, vanilla, and lemon juice until well combined. Cover the bowl and place it in the fridge while you prep the dough, or for at least 30 minutes.

2. Roll out two pie crusts and place one in a pie dish. Put the other one aside for the top crust.

3. Remove the fruit mixture from the fridge and use a slotted spoon to transfer the fruit from the bowl into the pie shell so any juices remain in the bowl.

4. Preheat the oven to 400°F.

5. Pour any juices that remain in the bowl, up to 3 tablespoons, into a small saucepan and cook over low heat. Stir constantly for 3-4 minutes, or until the juice has reduced and thickened slightly.

6. Cool for 5 minutes and then pour over the fruit in the pie shell. Toss if possible, but it doesn't have to be fully mixed.

7. Add dots of butter to the top of the filling and then add the remaining pie crust to the top. Crimp the edge as desired.

8. Place the pie on a large baking sheet in case of spillovers and bake for 20 minutes. Reduce the temperature to 375°F and bake for another 30–40 minutes, or until the top crust is golden brown and the filling is bubbling around the edges.

9. Remove from the oven and allow the pie to cool for at least 3–4 hours before slicing; otherwise, the filling will be too runny.

10. Serve alone or with ice cream and enjoy!

Old-Fashioned Banana Pudding

A Southern classic, banana pudding is a dessert I grew up with on every special occasion. You can make this in a 9" × 13" baking dish or omit the meringue and serve in individual jars for a crowd-pleasing treat.

Ingredients

1 cup sugar

⅓ cup (40g) all-purpose flour

Dash of salt

5 eggs, separated

4½ cups milk

2 teaspoons vanilla extract + 1 teaspoon for the meringue

2 tablespoons butter

16 ounces (about 120) vanilla wafer cookies

5–6 ripe bananas, sliced

⅓ cup powdered sugar

Instructions

1. Whisk together sugar, flour, and salt in a heavy bottom saucepan.

2. Add in the egg yolks and 2 cups of milk to the saucepan. Whisk together until smooth. Add the remaining 3 cups of milk and whisk until well combined.

3. Cook over medium heat, stirring constantly until the pudding comes to a simmer and thickens, about 10–15 minutes.

4. Once the pudding thickens, remove from heat and add butter and 2 teaspoons vanilla.

5. In the bottom of a 9" × 13" casserole dish, layer half the vanilla cookies. On top of the cookies add half the pudding, then all of the bananas. Repeat with remaining cookies and pudding.

6. Preheat the oven to 325°F while you make your meringue.

7. For meringue, beat the egg whites with an electric mixer or handheld mixer with a whisk attachment until foamy. Increase the mixer to high speed, gradually add the powdered sugar, and keep beating until stiff peaks form.

8. Briefly mix in 1 teaspoon vanilla extract.

9. Top the banana pudding with the finished meringue, fully covering the entire dish.

10. Bake for 12–15 minutes or until the meringue is golden brown.

11. Serve warm or chilled.

Enjoy a classic banana pudding with meringue on top, or serve in single-serving dishes such as half-pint mason jars.

Fruit Cobbler

Just like the fruit pie I shared on page 87, this recipe for fruit cobbler can be enjoyed with many different fruits, such as apples, peaches, grapes, pears, cherries, or plums. The cobbler batter is dolloped over the top of the fruit and topped with slices of butter. Serve alone or with ice cream. Yields 6–8 servings.

Ingredients

5 cups fruit of choice

1 cup + 2 tablespoons sugar, divided

1 teaspoon ground cinnamon (optional)

¾ cup butter, divided

1 cup flour

1 cup milk

1 teaspoon baking powder

Instructions

1. Preheat the oven to 350°F and grease a 9" × 9" square or a deep 9" round baking dish.
2. Clean and chop the fruit as desired, then toss with 2 tablespoons of sugar and 1 teaspoon of cinnamon (optional). Pour the fruit mixture into the prepared baking dish and set aside.
3. In a medium saucepan, melt 4 tablespoons of butter and remove the pan from the heat.
4. Stir in remaining ingredients, except for the reserved butter, and mix until well combined.
5. Dollop the cobbler batter over the fruit as evenly as possible. Slice the remaining ½ cup of butter into 12–15 pieces and space them evenly on top of batter.
6. Bake for 35–40 minutes or until the cobbler is golden brown. Allow to cool for 30–60 minutes before serving.

Note: This recipe also works well for the other traditional manner of making fruit cobbler. You can place the cobbler batter in the pan first and place the fruit on top. The batter will rise to the top by the end of the baking time, and will have soaked up the fruit juices as well. If this method is used, the additional ½ cup of butter dotted on the top is not needed.

Classic Pound Cake

My great-aunt Annie made the best pound cake known to man, and she shared her recipe with me. This classic pound cake is light and fluffy, but still has that delightfully dense quality that all the best pound cakes share. Eat this on its own, or top with strawberries and whipped cream for an easy strawberry shortcake. Yields 10 servings.

Ingredients

- 1 cup butter, room temperature
- 1¾ cups sugar
- 5 eggs
- 1 teaspoon vanilla extract
- 1 teaspoon lemon extract
- 2 cups (240g) all-purpose flour

Instructions

1. Preheat the oven to 350°F.
2. In the bowl of an electric mixer, cream the butter and sugar together until light and fluffy. Add eggs one at a time, beating well after each addition.
3. Add the extracts and flour and mix well. The batter should be completely smooth after mixing.
4. Grease a loaf pan with butter and pour the batter into the prepared pan. Bake for 55–60 minutes, or until the top is golden brown and the loaf passes a clean toothpick test.
5. Allow to sit for about 10 minutes before removing from the pan. Cool before cutting for best results.

Fudgy Brownies

These brownies have a thin layer of crunch on top and a dark, gooey center. With a rich dark chocolate flavor and chewy edges, these homemade brownies check all the boxes! Enjoy fresh or freeze them for later. Yields 9–18 servings, depending on serving size.

Ingredients

- 1 cup butter
- 3 eggs
- 2 cups sugar
- ⅔ cup (84g) all-purpose flour
- ½ cup unsweetened cacao, regular cocoa (not Dutch cocoa)
- ½ cup black cacao (Dutch or dark cocoa will also work)
- 1 teaspoon sea salt or ½ teaspoon table salt
- ½ teaspoon baking powder
- 1 teaspoon vanilla extract

Instructions

1. Preheat the oven to 350°F. Melt butter in a small pan over medium heat. You can use the microwave, but it will likely get too hot. You want it to be bubbling but not boiling.
2. While the butter is melting, add the eggs and sugar to the bowl of an electric mixer (or use a hand mixer). Whip until light and fluffy. Scrape down the bowl as needed.
3. Add melted butter to the egg and sugar mixture and whip again for about 2 minutes.
4. Add all remaining ingredients to the mixing bowl and mix until smooth. Scrape the sides of the bowl and remix to incorporate fully.
5. Line a square (8" × 8" or 9" × 9") baking dish with aluminum foil. This helps the brownies cook just fast enough to form the crunchy top while keeping its gooey center. No buttering is needed; the batter goes right against the foil.
6. Pour the batter into the lined baking pan, evening the top as best you can.
7. Bake for 35–40 minutes, or until you get a clean toothpick in the middle.
8. Allow to cool fully before removing the foil. If you can, cover the brownies with plastic wrap overnight. The brownies will be perfectly soft and chewy, and much easier to cut, the next day. If you can't, it's okay. Cut into 16 pieces and enjoy!

Lemon Chess Pie

Straight from my great-grandmother's personal collection, this recipe for lemon chess pie has been in my family for more than seventy years. It's the perfect combination of sweet and tart, and it makes a great addition to any potluck.

Ingredients

1 unbaked pie shell (see the recipe for flaky pie crust on page 80)

2 cups sugar

1 teaspoon flour

¼ cup butter, melted

¼ cup lemon juice

1 teaspoon grated lemon peel

4 eggs, beaten

¼ cup milk

1 teaspoon vanilla extract

½ teaspoon salt

1 tablespoon cornmeal

Instructions

1. Preheat the oven to 425°F.

2. In a medium bowl, combine the sugar and flour well. Add the melted butter, lemon juice, and grated lemon peel to the mix and combine well.

3. Add the blended eggs, milk, vanilla extract, and salt to the medium bowl and mix again until well combined.

4. Add the cornmeal and mix briefly. Pour mixture into the unbaked pie shell.

5. Bake for 15 minutes, then reduce the heat to 350°F and bake for about 35–40 minutes, or until the pie is set and the top is browned. The pie crust should also be golden brown.

Molasses Cookies

Also known as gingersnaps, these spiced cookies are packed with flavor and perfect for the fall and holiday seasons. Crispy on the edges and chewy in the middle, you'll want to make them over and over again! This recipe makes 40 average-sized cookies, or 28 large cookies. You can halve the recipe, if desired, or portion and freeze the dough to bake later.

Ingredients

- 3¾ cups (460g) flour
- 2 teaspoons baking soda
- 1 teaspoon ground cinnamon
- 2 teaspoons ground ginger
- ¾ cup butter, room temperature
- 1 cup sugar
- 1 egg
- ¾ cup molasses

Instructions

1. Preheat oven to 375°F.
2. In the bowl of an electric mixer, combine flour, baking soda, and spices.
3. Add the butter, sugar, egg, and molasses to the dry mixture and mix until well combined.
4. Allow dough to rest for about 15 minutes before assessing how sticky it is for rolling. If the dough is still very sticky, add additional flour. Dough will still be sticky but shouldn't coat your palms when rolled into a ball.
5. Roll dough into tablespoon-sized portions and roll portions in bowl of sugar to coat. If freezing for baking later, flattening the portions slightly after rolling in the sugar will help them bake more evenly straight from the freezer.
6. Bake for 10–12 minutes. Allow to cool completely before storing.

Bulk tip: Dough portions, rounded and coated in sugar, freeze very well for easy baking later.

Freeze in a single layer, then transfer to a bag once frozen. Bake straight from the freezer at 375°F for 12 minutes.

Soft and Fluffy Churros

Best when fresh and warm, these churros are fried to perfection and coated with cinnamon sugar. This batch yields 12 large churros and can be doubled if desired.

Ingredients

¼ cup butter, room temperature

1 tablespoon sugar

¼ teaspoon salt

1 cup water

1 cup and 3 tablespoons (140g) all-purpose flour

1 egg

1 teaspoon vanilla extract

Coconut oil (or frying oil of choice)

Coating

½ cup sugar

1 teaspoon ground cinnamon

Instructions

1. In a medium saucepan, melt butter over medium heat. Add the sugar, salt, and water, and stir until combined. Once the mixture starts to simmer, reduce the heat to low and stir in the flour. Mix the dough until a smooth ball forms and pulls away from the sides of the pan.

2. Remove from heat and let the dough cool for a few minutes.

3. Add the egg, stirring vigorously to fully incorporate. (If you are doubling the recipe, add the eggs one at a time, stirring vigorously after each addition.) The dough may look a little curdled at first, but keep stirring!

4. Add in the vanilla extract and continue stirring until the dough is smooth and glossy.

5. In a large, deep pan, heat the oil to 350°F. You'll need enough oil to submerge the churros, so be generous! While the oil heats, prepare a piping bag fitted with a star tip or use a churro press. Transfer the dough to the container of your choice.

6. Pipe 4–5-inch strips of dough directly into the hot oil, using scissors or a knife to cut each strip. Fry the churros in batches, turning them occasionally, until golden brown, about 2–3 minutes per side. *Note:* The larger the churro, the longer it needs to fry to cook through. Test the first churro for doneness to see if the time was long enough before continuing.

FROM SCRATCH COOKING

7. Remove the churros with a slotted spoon and drain on a paper towel–lined plate.
8. Mix the coating ingredients together in a dish that will accommodate the size of the churros.
9. While the churros are still warm, roll them in the sugar/cinnamon mixture. Make sure each churro is evenly coated for maximum deliciousness!

Graham Crackers

Every fall, I make a large batch of graham crackers to enjoy as s'mores or to use in graham cracker crusts during the holidays. They are easy to make and store for up to 6 months, making them perfect for bulk baking, especially if you have kids in the house. Yields 12 crackers.

Ingredients

Crackers

2¾ cups (330g) all-purpose flour

2 teaspoons baking soda

2 teaspoons ground cinnamon

⅓ cup butter, room temperature

⅓ cup brown sugar

⅛ cup sugar

1 tablespoon vanilla extract

2 tablespoons honey

½ cup milk

Topping

¾ teaspoon ground cinnamon

⅛ cup sugar

Instructions

1. Preheat the oven to 350°F and line two baking sheets with parchment paper.

2. In the bowl of an electric mixer, combine the flour, baking soda, and cinnamon. Next, add butter, brown sugar, sugar, vanilla, and honey. Process until the dough looks like small peas, then add the milk and process until a dough ball forms.

3. Divide the dough into two balls.

4. Prepare a piece of parchment the same size as your baking tray. Sprinkle with flour and roll the dough directly on the parchment.

5. Working with one piece of dough at a time, roll the dough as thin as you can, no thicker than ¼" thick, but preferably ⅛" thick (about the thickness of a quarter).
6. With a pastry cutter, pizza cutter, or very sharp knife, cut into 3" × 5" pieces and pierce each square with a fork several times.
7. Remove any excess dough and set aside to re-roll.
8. Sprinkle cinnamon and sugar over the top of the dough. You may need to use your hands to even out the coverage.
9. Repeat with the remaining dough until all the dough has been used.
10. Bake for 9–13 minutes or until lightly golden brown on top (watch closely). Cool completely and store in an airtight container with a silica pack for up to 6 months.

Ice Cream Base

Whether you love chocolate, mint chocolate chip, or classic vanilla, this recipe will allow you to turn fresh milk into creamy ice cream. Store this ice cream for 1–2 months for best results. Yields 1 quart.

Ingredients

- 3 cups heavy cream
- 1 cup milk
- ¾ cup sugar
- 1 tablespoon vanilla extract
- ½ teaspoon salt
- 5 large egg yolks

Instructions

1. In a medium saucepan, whisk the cream, milk, sugar, vanilla, and salt together. Bring mixture to a low simmer over medium heat.
2. In a separate bowl, whisk the egg yolks. While whisking, slowly add 1 cup of the hot cream mixture into the yolks, being careful not to scramble the eggs.

3. Add the cream and yolk mixture to the saucepan, whisking the whole time. Bring back up to a medium heat.

4. Stirring constantly with a wooden spoon, continue cooking until the mixture thickens and coats the spoon, about 6–8 minutes.

5. Remove from heat and strain the custard through a fine-mesh sieve into a large bowl. Do NOT skip this step, or the ice cream will be gritty! Discard the solids.

6. Transfer the custard to a fresh bowl. Stir the mixture every 10 minutes until the mixture cools to room temperature. Cover bowl with plastic wrap and chill for about 3 hours (or until cold).

7. Remove custard from the fridge and stir well to loosen. Follow your ice cream maker's directions to freeze the custard. If you don't have an ice cream maker, just pour the cooled custard into a freezer-safe dish and freeze for 2 hours. Remove from the freezer and stir in any mix-ins, then freeze again for about 2 hours.

FLAVOR VARIATIONS

Except for the chocolate, these additional ingredients will be added during the freezing stage. If you aren't using an ice cream maker, stir well to combine before freezing, and stir again after 2 hours to ensure an even mix.

- **Chocolate:** ¼ cup unsweetened cocoa powder, 6 ounces semisweet chocolate, chopped. Add these ingredients to the warm cream before adding the egg yolks and whisk until smooth.

- **Mint Chocolate Chip:** ½ teaspoon peppermint extract, 2 tablespoons chopped chocolate, 10-15 drops natural green food coloring (optional).

- **Cookies and Cream:** ½ cup crushed chocolate sandwich cookies

CHAPTER 2

KEEPING A DEEP PANTRY

Whenever I start talking about building a food supply, most people assume I am a doomsday prepper with iron rations hidden in every crevice and gas masks in the closet. But the truth is that our food supply is more easily disrupted now than at any other time in history and having a food supply is truly important to surviving the day-to-day realities of our society.

More often than not, the food in our grocery stores doesn't come from local farms or dairies like it once did, even as recently as the 1950s. Instead, it's brought in from all over the world. Our food supply chain runs on a fine-tuned system; however, the smallest glitch can disrupt it. Did you know that most modern grocery stores only have enough food on hand to serve their area for about three days at any given time?

You may have noticed bare shelves at the grocery store during pro-sporting event weekends, holidays, or even right before a big storm. Still, you didn't worry because you knew those shelves were going to be refilled in a day or two and things would go back to normal. But what if they didn't?

Economic woes run high in our country right now, and across much of the world. You never know what tomorrow might—or might not—hold. Things may continue for decades just as they are now—but they may not.

Beyond the possibility of supply chain interruptions, there are things in everyday life that might cause you to rely on your personal food stores: prolonged illness for you or a loved one, a sudden job loss that leaves you strapped for cash and needing to choose between purchasing food or paying the electric bill, or even the all-too-common natural disaster that leaves your area without supplies for an extended period of time. By having a solid food supply in place for you and your family, you can easily survive any of these possibilities without the additional stress of worrying about keeping everyone fed and well. Not only that, but having a food supply will help your community as well, because it will remove you from relying on the food chain during times of mass crisis, leaving the food in the stores available for others in need.

It's possible that you have already been purchasing some food in bulk, such as flour and other grains. Maybe you even have a garden and have been canning some or a lot of the harvest. That's an amazing start!

But I have found that while most homesteaders have some amount of food stored, whether from their own homesteading efforts or from bulk food purchases, most of the time it's not as much as they think. While many people *think* they have a complete food supply, they may find that on closer examination, all they really have is canned vegetables, frozen meat, and some flour in buckets.

Don't get me wrong, you could definitely live off of those rations. And it's a great place to start. However, an incomplete food supply can leave you feeling trapped and frustrated as your meals end up being the same every day, meal after meal, week after week. Instead of being forced to live on simple rations, creating a deep pantry is all about making food choices before the choice is taken away from you. A well-stocked pantry isn't just a collection of canned goods and boxed foods; it's a strategic reserve of quality ingredients that will allow you to cook nourishing meals, no matter what's going on outside your door.

CREATING A FUNCTIONAL FOOD SUPPLY

Whether you are homesteading or not, having a full pantry doesn't necessarily equal a sufficient and comprehensive food supply for your family. Yes, you can live off peanut butter, crackers, and canned tuna if you have to. But I want you to be able to thrive on your food supply in a way that is enjoyable, sustainable, and will help remove you from the food supply lines in a more permanent way.

Building a deep pantry is about stocking the food you and your family love, rotating it effectively, and making sure you have the essentials beyond food on hand to weather any storm—big or small.

When my family lived in the city but decided that we wanted to live a more sustainable life, we started buying some items in bulk: things like flour and sugar, bulk produce that I would can, and a few other things such as chocolate, coffee, and tea. I thought we had a huge food supply that would allow me to make many different items in the event of a crisis. After all, we had 200 pounds of flour in the pantry, and flour makes tortillas, biscuits, bread, pizza, and more.

Except I hadn't planned for any of the other things that were required for making those recipes. I didn't have any butter or tallow, no powdered milk, and certainly no cheese for pizza. I had fallen into the trap of believing that we had a large food supply, but upon closer examination we discovered we were missing quite a lot of items that would make our supply truly functional.

Where to Start: An Emergency Supply

Our very first attempt at building a food supply was packed into this tiny pantry. This is two corners, and each shelf was about a foot deep.

You may or may not have any food on hand yet, so let's start with a minimum emergency food supply of thirty days for your family. No matter how much food you have available in your supply already, it's important to have a plan for how you will use those stores if the power goes out, if you have no water, and if you don't have access to the recipes online.

First, let's make a meal plan for your family for thirty days. You can limit repeating meals if you'd like, but I prefer to make a weekly meal plan and then duplicate it for the rest of the month. That way I can buy more items in bulk, plan more effectively, and know that I'm not going to end up with half boxes of various items. This not only helps lower costs but also helps keep the space required for your first emergency food supply to a minimum.

I'll also add that for my crisis meal plan, I try to keep everything on the list as shelf stable as possible. This is really to protect you and your family during times of natural disasters when the power may go out. It's great to have thirty frozen lasagnas, but if the power's off, you don't want to open the freezer three times a day. Instead, you want to keep the freezer shut so that your food has the best chance of survival

KEEPING A DEEP PANTRY 103

This is enough food to feed my family for a full thirty days. Only five items require refrigeration, and they can be used first if the power goes out.

(assuming the power does come back on within a few days). Of course, having a generator for backup power would be ideal.

Grab a piece of paper or print a blank calendar and create at least a week of meals (breakfast, lunch, dinner, and snacks, as needed) that you know your family enjoys, keeping an eye to recipes that have shelf-stable ingredients, if possible. Also consider items that can be put together without any power, such as foods that could be cooked over a fire or that don't require heating at all. Canned meat and vegetables, canned fruit, crackers, cured meats, and so on can all be consumed without additional heat or water.

If you are using recipes (rather than cooking from memory), make sure they will make enough to feed your family, and indicate whether you will need to make a single or double batch in order to have enough food for a single meal. I would also recommend keeping a hard copy of any recipes you may need for your emergency supply, so that you can easily make your food even if the power (and internet) is out.

I'll also add that in the event of a power outage, you won't be able to keep leftovers, so try to develop or adapt recipes so that only a single meal is made from the ingredients. You don't want to open a large can of tuna only to leave half of it unused because the recipe didn't call for the full amount. Remember, this thirty-day plan isn't the way you would live all the time!

Once you have your meal plan created, break down each meal by its ingredients and combine like ingredients to determine the total amount needed for the week—then multiply that by 4 for the month. Or, if you did a whole month of varied meals, just add everything up to find the ingredient totals. For example, if you need 2 cups of flour for one recipe and 4 cups of flour for another, you will add up all of those requirements for the whole month of meals to find your total flour requirement.

After you know how much you need of the various items, you can head to your pantry and start crossing things off the list, based on what you already have. If you have a 10-pound bag of flour in the pantry and you only need 5 pounds for your meal plan, then you don't need to buy more flour. Repeat this process with every item on the list until you have just the final amounts still needed of the various items to complete your full meal plan.

You can simply print recipes from online sources and store them in a binder. If you are using your own recipes that aren't written down anywhere, be sure to type them up or write them out so that anyone in the family can use them if you aren't available.

> If you want to build up to a twelve-month food supply, you'll need to approach those meals much differently. Because you'll want to make sure you have food on hand in times of true crisis, where power and water may not be available for extended amounts of time, the meals you plan for a month's deep pantry will be different from those planned for in a long-term food supply.

KEEPING A DEEP PANTRY

Then all you need to do is purchase those remaining items. Later in this chapter I'll share some tips for building your food supply on a budget, but for now, try to stick to one hundred dollars per person for the thirty-day meal plan.

Testing Your Emergency Supply

Before we move on, I also want to mention the importance of testing this food supply. You don't want to buy a bunch of canned goods and stick them under your bed with the idea that you won't touch them for the next fifteen years unless there is an emergency.

Instead, it's crucial that you do a trial run of the plan before you actually need to put it into action. This means pretending that the grocery store doesn't exist for a full thirty days. Print your meal plan, put it on the fridge, and then live by it until the end of the trial period. This will not only allow you to identify any gaps in your plan, but also let you test the food itself too: Were the meals filling enough? Did you hate the tuna casserole recipe? Did you plan enough protein? You may have other questions as well, but those are a few examples.

Keep notes throughout the month and then make changes accordingly when you restock the supplies. Given our current climate, I would recommend restocking your supplies each week so that you still have that emergency supply if something happens during the testing period.

Remember, no cheating. If it's not on the list, don't eat it! This is the only way to know for sure that your supply will truly work for your family.

Understanding Storage Limitations

Depending on your home, the size of your family, and the length of time you want your food supply to cover, storage is something very important to consider. For a thirty-day supply, finding places to tuck food will likely not be an issue. However, if you are trying to build a twelve-month food supply for a family of seven, it's going to take quite a bit of space to store the grains, canned goods, and especially frozen goods that you'll need.

All food items need to be stored in a cool, dry place, away from the sun for best results. This will ensure the food doesn't spoil before it should and will help you get the most out of your supply. Nonfood items, such as toiletries, paper goods, batteries, and so on, can be stored in spaces that may get up to 85°F. Here is a brief look at some of the places in your home that you can use to store supplies, as well as ways to maximize those spaces:

When we lived in a tiny house, we even had food storage in the dining room. These shelves were in place behind our table and made a lovely backdrop to any meal.

- *Pantry:* Depending on the size of your pantry, this is a great place to store one to three months of food for immediate usage. Dry goods and canned food as well as tea, coffee, and spices can be stored in this space. Optimize your pantry space by rearranging the shelves to fit canning jars, flats of store-bought canned items, or buckets, without leaving much space above the items. This will increase the number of shelves in the pantry and fill the available space much better.

- *Closets:* Five-gallon buckets of dry goods are a great option for closets. Tuck a few stacked buckets behind clothes for a convenient way to store hundreds of pounds of food even in the smallest home.

- *Under beds:* We have found that flat underbed boxes are also a good option for storing mylar bags of dry goods, as well as flats of canned food.

- *Non-air-conditioned spaces:* If you have a large attic, garage, or outbuilding, be sure to only store nonfood items in these areas, unless the spaces are well sealed and air conditioned. Rodents and other animals are more likely to find food here as well, so make sure that any food items are double sealed in mylar bags and placed inside airtight plastic containers.

- *Freezers:* Carefully consider your freezer's capacity to store food items. Before you start buying meat or frozen goods in bulk, you need to make sure you have enough freezer room to accommodate the purchase before you bring it home.

CREATING AN EXTENDED FOOD SUPPLY

Now it's time to start shaping your extended food supply. This is where your real food choices come into play. For the one-month food supply, you are just trying to make sure you have shelf-stable food on hand to survive in the immediate aftermath of a natural disaster or some other emergency. And really, you can stand eating just about anything for four weeks. But once you get past that point, you want to make sure that the food you are eating is something that you and your family will legitimately enjoy.

At first glance, it might seem overwhelming to estimate and plan how much food you should have on hand in order to feed your family in extended times of need. However, this process is very straightforward and will be the same whether you are planning a three-month supply or a twelve-month supply. I recommend starting with a three-month supply so that you can understand the process, test your storage methods, and evaluate your food choices before moving into larger storage quantities.

The process is not all that different from creating a thirty-day supply, so I'm not going to go into great detail on the extended food supply. Rather, here is a quick overview of the process, with some expanded information in areas where it does vary from the process of building an emergency food supply:

1. *Create a meal plan.* When you created your thirty-day food supply, the focus was on foods that were shelf-stable and required little to no water or electricity to store or

cook. With an extended food supply, you instead can—and should—consider any and all foods that your family enjoys. You can create a rotating weekly or monthly meal plan, or you can create a full three- to twelve-month meal plan without a single repeating meal. That is up to you; however, I recommend some amount of repeating in your plan so that you can take advantage of bulk-buying sales.

This is over sixty crockpot meals from our meal plan, ready to freeze.

2. *Break down the recipes.* Just like before, break down each recipe into its ingredients, then add all similar ingredients together to understand the total need for the given time period. For example, on my monthly meal plan I have bone broth rice and vegetables as one of the meals that repeats twice per week. We cook 1 cup of dry rice in 2 cups of bone broth and pair it with a pound of green vegetables for a heathy, filling, and delicious meal. So, two times a week times four weeks gives me my total for the month, but then I also need to multiply that by three to get the total number of meals for this three-month period I'm working on filling. Doing the math, I know that I'll need about 24 cups of rice, 48 cups of bone broth, and 24 pounds of green vegetables in order to fulfill my needs for that one meal. I also need to make sure I have the ingredients to make the bone broth, or that I have enough purchased broth on hand.

3. *Consider your homestead.* If you are gardening or raising animals, the thought process behind this exercise will be a little different because you will also need to consider seasonality. As you're going through this planning process, pick the first season you want to build up a supply for and fill out a sheet for that particular season, then follow the same steps I laid out before for finding your full ingredients needs, multiplied by three for your three-month supply. When you move into creating your twelve-month supply, you'll again fill out one sheet for every season. That will allow you to incorporate the seasonality of your production, since meals

KEEPING A DEEP PANTRY   109

Even without any food storage on hand, we can make spinach and eggs from what we gather daily. Never discount what you produce on your homestead, no matter how small you think it is.

and needs will look very different in the winter versus in the spring. For example, we know that in the spring we have a bounty of eggs and cold weather crops, but in the winter, we will be living off canned vegetables, water glassed eggs, and grains much more heavily than we did in the spring. This means we plan a lot of egg-based dishes in the spring, but in the winter, we plan for more meals of soup and bread.

4. *Find the totals for purchasing.* After you have your meals planned, each recipe broken down into ingredients, and all like ingredients totaled, you'll want to subtract from the list anything that you already have on hand and things that you produce yourself. At that point, you will be left with a final list of items and amounts that still need to be purchased.

Purchasing Supplies in Shelf-Life Order

Regardless of how your supplies are being secured, whether by growing or by purchasing, once you have the list whittled down to the things you still need, set about purchasing the items with the longest shelf life first. This enables you to take a little longer to build up your total supply, without your first purchases going bad, before you can use them. Here is the order I recommend you go about acquiring supplies:

- *Dry goods.* Grains, sugar, spices, and so on, when stored properly, can last ten to fifteen years, so buying these very long-term food items first is a great place to start.
- *Meat.* If possible, purchase whole cuts of meat or whole birds. They will last longer in the freezer than ground beef, for example. For the longest shelf life, I recommend pressure canning as much of it as possible, based on the ratio of canned to fresh meat you are willing to consume. We like to make chili, sloppy joe mix, and stew with our beef, and then soups of various types out of other meat. Another

option is to can chicken or stew chunks in water for use in recipes later on. This alleviates some of the pressure on your freezers and drastically extends the life of the meat. In case of a power outage, canned meat allows you to open the jars and eat the food right away, since it's already cooked. Even if you don't have a way to heat it up, it's still safe and quick for your family to consume.

- *Fruits and vegetables.* These items will need to be canned or frozen, but they last up to five years when canned. Vegetables can be pressure canned in salted water, and most will taste just like the cooked version of the fresh vegetable, even years later. Water bath canning non-melon fruit in plain water is another way to preserve it, although the result is fairly bland once the fruit is removed from the water, since a lot of the flavor leaches out during the canning process. Instead, I like to can my fruits in a very light syrup made with maple syrup and water so that it is as close to eating fresh fruit, taste-wise, as possible. (See pages 130–45 for my favorite recipes.) This also allows you to reduce the juices by boiling them once the fruit is gone and then use them as a flavored syrup, which goes really well on pancakes, waffles, and biscuits. I err on the side of canning my fruits and vegetables so that they are ready to eat without additional water or heat, although freeze-dried fruits do make a delicious snack or meal if water is available and can also last for up to twenty-five years when stored properly.

Get the recipe for canning berries in light syrup on page 130 in chapter 3.

- *Fats.* If you are purchasing these items instead of making them fresh on your homestead, then having enough space to freeze them is important. As I mentioned earlier, it's important to take stock of how much freezer space you have and prioritize things that cannot be canned or freeze-dried. Butter, for example, can't be canned or freeze-dried, sadly, but it does freeze well for several years. Some

KEEPING A DEEP PANTRY 111

PROPERLY STORING DRY GOODS

There are a few different ways to store your bulk grains and room-temperature items to keep them fresh, bug-free, and safe from rodents. Having stored bulk grains for more than twenty years in various climates and methods, I'm only going to share the method that has worked the best for me, regardless of climate:

1. **Gather supplies.** You'll need a plastic five-gallon bucket with lid, a food-safe five-gallon mylar bag, silica packets, oxygen absorbers, and an iron.

2. **Freeze it.** Place your new dry goods in the freezer for four days, then remove them and let them fully come to room temperature on the counter before proceeding. I usually wait a full day before continuing, since you don't want to add cold items to a sealed bag and have condensation build up and ruin your food or overtax your moisture absorber.

3. **Fill it.** Place the mylar bag into the bucket and add your food to the bag. While food-grade buckets are available, they are not needed since the food never touches the plastic. Note that a five-gallon mylar bag will hold about twenty to twenty-five pounds of dry goods.

4. **Protect it.** Add to the bag, on top of the food, a silica packet and an oxygen absorber. You'll need 100cc of silica and 2g of oxygen absorber packets per gallon of food. For example, in a five-gallon bucket or bag, you will need 500cc of silica and 10g of oxygen absorber.

5. **Seal it.** Use an iron or heat sealer to seal the bag. If you use an iron, place a piece of wood under the bag to absorb the heat from the iron, seal about three-quarters of the bag, push as much air out as possible, and then seal the rest quickly. Be careful of the bag's edges; they will stay hot for a bit after sealing. When the edges of the bag have cooled off, just push the excess down into the bucket and add the lid, securing it fully. Write the item and the date on the top of the lid and store.

fats, such as nut butters, are shelf-stable for several years, making them a great choice in this category for your food supply.

- *Luxury items.* This category refers to food items that are not necessary for survival, or even satisfaction, but will make your food supply more enjoyable and will elevate it from survival rations to a way of eating that can be enjoyed year after year. For us, these items include things like chocolate chips, vanilla extract, and organic teas. A few other luxury items might be coffee, boxed macaroni and cheese, candy, soda, or bottled juice.

Money Management While You Grow Your Supply

Depending on how long you are planning for, you may be looking at the cost of your supply with some concern. Or maybe it has given you a new appreciation for how much you truly produce on your own and there's not much left to purchase. Either way, you will need to buy the remaining items on your list in a measured way that doesn't leave you strapped for cash.

When our favorite chocolate chips went on sale, we stocked up for a year with the funds we had set aside.

Since every family is going to have a different budget, I can't give you a hard and fast rule for building your supply. It's possible that you may have been blessed to the point that you could simply go out and purchase everything you need over the course of a few weeks. Or you may be in a similar situation to what my family faced when we were building our initial food supply, which was that we really had to save and pinch our pennies to be able to buy anything beyond our current needs.

Here, 120 pounds of flour purchased during a sale waits for its turn in the freezer before being stored in mylar bags.

Here are a few guidelines that will help you budget for your growing food supply:

- *Make a plan.* Be sure to actually create a plan as outlined earlier; don't just guess what you might need. Then stick to the plan as much as possible so you don't end up with perishable items that go bad before you purchase your dry goods.

- *Buy in bulk.* Dry goods can often be purchased at a deep discount if they are bought in bulk. For example, 2 pounds of oats may be reasonably priced, but buying 50 pounds at a time will save you 30 percent! If you know that you will need 50 pounds for the year (thanks to your food plan and ingredients list), you can purchase it all at once and save!

Each basket in our pantry holds a different type of food for easy access in a single place. There is a basket for sugar, spices, teas, and so on.

KEEPING A DEEP PANTRY 115

- *Shop seasonally.* You can save up to 50 percent on food items if you buy them "in season." For example, fresh organic strawberries are $2.50 a quart in my area in the spring, but in the winter, those same strawberries are $5.00 a quart. I buy them in the spring and preserve them for winter, which saves me 50 percent on strawberries. Likewise, during the holidays turkey is put on sale for a deep discount, so that's when we stock up for the year. Keep an eye on the seasonality of each item on your list to find the lowest price. For bulk items, look for holiday sales and buy during the sale. For example, einkorn berries go on sale several times a year at 20 percent off with free shipping. I only buy during those sales.

- *Build up a cash supply.* Put aside what you can, either in cash for easy spending or in a dedicated bank account, in order to keep a supply of available funds so that if

CAUTION WHEN BUYING IN BULK

With most brick-and-mortar stores as well as online retailers and food co-ops offering deep discounts on bulk purchases, buying in bulk is a great way to save money as you grow and maintain your food supply. However, as with most things in life, buying in bulk needs to be approached with some caution and an eye to whether it's a value or not. You'll want to compare not only the price but also the quality of the food.

For the price point, if sources are selling an item in different quantities, you'll want to make sure you break it down so you can see what the price per item, pound, or ounce is. For example, I recently purchased a large quantity of bacon from our favorite producer. They had a 10-pound item listed in their shop, so I was going to grab a few and call it good. But when I broke down the price per ounce, it was 15 percent less expensive to buy bacon in 1½-pound increments than it was to purchase 10 pounds at a time. I'm not sure why that was the case, but this wasn't an isolated incident—it happens all the time.

You may even find that your local grocery store sells small increments of an item for the best price per pound. When that happens, you can buy smaller bags to combine into larger mylar bags for bulk storage. It's well worth the effort to take a few moments to really understand not only which suppliers but also which version of an item, even from the same seller, is the best deal. Be sure to take into account shipping or other fees if you're buying online, so that you know the true cost of the items.

you do see something from your list on sale, you can grab it (and maybe even order more than you had planned due to the discount). It doesn't matter whether you have $1,000 a month to spend or an occasional $20. When you follow my suggestions for purchase order, you will be able to take longer to build up your supply without sacrificing quality. So, even if you can only spare $20 a week, you will eventually be able to build up your supply to the level you want to have on hand. And remember, once you have your food supply built up, it's not going to just sit there while you buy food from the grocery store each week. Instead, you will be eating from your supplies regularly and then buying more to replenish the stock as you go.

Rotating Your Food Supply

The easiest way to rotate food is a simple first-in, first-out system. By that I mean when you bring new food into your supply, you put it at the bottom or the back of the stack. That way, when you go to pull out a jar of food or a mylar bag of flour, you're getting the oldest item first.

It can be really tempting to just shove something in the front of the shelf and not worry about which items are the oldest. After all, you'll be using this supply fully each year, right? But while that *may* be true, it's often not the case for every single thing in your pantry. One year, we had a ton of canned black beans. I went on a kick where I wanted to eat them every day alongside our fresh vegetables—it was amazing. But, when that waned, I ended up with quite a few cans left on the shelf at the end of the year. You'll likely encounter similar ebbs and flows in what you're hungry for, which is why it's important to do a full inventory of your supply once a year.

Not only will doing such an inventory allow you to see what you ran out of and what you have left over from the year before, but it will also let you clean out anything that has expired. You'll also be able to take this information and use it as you plan your next year. For example, it's been several years since we turned any of our dried black beans into canned beans, because we just haven't wanted them the same way again. Instead, we keep them as dried beans in case a need arises, but there isn't a ticking timer for their shelf life.

WATER SUPPLY

One thing that often gets overlooked when planning your food supply is water. We all need a decent amount of water each day, not only for drinking but also for cooking, bathing, washing clothes, and so on. FEMA recommends a gallon of water per day per person: half for drinking and half for cooking and washing. If you have pets and livestock, you'll need even more. This water requirement is one of the reasons I really like to can as much food as possible, not only to increase its shelf life and reduce my dependence on my freezers but also because it means that all the cooking and water consumption is already done for the food in the jars!

Now, if you're on well water, water shortage likely won't be a problem for you. Just make sure you have a solar backup power supply for your pump, if you don't already.

Our water filter removes bacteria, as well as pharmaceuticals, fluoride, heavy metals, and chlorine that may be in the water supply.

But if you aren't on well water, canning water is a great way to ensure that you have clean water for when the supply may be down, or the power is out. Fortunately, canning water is a super simple process and doesn't require a pressure canner, so even if you aren't canning on a regular basis, you can still put a good supply of water away for later.

Of course, you may be wondering why you can't keep a supply of bottled water or water jugs on hand instead. And you can, but only for a relatively short period of time. In fact, bottled water only lasts about a year in plastic, though the bottles start to degrade right away. Depending on how long it has been in the bottles when you purchase your water, the shelf life may be very short. Instead, clean water stored in glass jars and fully canned can last for decades!

Canning Water

The process for canning water is simple—just see the water bath canning process on page 129 and process your jars of clean, filtered, and boiled water for 10 minutes at sea level. If you are canning between one thousand and six thousand feet above sea level, set the timer for 15 minutes; if you are above six thousand feet, you'll want to can the jars for 20 minutes.

You also don't have to can a dedicated batch of water. Instead, you can process jars of water anytime you are canning, either in a water bath canner or a pressure canner. Sometimes I only have five jars of potatoes at the end of a day of canning, so I'll add two quarts of water. This is a great way to slowly build up a water supply. If you are water bath canning, just make sure that the recipe you are canning requires at least ten minutes of processing time. For pressure canning, any recipe will be enough time.

If you want to quickly build up a large water store for your family, canning dedicated batches of water is a great way to do it. Keep in mind that if you have a water supply nearby, you wouldn't necessarily need as much water on hand since you could gather and filter the water around you as needed. However, if you live in an area that doesn't have a fresh water source, you will likely need that full gallon of water per day per person. That can add up to a lot of water jars!

Be sure to plan for your water needs when you're considering how much storage you have available in your home. Keep the cardboard boxes your

A quart of water going into the pressure canner.

jars come in, as they are a great, easy way to store and stack your water jars. One flat of quart jars is the equivalent of 3 gallons, and you can stack the flats as needed. Water jars are great for underbed storage as well, allowing you to reserve closet and pantry space for food items. Aim for a thirty-day supply of water first, then consider if you have room for a larger supply. If not, you'll want to make sure you have plenty of water filters on hand and arrange for some rainwater collection around your property.

BEYOND FOOD

In addition to your actual food supply, it's important to remember that you and your family, your pets, and any other animals you have consume many other things on a daily, weekly, and monthly basis. This may include immediately recognizable items like toilet paper, bar soap, and shampoo, as well as items such as laundry detergent and dish soap, supplements, medications, feminine supplies, canning supplies, and so on. I recommend taking a tour through your home and making a note of everything that you, your family members, and your pets or livestock use regularly, as well as how much is used and whether it's on a daily, monthly, or weekly basis. Write it all down *without* editing as you go. And don't forget kitchen items like plastic wrap or parchment paper, if you use them regularly. Also include seasonal items: canning lids, freezer bags, wrapping paper, and so on.

Once you have everything listed, go through and decide what you can, or just want, to live without for a period of time, if needed. For example, like most people, we use toilet paper. But we don't stockpile it. It's a luxury that we enjoy while it's available, but we also have a plan for using family cloth in case toilet paper is not available in the future. On the other hand, having essential oils and various tinctures available is very important to us. As a result, we make sure we have a constant supply of those items, replacing each bottle before it fully runs out, so that our supply never changes. You will have similar things on your list—things that you don't care about as much and other things you can't live without—so remove anything that is optional, and then organize the rest by priority and determine how much you will need for your chosen period. Just like food, I recommend having at least a thirty-day supply before building up to a full twelve-month supply of each item.

Finally, in addition to having at least three months of ready-to-use food on hand, I recommend storing seeds for your favorite vegetables, as well as having seeds to sprout. Sprouts are high in nutrients and can be ready to eat in just a few days. In times of great crisis, no matter where you live, you would likely be able to plant a garden in an area where it might not have previously been allowed. So, having seeds stored alongside your food supply means you could start a garden and have food to eat while it grows to maturity.

CHAPTER 3

FOOD PRESERVATION, PART I

Canning and Freezing

While growing your own food can help keep costs down and nutrients high, you don't need a garden to be able to preserve food long term for your family. Food preservation methods like canning and freezing are a great way to take advantage of lower food costs throughout the year while also increasing your family's food security.

Just imagine being able to buy strawberries on sale in the spring, properly preserve them, and then enjoy them in the winter when they're typically double the price! Or maybe you have a garden, and you want to preserve all the green beans and corn that you have been harvesting during the summer months.

In this chapter, I'm going to show you how to safely can food for your family using the water bath and pressure canning methods. While pressure canning allows you to store low-acid foods such as meats and vegetables, water bath canning is used for high-acid foods such as pickles, jams, jellies, pie fillings, tomato-based products, and more. These two options provide shelf-stable food items that last anywhere from two to five years and require no electricity to maintain once they are processed. Additionally, we will discuss freezing foods for short-term food storage.

CANNING PREPARATION AND SAFETY

Before you dive into either method of canning, there are a few things you need to know in order to safely and correctly process your food. Even if you have canned food in the past, this information is still important to review, as many canning recipes found online disregard many of these crucial guidelines.

Boiling Water Canner

You can use a pot made specifically for water bath canning. They are deeper and usually come with a rack to stack the jars inside for more processing space. However, you can also just use a large soup pot, which is my preferred method as it doesn't require me to store an additional large pot. Before you start canning, be sure to check the depth of the pot you will be using by placing the empty jars inside and confirming that there is at least 3 inches of space from the top of the jar to the top of the pot. This will allow you to have 1–2 inches of water above the jars without it spilling over. You will also want to check that the jars will not touch each other inside your pot. If they touch during the canning process, they could shake too much and break.

Pressure Canner

It's important to note that pressure *canning* and pressure *cooking* are two different things. While some pressure canners can also be pressure cookers, the opposite is not always true. Be sure that you are using a pressure *canner* when processing your low-acid vegetables and meats. Additionally, check all rubber seals each time you use this method and ensure that all valves are free of debris so that the pressure can build safely during the canning process. Follow the manufacturer's recommendations for internal water levels.

Canning Tools

In addition to a large pot or a pressure canner, you will also need a set of canning tools. This includes a jar lifter and a plastic canning knife at a minimum. Both are necessary for safe canning. The jar lifter allows you to lift the jars in and out of the canner while keeping them straight upright. This will prevent burns, reduce the risk of the jars slipping and breaking, and lower the risk of the glass breaking under the pressure that may result from using other tools. The plastic canning knife is used to remove air bubbles, as discussed later in this section.

Stovetop Recommendations

Many modern homes are equipped with glass-top stoves in the kitchen. While these are very sleek, they can cause issues when attempting to can food, because the pressure canner plus the necessary water is very heavy and can break the glass. Instead, consider purchasing a standalone burner that can be plugged in and utilized just for pressure canning. Gas and electric coil burner stoves are fine for all types of canning. For water bath canning, any stovetop surface is typically fine as long as you are not using a pressure canner to process a water bath canning batch.

Jar Selection

Use only clean jars that are free of any chips or cracks. All jars, new or used, must be washed with hot soapy water before filling. Never fill a chilled jar with hot food, as the jar may crack or explode. Likewise, never put a cold jar into a boiling water bath or the same situation may occur.

Lid and Ring Selection

New lids should be used for every canning batch. Old lids that have been used for non-canning purposes can be considered new as long as they don't have any dents or deformations and the rubber sealing ring is intact. Old or new rings may be used, as long as they are also free of any dents or deformations. Anything that mars the original shape of the lid or the ring can interfere with the seal forming during the canning process.

Removing Air Bubbles

After filling the jars, it's important to remove any air pockets to prevent bacteria growth. To do this, simply take a plastic canning knife (metal can score the glass and lead to breakage) and push it all the way to the bottom of the jar. Then, work the knife along the inside wall of the jar, pushing in slightly to force any air in the food to release and move up the side. This may cause the food to settle, leaving room for additional food to be added.

Applying the Lids

Before adding the lids and rings to each jar, take a clean dishcloth or paper towel, dipped in boiling water, and clean the top rim of the jar to remove any excess grease, sugar, or other food particles that would block a proper seal from forming. Be careful not to drip water into the food within!

Match rings and lids and place them on each jar. Hand-tighten only until the ring stops spinning, then go just a little bit tighter. The rings should be tight, not loose enough to remove without effort, but not tightened with all your might.

Cooling after Canning

Many online recipes call for flipping the jars upside down while they cool to ensure a tight seal. I do not recommend this, nor does the USDA, as it can actually cause seal failure. Instead, remove the jars from the canner and place them upright on a towel or wooden cutting board about an inch apart. Allow them to cool to room temperature before moving.

Seal Testing

Once your jars have cooled completely, press the center of the lid to confirm that the metal is concave. If it's not, the food will need to either be reprocessed or refrigerated. If the metal is concave, you will need to remove the ring and attempt to lift the jar by the lid alone. If the lid stays in place, the seal was successfully formed.

Reprocessing

If the seal has not formed once the jars are completely cooled, you can fully reprocess it by removing the lid and reheating the contents as done in the original recipe. Then place the hot food into a new, clean jar, with a new lid and ring set, and process for the full time indicated in the original recipe.

Canning at High Altitude

Both water bath and pressure canning recipes are written with the processing times for canning at sea level. If you are canning at a higher altitude, you will need to increase the processing time to account for the elevation difference as follows:

Altitude in Feet	Increase Processing Time
1,001–3,000	5 minutes
3,001–6,000	10 minutes
6,001–8,000	15 minutes
8,001–10,000	20 minutes

CANNING TERMINOLOGY

You will see the following important canning terms often as you move along your canning journey. Understanding them will help you safely can food year after year.

Raw Pack. This refers to putting uncooked food into a clean jar and covering it with hot liquid before canning. No cooking required! For foods that are delicate, such as peaches, the raw pack method helps maintain the shape and texture of the produce. While the raw pack method is preferred for whole or cut fruits, you can also use the hot pack method instead.

Hot Pack. When food is heated or cooked prior to filling your jars, this is called hot packing. Many foods like jams, jellies, and salsas are hot packed by default since they are cooked before canning. However, you can also heat whole or cut fruit in syrup before canning if you prefer the hot pack method.

Headspace. This term refers to the amount of room between the top of the food inside the jar and the top rim of the jar itself. Most water bath canning recipes require a ¼-inch or ½-inch headspace but double-check each recipe before placing the lid. Pressure canning tends to call for a 1-inch headspace but should be confirmed in the specific recipe you are canning.

Gelling Point. When making jams or jellies without pectin, you will need to test if the gel has set by taking the temperature with a candy or jelly thermometer.

- *At sea level:* The gelling point is 220°F, or 8°F above boiling.

- *Above sea level:* For each one thousand feet of altitude above sea level, subtract 2°F. For example: at one thousand feet of altitude, the jelly is done at 218°F; at two thousand feet, 216°F, etc.

A canning knife that is used to remove air bubbles also has a headspace depth tool on the other side.

128 CREATING A MODERN HOMESTEAD

A NOTE ON PECTIN

While pectin is often used in canning, I try not to rely on it since it's not always available. Sugar, honey, and maple syrup tend to be readily available and can be purchased in whatever quality level you prefer. For example, organic pectin does not currently exist, but organic sugar does. Therefore, I am not including any recipes using pectin in this book.

WATER BATH CANNING FRUITS AND VEGETABLES

As I mentioned earlier, water bath canning is used for high-acid foods such as pickles, jams, jellies, pie fillings, tomato-based products, and more. I personally love water bath canning, as it lets me save my freezer space for foods that can't be canned safely, like melon chunks or okra for frying. In this section you will find recipes for canning fruits and tomatoes safely in a variety of ways. You'll also find recipes that combine high- and low-acid foods but call for adding acid, which raises the pH and makes them safe for water bath canning.

SYRUPS FOR CANNING FRUIT

Sugar is not required to safely can fruit; however, in order to retain the natural sweetness of the fruit, which would otherwise leach into the water, many canners often use a sweet syrup. Thankfully, you can customize the strength of the syrup to your liking. We tend to use an extra-light syrup ratio made with maple syrup for most of our fruit canning efforts.

Fruit juice, sweetened or unsweetened, can also be used in place of syrup; however, alternative sugars such as stevia or monk fruit are not recommended for canning, as they tend to drastically change their flavor during the process and can become very bitter.

FOOD PRESERVATION, PART I　129

Use the table below to create the syrup strength you enjoy for canning by mixing the amount of sweetener listed into the amount of water listed, then heating the solution over medium heat until the sugar dissolves fully. The "Sweetener" can be sugar, honey, or maple syrup. If you use fruit juice, simply leave it at full strength and do not mix it with water.

Type of Syrup	Sweetener	Water	Syrup Yield
Extra Light	1¼ cups	5½ cups	6 cups
Light	2¼ cups	5¼ cups	6½ cups
Medium	3¼ cups	5 cups	7 cups
Heavy	4¼ cups	4¼ cups	7 cups

CANNING STRAWBERRY JAM

With a firm grasp on safety, terminology, and basic guidelines, it's time to start canning! One of the best recipes to start with is this easy and delicious strawberry jam. Note: You will need six pint-sized canning jars with lids and rings. This recipe yields 6 pints.

Strawberry Jam

Ingredients

3 quarts (12 cups) strawberries

9 cups sugar (honey or maple syrup can be substituted; however, then you will also need pectin to cause the jam to gel)

Instructions

1. Wash the jars using soap and hot water. Jars can be washed by hand or in the dishwasher. Rings and lids *must* be washed by hand in hot soapy water, as the heat of the dishwasher will ruin the adhesive on the lids.

2. Wash and slice the strawberries. Add one layer of strawberries at a time to the bottom of a large pot. Mash them well before adding another layer. Continue to layer and mash until all strawberries are mashed. I use a sturdy whisk or a potato masher for this step. Remember that any chunks of strawberry you leave will end up in your jam. That's not a bad thing, just be aware!

3. Fill your canning pot a little less than halfway with water and start bringing to a low simmer over medium heat.

4. Place the pot with the mashed strawberries on the stove and add the sugar. Stir until mixed well. With heat on medium-high, stir until the sugar is dissolved. Once the sugar is dissolved, turn the heat up to high and stir constantly.

5. After 15–20 minutes, the jam will start to thicken and coat the spoon. Fill the clean jars with the hot jam. Leave a ¼-inch headspace.

6. Once all jars are full, place a bubble remover all the way into one of the jars until it touches the bottom and then run it along the entire wall of the jar. This will remove any air bubbles that might cause bacterial growth. Repeat with the remaining jars.

7. Take a clean dishcloth or paper towel, dipped in boiling water, and clean the top rim of each jar. Be careful not to drip water into the jam. Match rings and lids and place them on each jar. Hand-tighten only. The rings should be tight but not tightened with all your might.

8. Using the jar lifter, place five jars into the canning pot. Make sure they do not touch. If they touch during the canning process, they could shake too much and break.

9. Once all the jars are in place, confirm that there is at least 1½–2 inches of water covering the tops of the jars. If there's not, add more hot water. Turn the heat up to high until a full boil is achieved. Once a full boil starts, set a timer for 15 minutes.

10. After 15 minutes, use the jar lifter to remove the jars from the boiling water. Place them on a towel and do not move them for at least 6 hours.

Cooked jam is added to clean jars and then the rims are wiped to help ensure a good seal.

Make sure the water level is at least one and a half inches above the jars for processing.

Lift the finished jar of properly canned jam and bask in the glow of a job well done.

FOOD PRESERVATION, PART I 131

Listen for a popping noise over the first hour. That little popping you hear is the sound of the jar fully sealing.

11. Allow the jars to sit in place until fully cooled. Once cooled, check that each jar has sealed by removing the ring and picking the jar up by the lid. Keep one hand on the jar itself lightly in case the lid doesn't hold! As long as the lid holds, you can replace the ring (or not) and store it in the pantry for up to five years. If any jars haven't sealed, you can try to process them again in the water bath, or simply place them in the refrigerator and use them first.

MORE WATER BATH CANNING RECIPES

Now that you're familiar with the general process of water bath canning, it's time to fill out your pantry with all sorts of jams, jellies, pie fillings, pickles, tomato-based products, and more!

DO NOT double or triple jam or jelly recipes, as it will result in the final product not setting up properly.

Apples for Baking (Pie Filling)

Yields about 8 pints or 4 quarts

Ingredients

- 10–12 pounds apples (about 16–20 cups, sliced)
- 3¼ cups water
- 5 cups sugar

Wash, core, and peel (optional) apples. Slice apples in ¼"-thick pieces. Combine water and sugar in a large pot and bring to a boil over high heat. Reduce heat to medium and boil apples in their syrup for 5 minutes. Pack hot apples into hot jars, leaving ½" headspace. Ladle syrup over apples, leaving ½" headspace. Remove air bubbles and adjust two-piece caps. Process pints and quarts for 20 minutes according to general water bath canning directions.

Apple Butter

Yields about 6 half-pints or 3 pints

Ingredients

 4 pounds apples (about 8–10 cups, sliced)

 4 cups sugar

 2 teaspoons ground cinnamon (optional)

 ¼ teaspoon ground cloves (optional)

Wash, peel, and core apples. Chop roughly and place in a large pot with just enough water to keep them from sticking to the pan, about ¼". Place a lid on the pot and cook over medium heat until the apples are soft. Use an immersion blender to blend the apples until smooth (if you don't have an immersion blender, place the cooked apples in a standard blender and, once blended to a pulp, place back in cooking pot). Add sugar and spices to the apple pulp and cook over low heat for 4–8 hours, or until very thick and dark brown. Ladle into hot jars, leaving ½" headspace. Remove air bubbles and adjust two-piece caps. Process half-pints and pints for 10 minutes and quarts for 15 minutes according to general water bath canning directions.

Apple Juice

Yields about 6 pints or 3 quarts

Ingredients

12 pounds apples (about 24 cups, chopped)	1 quart water

Wash and chop apples and place in a pot large enough to accommodate all the apples. Add water and cook until tender. Stir to prevent sticking. Strain the cooked apples through cheesecloth into a large bowl. Pour the apple juice into a large pot. Over medium heat bring to 190°F (this takes about 5 minutes) but do not boil. Ladle hot juice into hot jars, leaving ¼" headspace. Remove air bubbles and add two-piece caps. Process for 10 minutes according to general water bath canning directions.

Applesauce

Ingredients

2½–3½ pounds apples, per quart (about 3–5 cups, quartered)

Water

Sugar (optional)

Wash, core, peel, and quarter apples. Place apples in a large pot and cover with just enough water to prevent sticking, about ¼". Cover pot and cook over medium heat until cooked through and soft. In a blender or food processor puree apples then return pulp to cooking pot. Add sugar to taste, if desired. Over medium heat, bring mixture to a boil, stirring often to prevent sticking. Ladle boiling apple sauce into hot jars, leaving ½" headspace. Remove air bubbles and adjust two-piece caps. Process for 20 minutes according to general water bath canning directions.

Apricot Preserves

Yields about 4 half-pints or 2 pints

Ingredients

5 cups apricots, pitted and halved (about 2 pounds)

4 cups sugar

¼ cup lemon juice

Combine apricots, sugar, and lemon juice in a large saucepot. Cover and let stand for 4–5 hours in a cool place. Over medium heat, bring to a boil, stirring until sugar dissolves. Cook almost to gelling point, stirring frequently to prevent sticking. Remove from heat and skim foam if necessary. Ladle into hot jars, leaving ¼" headspace. Remove air bubbles and add two-piece lids. Process for 15 minutes according to general water bath canning directions.

Berry Juice

This recipe is intended to allow you to process berries in whatever quantity you have on hand, be it a few cups, or many pounds. Unlike jam and jelly recipes that cannot be doubled, you can process juice in larger quantities. There are no set measurements as the amount of sugar will vary by preference. Once your juice is strained, sweeten to taste, using at least 1 cup of sugar per gallon of juice (or 1 tablespoon per cup of juice).

Ingredients

Berries of choice

Sugar

Water

Wash berries and place them in a cooking pot and crush the berries well with a whisk or potato masher. Simmer berries over medium heat until cooked through. Use enough water in the pot to prevent sticking, about ¼". Strain through cheesecloth and add back to pan. Add 1–2 cups sugar per gallon of juice. Heat juice over medium heat to 190°F for 5 minutes, but do not boil. Ladle juice into hot jars, leaving ¼" headspace. Remove air bubbles and add two-piece lids. Process pints and quarts for 15 minutes according to general water bath canning directions.

Blackberry Jam

Yields about 12 half-pints or 6 pints

Ingredients

9 cups crushed blackberries

6 cups sugar

Combine berries and sugar in a large saucepot. Bring to a boil, stirring to prevent sticking, until mixture reaches gelling point. Remove foam if needed. Ladle into hot jars, leaving ¼" headspace. Remove air bubbles and add two-piece lids. Process for 15 minutes according to general water bath canning directions.

Blackberry Jelly

Yields about 8 half-pints or 4 pints

Ingredients

4 cups blackberry juice (see berry juice recipe on opposite page, no sugar added)

7½ cups sugar

2 tablespoons lemon juice

Combine all ingredients in a large saucepot. Bring to a boil over high heat, stirring to prevent sticking, until mixture reaches gelling point. Skim foam if needed. Ladle into hot jars, leaving ¼" headspace. Remove air bubbles and add two-piece lids. Process for 10 minutes according to general water bath canning directions.

Blueberry Pie Filling

Ingredients

1½–3 pounds blueberries, per quart (about 4–6 cups)

Sugar

Water

Wash and drain blueberries. Make a light or medium syrup (30%–40% sugar-to-water ratio). Ladle ½ cup of hot syrup into each jar, then pack with berries, leaving ½" headspace. Add additional syrup if needed. Remove air bubbles and adjust two-piece caps. Process pints for 15 minutes and quarts for 20 minutes according to general water bath canning directions.

Cherries, Brandied

Yields about 6 pints

Ingredients

6 pounds dark, sweet cherries

1 cup sugar

1 cup water

½ cup lemon juice

1¼ cups brandy

Wash and pit cherries. Combine sugar, water, and lemon juice in a large pot. Over medium heat, bring to a boil, then reduce to simmer. Add cherries and simmer until hot. Remove from heat and stir in brandy. Pack cherries into hot jars. Ladle syrup on top, leaving ½" inch headspace. Remove air bubbles and adjust two-piece caps. Process for 10 minutes according to general water bath canning directions.

Cherry Pie Filling

Ingredients

2–2½ pounds cherries, per quart (about 4–6 cups)

Sugar

Water

Wash and pit cherries, then drain. Make a syrup with sugar and water to your desired strength. Ladle ½ cup of hot syrup into each jar and pack with cherries, leaving ½" headspace. Add additional syrup if needed. Remove air bubbles and adjust two-piece caps. Process for 25 minutes according to general water bath canning directions.

Cranberry Juice

This recipe is intended to allow you to process cranberries in whatever quantity you have on hand, be it a few cups, or many pounds. There are no set measurements as the amount of sugar will vary by preference. Once your juice is strained, sweeten to taste.

Ingredients

Fresh cranberries

Water

Sugar (optional)

Wash and drain cranberries. Combine equal parts cranberries and water in a large saucepot. Over high heat, bring to a boil, reduce heat to medium-low, and simmer until cranberries burst. Strain through damp jelly bag or cheesecloth. Add sugar to taste, if desired. Heat the cranberry juice to 190°F for 5 minutes. Ladle into hot jars, leaving ¼" headspace. Remove air bubbles and adjust two-piece caps. Process for 15 minutes according to general water bath canning directions.

Cranberry Sauce, Jellied

Yields about 4 half-pints or 2 pints

Ingredients

4¼ cups fresh cranberries

1¼ cups water

2 cups sugar

Wash and drain cranberries. Combine cranberries and water in a large pot and boil until skins burst. Transfer cranberries to food processor and puree. Add sugar to pulp and juice. Place cranberry puree back into the pot and boil almost to gelling point. Ladle into hot jars, leaving ½" headspace. Remove air bubbles and add two-piece lids. Process for 15 minutes according to general water bath canning directions.

Cranberry Sauce, Whole Berry, with Port Wine and Cinnamon

Yields about 12 half-pints or 6 pints

Ingredients

10 cups fresh cranberries

4 cups sugar

4 tablespoons red wine vinegar

1 cup water

2 cups port wine

8 cinnamon sticks

Wash and drain cranberries. Combine sugar, vinegar, and water in a large pot and boil over medium heat for 5 minutes. Add cranberries and boil, without stirring, until skins burst. Remove from heat, add port wine, and stir well. Add two cinnamon sticks to each jar. Ladle mixture into hot jars, leaving ½" headspace. Remove air bubbles and add two-piece lids. Process for 15 minutes according to general water bath canning directions.

Figs, Whole

Ingredients

2½ pounds fresh figs, per quart (about 5–6 cups)

Water

Sugar

Bottled lemon juice

Wash and drain figs. Do not stem, peel, or cut them. Blanch whole figs for 2 minutes in boiling water, then drain. Gently boil figs on medium heat in a light or medium syrup (30%–40% sugar-to-water ratio) for 5 minutes. Add 1 tablespoon lemon juice to each pint, or 2 tablespoons per quart. Pack hot figs into hot jars, leaving ½" headspace. Ladle hot syrup over figs. Remove air bubbles and add two-piece lids. Process pints for 45 minutes and quarts for 50 minutes according to general water bath canning directions.

Grape Jelly

Yields about 4 half-pints or 2 pints

Ingredients

4 cups concord grape juice

3 cups sugar

Add grape juice and sugar to large pot over medium heat and stir until sugar is dissolved. Bring to a boil over medium heat, stirring constantly. Cook to gelling point, then remove from heat. Skim foam if desired. Ladle into hot jars, leaving ¼" headspace. Remove air bubbles and add two-piece lids. Process for 10 minutes according to general water bath canning directions.

Grape Juice

This recipe is intended to allow you to process grapes in whatever quantity you have on hand, be it a few cups, or many pounds. There are no set measurements as the amount of sugar will vary by preference. Once your juice is strained, sweeten to taste.

Ingredients

Grapes

Water

Sugar

Wash and drain grapes. Stem, crush, and measure crushed grapes. Place crushed grapes into a cooking pot large enough to accommodate all the grapes. Add 1 cup water to each gallon of crushed grapes. Heat grapes for 10 minutes at 190°F over medium-low heat. Do not boil. Strain juice through a damp jelly bag or cheesecloth. Measure juice and add 1–2 cups sugar per gallon. Reheat to 190°F for 5 minutes over medium-low heat. Ladle into hot jars, leaving ¼" headspace. Remove air bubbles and adjust two-piece caps. Process for 15 minutes according to general water bath canning directions.

Peaches, Brandied

Yields about 4 pints or 2 quarts

Ingredients

4 pounds small peaches (about 10–12 cups)

6 cups sugar, divided

4 cups water

1 teaspoon salt

3–4 tablespoons brandy, per jar

Wash and peel peaches; leave whole. Combine 3 cups sugar, water, and salt in a large pot. Bring to a boil over medium heat then reduce to simmer. Add enough peaches to cover the bottom of the pot and simmer until hot (about 5 minutes). Remove peaches from syrup and place in a deep bowl. Repeat until all peaches are heated. Once all peaches are heated, boil syrup for 5 minutes and pour over peaches. Cover and let stand 12 to 18 hours in a cool place. Remove peaches from syrup.

Combine syrup with last 3 cups of sugar, boil for 5 minutes over high heat, and pour over peaches. Pack peaches into hot jars, then pour 3–4 tablespoons brandy into each jar. Ladle syrup over peaches, leaving ½" headspace. Remove air bubbles and adjust two-piece caps. Process for 10 minutes according to general water bath canning directions. Peaches are ready to use after about 4 weeks, by which point the brandy will have fully soaked into the fruit for the full flavor experience.

Peach Pie Filling

Ingredients

2–3 pounds peaches, per quart (about 4 cups, sliced)

Water

Sugar

Wash, halve, pit, and drain peaches. Make a light or medium syrup (30%–40% sugar-to-water ratio). Pack peaches cut side down, layering to save space. Ladle hot syrup into jars, leaving ½" headspace. Remove air bubbles and adjust two-piece caps. Process pints for 25 minutes and quarts for 30 minutes according to general water bath canning directions.

Pears

Ingredients

2–3 pounds pears, per quart (about 4 cups, sliced)

Water

Sugar

Wash, halve, core, peel, and drain pears. Make a light or medium syrup (30%–40% sugar-to-water ratio). Cover the bottom of a large pot with the pears one layer at a time and simmer on medium heat until hot (about 5 minutes). Pack hot pears into hot jars. Ladle ½ cup of hot syrup into each jar, leaving ½" headspace. Remove air bubbles and adjust two-piece caps. Process pints for 20 minutes and quarts for 25 minutes according to general water bath canning directions.

FOOD PRESERVATION, PART I

Pickles, Dill

Yields about 7 pints or 3 quarts

Ingredients

- 8 pounds (4–6-inch) cucumbers
- ¾ cup sugar
- ½ cup canning salt
- 4 cups vinegar
- 4 cups water
- 3 tablespoons mixed pickling spice
- 4 fresh dill sprigs (1 sprig per jar)

Wash cucumbers. Cut into rounds, ¼" thick, or into spears, depending on your preference. Combine sugar, canning salt, vinegar, and water in a large pot. Tie up pickling spice in a spice bag, then add bag to vinegar mix. Simmer for 15 minutes over medium heat. Pack cucumbers into hot jars. Add 1 sprig of dill to each jar. Ladle hot syrup into jars, leaving ½" headspace. Remove air bubbles and adjust two-piece caps. Process for 15 minutes according to general water bath canning directions.

Pickles, Sweet

Yields about 3 pints or 2 quarts

Ingredients

- 4 pounds (4–6-inch) cucumbers
- Water
- 4 cups sugar
- 3 tablespoons canning salt
- 3¾ cups white vinegar
- 4 cinnamon sticks
- 4 teaspoons whole cloves
- 2 teaspoons diced fresh ginger
- Pickle Crisp granules

Wash and cut the blossom ends off the cucumbers. Place cucumbers in a large bowl, cover with boiling water and let stand 2 hours. Drain. Combine sugar, canning salt,

Small, whole cucumbers work best for making sweet pickles. Choose produce that will fit fully in the jars without cutting.

and vinegar in a large pot and bring to a boil over medium heat. In each quart jar, place 1 cinnamon stick, 1 teaspoon whole cloves, ½ teaspoon fresh ginger, and ¼ teaspoon of Pickle Crisp. Pack cucumbers into hot jars. Ladle hot syrup into jars, leaving ½" headspace. Remove air bubbles and adjust two-piece caps. Process for 15 minutes according to general water bath canning directions. Allow to rest in the pantry for at least 2 weeks before eating to let the flavors mature.

Pineapple

Ingredients

3 pounds pineapple, per quart

Water

Sugar

Peel, core, cut, and drain pineapple. Make a light or medium syrup (30%–40% sugar-to-water ratio). Simmer pineapple over medium heat in syrup until tender. Pack hot pineapple into hot jars. Ladle hot syrup into jars, leaving ½" headspace. Remove air bubbles and adjust two-piece caps. Process pints for 15 minutes and quarts for 20 minutes according to general water bath canning directions.

Plum Jam, Red (*Damson*)

Yields about 6 half-pints or 3 pints

Ingredients

5 cups red plums (about 2 pounds)

3 cups sugar

¾ cup water

Wash, pit, and chop plums. Combine all ingredients in a large pot. Gently boil over medium-low heat, stirring until sugar is dissolved. Bring to gelling point. Remove from heat and skim foam if needed. Ladle into hot jars, leaving ¼" headspace. Remove air bubbles and adjust two-piece caps. Process for 15 minutes according to general water bath canning directions.

Raspberry Jam

Yields about 8 half-pints or 4 pints

Ingredients

4 cups crushed raspberries

6 cups sugar

Combine berries and sugar in a large saucepot. Bring to a boil over medium heat, stirring to prevent sticking, then to gelling point Remove foam if needed. Ladle into hot jars, leaving ¼" headspace. Remove air bubbles and add two-piece lids. Process for 15 minutes according to general water bath canning directions.

Salsa

Yields about 8 pints

Ingredients

- 10 cups tomatoes
- 2 cups tomato paste
- 2 cups water
- 1¾ cups chopped green bell pepper
- 5 jalapeños, finely chopped, membranes/seeds removed
- 3 cups chopped onion
- 7 cloves garlic, minced
- ⅓ cup chopped fresh cilantro
- 1¼ cups apple cider vinegar
- 2½ teaspoons ground cumin
- 2½ teaspoons black pepper
- 2½ tablespoons canning salt
- ⅓ cup sugar (optional)

Wash, halve, and roast tomatoes. Roast tomatoes by washing and cutting tomatoes, if desired, then drizzle with oil and season to taste. Roast at 425°F for 45 minutes, or until skins

Our fresh tomatoes roasted and ready to turn into salsa!

are wrinkled and juices start to release. Remove peels if desired, but it is optional. Allow tomatoes to drain for 30 minutes in strainer above bowl to remove excess liquid. Mix tomato paste and water in bowl until smooth and transfer to a large pot along with the rest of the ingredients. Bring to boil over high heat, reduce to medium and simmer for 10 minutes. Stir often. Ladle into hot jars, leaving ½" headspace. Remove air bubbles and adjust two-piece caps. Process for 15 minutes according to general water bath canning directions.

Marinara Sauce

Yields about 4 pints or 2 quarts

Ingredients

10 pounds tomatoes	¼ tablespoon black pepper
2 tablespoons olive oil	1 bay leaf
1½ cups chopped onion	1 tablespoon salt
4 cloves garlic, minced	2 tablespoons minced fresh basil
½ tablespoon oregano	Bottled lemon juice

Peel, core, and cut tomatoes into small pieces and set aside in a large bowl. In a large cooking pot, sauté onion and garlic in oil until transparent. Add tomatoes, oregano, black pepper, bay leaf, and salt and simmer for 20 minutes. Stir occasionally. Remove bay leaf and puree mix in food processor in batches, if needed. Strain to remove seeds, if desired. Add puree back to the large pot along with basil. Gently simmer over medium-high heat until reduced by half volume. Add 1 tablespoon bottled lemon juice to each pint (2 tablespoons per quart). Ladle hot sauce into jars, leaving ½" headspace. Remove air bubbles and adjust two-piece caps. Process for 35 minutes according to general water bath canning directions.

Strawberry Jam

Yields about 12 half-pints or 6 pints

Ingredients

3 quarts strawberries, crushed	9 cups sugar

Combine berries and sugar in a large saucepot. Bring to a boil, stirring to prevent sticking, then bring to gelling point. Remove foam if needed. Ladle into hot jars, leaving ¼" headspace. Remove air bubbles and add two-piece lids. Process for 15 minutes according to general water bath canning directions.

FOOD PRESERVATION, PART I 145

PRESSURE CANNING LOW-ACID VEGETABLES AND MEAT

You've seen how water bath canning preserves high-acid foods. Now let's take a look at pressure canning, which will allow you to preserve low-acid foods, such as meats and vegetables, due to the higher heat achieved by pressurizing the canner. I personally love pressure canning meat and vegetables for quick and easy meals that are shelf-stable and ready to heat. In this section, I'll walk you through the general process for pressure canning, and then share all my favorite recipes for vegetables, chili, and more!

Many pressure canners have an arrow on the side that allows you to easily align the arrow on the lid with the dent on the base.

PRESSURE CANNING WHITE POTATOES

I'm going to walk you through the pressure canning process using potatoes because I find them to be the fastest and easiest vegetable to pressure can. Tackling potatoes as your first foray into the art of pressure canning will give you the confidence to can more challenging items without wearing you out on your first attempt.

Ingredients

2½ pounds white potatoes, per quart (about 4 cups)

Water

Canning salt

Instructions

1. Wash and prep jars like you would for water bath canning. Place them in a cold oven and heat to 250°F.
2. Boil a pot of water to use for covering potatoes in jars. Also, fill your pressure canner with 3–4 inches of water and place on medium-low heat.
3. Wash, peel, and cut potatoes. I like to cut them in 2-inch chunks, but you can make them smaller, if desired. Note: Smaller potato pieces may turn out mushier than you like; you'll just have to try a few that way and see what you think!

4. Add 1 teaspoon salt to each quart jar (or ½ teaspoon per pint jar).

5. Fill jars with potatoes and pour boiling water on top. Leave a 1-inch headspace. Use a canning knife to remove all bubbles from the jars. Add additional potatoes or water as needed to reach a 1-inch headspace.

6. Wipe the rims of each jar with a clean dishcloth or paper towel, dipped in boiling water, to ensure a proper seal. Remove air bubbles, then fit and adjust two-piece lids and rings to finger tightness (don't torque down on lids too much).

7. Place jars in pressure canner and fit lid securely according to how your pressure canner seals. Bring canner to 10 pounds pressure (remember that if you are canning at a higher altitude, you will need to increase the processing time to account for the elevation difference. See the table on page 127).

8. Process quarts for 40 minutes, or pints for 35 minutes.

9. Once the timer goes off for the processing time, turn the heat off completely and allow the pressure canner to naturally reduce to zero pounds pressure. Remove canning weight and let sit for 5 minutes before removing the lid. Be careful—the lid will be VERY hot!

10. Remove jars and place them on a folded kitchen towel. Allow the jars to cool fully before moving again, usually 12–24 hours. Store in a cool dry place.

MORE PRESSURE CANNING RECIPES

Now that you're familiar with the general process of pressure canning, it's time to fill out your pantry with all sorts of vegetables, broths, meat, and more!

Beans, Dried

¾ pound dried beans, per quart   Salt (optional)

Water

Add beans to a large pot and add water to cover beans by 2 inches. Let soak overnight, drain, and rinse. Cover beans again with water, bring to a boil, and cook for 30 minutes, stirring frequently. Pack beans in hot jars, leaving 1-inch headspace. Add ½ teaspoon salt per pint, or 1 teaspoon salt per quart. Ladle hot water from beans or fresh boiling water over beans. Remove air bubbles and add two-piece lids. Process pints for 1 hour and 15 minutes or quarts for 1 hour and 20 minutes at 10 pounds pressure.

Beans, Lima or Butter

3–5 pounds beans, per quart   Salt (optional)

Wash and drain beans. Shell beans and wash again. Pack beans LOOSELY into jars, leaving a 1-inch headspace. Do not overfill (the beans expand!). Add ½ teaspoon salt per pint, or 1 teaspoon salt per quart. Ladle boiling water over beans. Remove air bubbles and add two-piece lids. Process pints for 40 minutes or quarts for 50 minutes at 10 pounds pressure.

Beef Broth

Yields about 4 pints or 2 quarts

4 pounds meaty beef bones   Salt to taste

2 quarts water

Place bones in a large pot, cover with water, and bring to a simmer. Cover and simmer for 2–18 hours, depending on how strong you want the broth to be. Add more water as needed and salt to taste. Drain bones and save (freeze) for additional broth, if desired. (You can use the bones up to three times.) Ladle hot broth into hot jars, leaving a 1-inch headspace. Remove air bubbles and add two-piece lids. Process pints for 20 minutes or quarts for 25 minutes at 10 pounds pressure.

It's especially important to thoroughly wipe the rims of high-fat items such as broth, since the fat will prevent a seal from forming.

Beef Stew

Yields about 14 pints or 7 quarts

4–5 pounds stew meat

1 tablespoon oil of choice

12 cups cubed potatoes, peeled

8 cups sliced carrots, peeled

3 cups chopped celery

3 cups chopped onions

1½ tablespoons salt

3 tablespoons minced garlic

1 teaspoon dried thyme

1 teaspoon black pepper

Cut meat into cubes and brown in oil. Combine all ingredients into a large pot, cover with boiling water, and bring to a boil. Remove from heat. Pack hot stew into hot jars, leaving a 1-inch headspace. Remove air bubbles and add two-piece lids. Process pints for 1 hour and 15 minutes or quarts for 1 hour and 30 minutes at 10 pounds pressure.

Carrots

2–3 pounds carrots, per quart

Water

Salt (optional)

Wash carrots, drain, and peel. Wash again. Slice or dice into desired sizes and pack carrots tightly into jars, leaving a 1-inch headspace. Add ½ teaspoon salt per pint, or 1 teaspoon salt per quart. Ladle boiling water over carrots. Remove air bubbles and add two-piece lids. Process pints for 30 minutes or quarts for 35 minutes at 10 pounds pressure.

Chicken Broth

Yields about 8 pints or 4 quarts

2 pounds chicken bones

4 quarts water

Salt to taste

Place bones in a large pot, cover with water, and bring to a simmer. Cover and simmer for 2–18 hours, depending on how strong you want your broth to be. Add more water as needed to keep the bones covered and salt to taste. Drain broth and place in the fridge until fat solidifies on top. Save bones (freeze) for additional broth batches, if desired. Remove fat and either save or discard. Reheat cooled broth on stove, bringing to a boil. Ladle hot broth into hot jars, leaving a 1-inch headspace. Remove air bubbles and add two-piece lids. Process pints for 20 minutes or quarts for 25 minutes at 10 pounds pressure.

Chicken Soup

Yields about 14 pints or 7 quarts

- 1 whole chicken (3–5 pounds)
- 1½ gallons filtered water
- 1 cup chopped carrots
- 2 small–medium onions, chopped
- 1 cup chopped celery

Roast chicken at 375°F until internal temperature reaches 165°F, about 45–60 minutes. Remove skin and chop the meat into small bite-sized pieces. Reserve bones and place them in a large pot and cover with water. Cover, bring to a simmer over medium-high heat and cook for 2–18 hours, depending on how strong you want your broth to be. Remove bones (strain). Place the bone broth in the fridge and cool until the fat rises to the top. Once the fat has solidified on the top, scrape it off and either save for a different dish or throw away. Place broth back on the stove and return to slow boil. Mix chopped vegetables in a bowl. Place 1 cup of vegetable mixture and 1 cup of meat into each quart. Cover contents with hot broth, leaving a 1-inch headspace. Remove air bubbles and add two-piece lids. Process pints for 1 hour and 15 minutes, and quarts for 1 hour and 30 minutes at 10 pounds pressure.

Chili

Yields about 10 pints or 5 quarts

- 4 cups tomato paste
- 1 gallon water
- 2 large yellow onions, diced
- 5 pounds ground beef (we use ground brisket)
- 8 tablespoons ground chili powder
- Salt, pepper, and garlic (to taste)

In a large bowl combine water and tomato paste and whisk until smooth. In a large soup pot, sauté onion and ground beef until brown, then add tomato mixture on top. Add spices and stir until well combined. Bring to a simmer over medium heat and cover for 5 minutes. Ladle hot chili into hot jars, leaving 1-inch headspace. Remove air bubbles and add two-piece lids. Process pints for 1 hour 15 minutes or quarts for 1 hour 30 minutes at 10 pounds pressure.

Corn, Whole Kernel

3–6 pounds of EARS of corn, per pint (about 2 cups of kernels)

Water

Salt (optional)

Husk corn and remove silk. Wash and cut kernels from the cob. Do NOT scrape cob. (For this recipe, you do not need to extract the pulp and milk from the cob.) Pack corn loosely into hot jars, leaving a 1-inch headspace. Add ½ teaspoon salt per pint, or 1 teaspoon salt per quart. Ladle boiling water over corn. Remove air bubbles and add two-piece lids. Process pints for 55 minutes or quarts for 1 hour and 25 minutes at 10 pounds pressure.

Corn, Creamed

1–1 ½ pounds of EARS of corn, per pint (about 2 cups of kernels)

Water

Salt (optional)

Husk corn and remove silk. Wash and cut kernels from the cob. Scape cob to extract pulp and milk. Measure kernels, pulp, and milk together. Add ½ teaspoon salt and 1¼ cups boiling water for every 2 cups of corn mix. Bring corn mix, salt, and water to a boil for 3 minutes. Ladle hot corn loosely into hot pints (only), leaving a 1-inch headspace. (*Note:* Don't can creamed corn in quarts, as the heat won't penetrate properly to kill the bacteria.) Remove air bubbles and add two-piece lids. Process pints for 1 hour and 25 minutes at 10 pounds pressure.

Depending on the size of your canner, you may be able to can a double batch of pint jars with the use of a canning rack between the layers.

FOOD PRESERVATION, PART I 151

Green Beans

2–3 pounds green beans, per quart (about 4 cups)

Water

Salt (optional)

Wash and drain beans. Remove strings and snap into 2-inch pieces. Pack tightly into jars, leaving a 1-inch headspace. Add ½ teaspoon salt per pint, or 1 teaspoon salt per quart. Ladle boiling water over beans. Remove air bubbles and add two-piece lids. Process pints for 20 minutes or quarts for 25 minutes at 10 pounds pressure.

Greens (beets, chard, kale, spinach, turnips, etc.)

2–6 pounds greens, per quart (about 4 packed cups)

Water

Salt (optional)

Triple wash greens, using clean water for each washing. Heat greens in a large pot until just wilted, using only enough water to prevent sticking. Cut greens several times to create smaller pieces (don't chop them finely) and pack hot greens into hot jars, leaving a 1-inch headspace. Add ½ teaspoon salt per pint, or 1 teaspoon salt per quart. Ladle boiling water over greens. Remove air bubbles and add two-piece lids. Process pints for 1 hour and 10 minutes or quarts for 1 hour and 30 minutes at 10 pounds pressure.

Ground Meat

2–3 pounds ground meat, per quart

Water

Broth of choice (optional)

Salt (optional)

Brown meat and drain fat. Pack meat into hot jars, leaving a 1-inch headspace. Add ½ teaspoon salt per pint, or 1 teaspoon salt per quart. Ladle boiling water OR boiling broth over meat. Remove air bubbles and add two-piece lids. Process pints for 1 hour and 15 minutes or quarts for 1 hour and 30 minutes at 10 pounds pressure.

Be sure to heat your jars before adding hot food to them; otherwise they can break from the temperature stress and ruin the food inside.

Mixed Vegetables

Yields about 14 pints or 7 quarts

7 cups sliced carrots

7 cups corn

6 cups diced zucchini

1 cup chopped sweet red pepper

7 cups lima beans

Combine all vegetables in a large pot and add water to cover. Over medium heat, boil for 5 minutes. Pack hot mix into hot jars and cover with liquid from the pot, leaving a 1-inch headspace. Remove air bubbles and add two-piece lids. Process pints for 1 hour and 15 minutes or quarts for 1 hour and 30 minutes at 10 pounds pressure.

Peas, Black-Eyed

About 2 pounds pea pods, per quart (about 4 cups shelled peas)

Water

Salt (optional)

Wash and drain peas. Shell peas and wash again. Pack peas LOOSELY into jars, leaving a 1-inch headspace. Do not overfill (the peas expand!). Add ½ teaspoon salt per pint, or 1 teaspoon salt per quart. Ladle boiling water over peas. Remove air bubbles and add two-piece lids. Process pints for 40 minutes or quarts for 50 minutes at 10 pounds pressure.

Peas, Green

3–6 pounds pea pods, per quart (about 4 cups shelled peas)

Water

Salt (optional)

Wash and drain peas. Shell peas and wash again. Pack peas LOOSELY into jars, leaving a 1-inch headspace. Do not overfill (the peas expand!). Add ½ teaspoon salt per pint, or 1 teaspoon salt per quart. Ladle boiling water over peas. Remove air bubbles and add two-piece lids. Process pints for 40 minutes or quarts for 50 minutes at 10 pounds pressure.

Potatoes, Sweet

2–3 pounds sweet potatoes, per quart (about 4 cups)

Water

Sugar (optional)

Peel and rinse potatoes. Cut to size desired. Pack tightly into jars, leaving a 1-inch headspace. Make syrup at a ratio of 2¼ cups sugar to 5¼ cups water. Bring to a boil. (You may need to double the amount of syrup, depending on how many pounds of sweet potatoes you are processing.) Ladle boiling syrup over sweet potatoes OR cover sweet potatoes with boiling water instead of syrup. Remove air bubbles and add two-piece lids. Process pints for 1 hour and 5 minutes or quarts for 1 hour and 30 minutes at 10 pounds pressure.

Potatoes, White

2–3 pounds white potatoes, per quart (about 4 cups)

Water

Salt (optional)

Peel and rinse potatoes. Cut to size desired. Pack tightly into jars, leaving 1-inch headspace. Add ½ teaspoon salt per pint, or 1 teaspoon salt per quart. Ladle boiling water over potatoes. Remove air bubbles and add two-piece lids. Process pints for 35 minutes or quarts for 40 minutes at 10 pounds pressure.

Stew Meat

2–3 pounds stew meat, per quart

Water

Broth of choice (optional)

Salt (optional)

Brown meat and drain fat. Pack meat into hot jars, leaving a 1-inch headspace. Add ½ teaspoon salt per pint, or 1 teaspoon salt per quart. Ladle boiling water OR boiling broth over meat. Remove air bubbles and add two-piece lids. Process pints for 1 hour and 15 minutes or quarts for 1 hour and 30 minutes at 10 pounds pressure.

FREEZING FOR SHORT-TERM STORAGE

In some cases, simply freezing food may be the right choice for your family, as canning can change the taste or texture in a way that isn't as desirable. However, freezer space is often limited in some homes. For that reason, I prefer to keep the items we freeze to a minimum when possible so that we have room for meat as well as vegetables that don't can well, like okra, broccoli, and corn on the cob. We also choose to freeze a portion of our fresh fruit for our son to enjoy during the winter months. If you have enough freezer space to allow for it, baked goods, ready-to-bake meals, and dairy products also freeze well.

Keep in mind, too, that frozen food storage has a much shorter life span than that of canned goods, which can store well for two to five years. Most frozen foods should be consumed within three to twelve months.

GENERAL GUIDELINES FOR FREEZING

It may seem like enough to simply place your food in a freezer bag with a label and call it good, but there are a few more nuances to successfully freezing your food. Here are some helpful guidelines to ensure that your frozen foods are of the highest quality when served.

Produce Quality

The single most important factor when freezing your food is the quality of the original produce. For best results, choose young, tender, and ripe produce with no signs of rotting.

Blanching

This process of quickly dipping the produce in boiling water and then placing in cold or ice water is recommended for most vegetables and for peaches before freezing to preserve their color, flavor, texture, and nutritional value. Each produce variety has its own blanching time; see pages 162–63.

Storage Containers and Bags

- *Plastic Freezer Bags.* Freezer bags are a readily available option that are easy to use and come in many different sizes. Be sure to use freezer bags and not just any zip-top plastic bag. If you are storing food for less than a month, any plastic bag will likely be fine, but for long-term storage and best results, use a thicker bag rated for freezing food.

- *Plastic Containers.* These are a great option if you want something stackable, but they can also make your food more susceptible to freezer burn if they aren't meant to be used for freezing food. Be sure to use proper containers and don't just reuse any plastic container you might have on hand.

156 CREATING A MODERN HOMESTEAD

- *Glass Jars.* Some canning and other glass jars can be used for freezing, but only when the opening of the jar is not smaller than the sides it connects with. When there are "hips" or "shoulders" on the jar, it creates a weak spot that can cause breakage during the freezing and thawing processes. Instead, only use "tapered" glass jars where there are no weak spots.
- *Vacuum-Sealed Bags.* These bags are much thicker than regular or freezer zip-top bags and can help prolong the life of your frozen foods. For this option, freeze your food on a baking tray lined with wax paper and then transfer the frozen foods into a vacuum-seal bag and seal with the vacuum sealer.

Freezing Positions

After filling your chosen containers, you will need to consider how your food should be positioned during the freezing process. If you choose to use a rigid option like a container or jar, you can stack the items right away. If you are using plastic bags, however, you will need to place the food flat on a baking sheet, in a single layer, until fully frozen before bagging and stacking.

Storage Life

Though technically you can consume frozen foods for many years, as long as they have been frozen the whole time, there is a loss of quality and nutritional value after a period of time. Here is a general overview of how long various types of foods can be stored in the freezer without a loss of quality.

I love making a triple batch of meatloaf and freezing the extra portions. Once the meat is baked and cooled, I slice it into portions and freeze it on a baking tray before moving the pieces to freezer bags.

Food Type	Length of Storage
Bread and Baked Goods	4–8 months
Citrus	3-4 months
Dairy (Butter, Cheese, Milk)	12 months
Dairy Products (Ice Cream/Sherbert)	2-4 months
Eggs	12 months
Fruits (Except Citrus)	12 months
Meat (Whole Cuts)	8-12 months
Onions	3-6 months
Pastries, Baked	3-6 months
Pastries, Unbaked	1-3 months
Poultry (Whole)	12-15 months
Prepared Meals	3-6 months
Seafood	3-4 months
Vegetables (Except Onions)	12 months

Specifics for Freezing Foods

In this section, I'm going to break down each type of food or produce variety and give you the details on exactly how to freeze each one for the best results. For example, while you can blanch your vegetables for a random amount of time and then freeze them, blanching for the proper amount of time for each variety will lead to the highest quality when the food is served later. The same principle holds true for non-produce items as well. So, let's get into the details!

Dairy Case Items

Freezing homemade dairy items is crucial for access during low production months. However, you can also buy dairy goods on sale and freeze them for later to reduce your overall spending throughout the year. Here are a few examples:

- *Butter:* Freeze store-bought butter in the box or wrapper without any additional packaging for up to 12 months. If the butter is fresh and homemade, wrap it in wax paper and then put the wrapped portions into a freezer bag.

- *Cream:* Pour cream into plastic bags and freeze flat or freeze in ice cube trays for smaller portions before placing in freezer bags. You can add 2–3 tablespoons of sugar to each pint of cream to help reduce ice formation and promote creaminess when it is thawed. It is optional but helps prevent the cream from separating after thawing.

- *Eggs:* Freeze whole eggs (yolks and whites together) or whites and yolks separated as needed for your preferred use. Either way, crack the eggs into a bowl and gently whisk to reduce the risk of air bubbles before packing into the desired containers. Leave a ½-inch headspace if freezing in jars.

- *Milk:* You can freeze milk in the plastic gallon jug it comes in, if desired. Simply leave sealed and freeze. To thaw, place the container on the counter and shake it vigorously every hour until the milk is fully thawed. This process will help reincorporate the cream and give a better finished quality. Milk can also be frozen like cream either in bags, jars, or preportioned cubes.

Since we buy raw milk from a dairy that is more than four hours roundtrip from our home, we buy in bulk and freeze it to reduce our trips.

Fruit: Whole, Cut, Jams, Jellies, and Pie Fillings

In general, fruits do not need to be blanched before freezing. Peaches are the exception, as blanching helps to easily remove the skin (if desired). You can also leave the skin on and simply freeze the cut peaches without blanching.

- *Whole fruit:* For small fruits such as berries, cherries, and figs, no cutting is required. You can simply wash and dry the fruit before freezing it on a baking tray lined with wax paper and then transferring the frozen fruit into the freezer container of your choice.

- *Cut fruit:* No matter what type of fruit you are freezing, wash and dry the exterior before cutting as desired. Freeze the pieces on a baking tray as indicated above before transferring to your choice of storage container.

- *Jams, jellies, and pie fillings:* You can use any canning recipe for the type of jam, jelly, or pie filling that you would like. Once your recipe is made, let the mixture cool to room temperature before filling your containers of choice. If you are using

FOOD PRESERVATION, PART I 159

jars, leave a half-inch headspace to account for expansion. Freeze in small enough portions so that you will be able to eat all of it within about a month of thawing. Store in the fridge after thawing.

Prepared Foods

If you're like me and enjoy having homemade food ready to eat at the last minute, then freezing prepared foods is a great option! These guidelines will allow you to bake or prep your meals in bulk and freeze them for later.

- *Bread and baked goods:* When I bake bread, I like to triple the batch and freeze the extra two loaves. This doesn't take much extra effort and reduces the amount of time I spend in the kitchen, while still allowing us to eat homemade, high-quality foods year-round. For all baked goods, whether tortillas, biscuits, or muffins, bake as normal and cool to room temperature before bagging to freeze. For sandwich bread, slice before bagging and freezing. Thaw bread overnight in the fridge to reduce condensation buildup inside the bag and then enjoy as normal. While the recommendation is to eat frozen baked goods within eight months, as long as the items don't have freezer burn, they are very likely still delicious. Even with freezer burn the items are safe to eat, they just may taste a little different.

- *Pastries (unbaked):* Pie shells, puff pastry, ready-to-bake biscuits, cookie dough, and more—unbaked pastry items are a must in our freezer! Simply prep the items and stop short of baking. Place them in a single layer on a wax paper–lined baking sheet and freeze completely. Remove them from the tray and place in freezer containers of your choice. You can then bake as normal directly from the freezer. In some cases, an extra one to three minutes is needed on the baking time.

- *Pastries (baked):* Bulk bake your favorite pastries and freeze them for enjoyment later. Simply bake as normal and allow them to cool completely at room temperature. Then store them in the freezer container of your choice. Thaw

Slicing bread before freezing it makes it easier to enjoy straight from the freezer.

overnight in the fridge, then remove and allow the items to come to room temperature or warm in the oven for best results.

- *Prepared meals:* Having ready-to-bake lasagna, casseroles, ravioli, or pizza is very useful when trying to eat homemade food more often while still balancing a busy modern life. Simply prep your food items as normal and freeze before cooking. To make thawing as easy as possible, freeze items in single-meal portions as needed for the number of people in your family. Note, however, that meals such as soups, meatloaf, and cottage pies do best if baked, cooled, and then frozen. To cook or reheat directly from the freezer, simply remove the packaging and cook/reheat in the oven or on the stove, as appropriate for the type of food—no need to thaw beforehand. In some cases, an extra minute or two may be required on the normal cooking time.

You can find oven-safe casserole pans with paper lids in bulk and at most dollar stores, as well as online. Write directly on the lid in a way you will understand (these are mashed butternut squash dishes)

Vegetables

Each vegetable type has its own blanching requirements to preserve the taste and texture without creating a soggy mess. Be sure to check each specific vegetable listing in the table on pages 162–63 for blanching timing by size, as well as other useful information about the freezing process. I prefer to freeze my vegetables on wax paper–lined baking trays before placing them in freezer containers to help avoid smashed vegetables.

Freeze dollops of mashed potatoes on a wax paper–lined baking tray, then remove them and store in plastic bags for a ready-to-heat side dish!

FOOD PRESERVATION, PART I 161

Asparagus	Wash and trim asparagus. Blanch small spears for 1 ½ minutes, medium spears for 2 minutes, and large spears for 3 minutes. Cool, drain, and store as desired.
Beans (Lima and Snap)	Wash and snap or shell the beans. Blanch small beans for 1–2 minutes, or large beans for 3 minutes. Cool and drain before freezing.
Beets	Remove the skin and leaves, and rinse. Dry the beets and either leave whole or cut up as desired. Beets do not require blanching so you can freeze them right away.
Broccoli and Cauliflower	Wash and remove leaves and cut into preferred sizes. Create a brine of 1 cup salt and 1 gallon water and soak pieces for 30 minutes. This helps to kill any bugs inside the tight pieces. Blanch for 3–4 minutes, cool, and drain before portioning to freeze.
Brussels Sprouts	Remove outer leaves and wash before sorting by size. Blanch small sprouts for 3 minutes, medium sprouts for 4 minutes, and large sprouts for 5 minutes before cooling. Drain and store in desired freezer containers.
Cabbage	Cabbage is very versatile and can be frozen in wedges, cut pieces, or shreds. For cut pieces or wedges, blanch for 3 minutes and cool quickly. For shreds, blanch for 1 ½ minutes or not at all. Cool and freeze as desired.
Carrots	Wash, peel, and rinse carrots before cutting into desired sizes. Small pieces or shreds can be blanched for 3 minutes, or larger pieces for 5 minutes, before cooling. Drain and freeze.
Corn on the Cob	Remove husks and silks and wash ears. Blanch small ears for 6 minutes, medium ears for 8 minutes, and large ears for 10 minutes. Cool and drain. Pat dry and tightly wrap in wax paper before placing in freezer containers.
Corn (Whole Kernel)	Prepare, blanch, and cool the same as for corn on the cob. Once cooled and drained, cut the kernels from the cob and pack into freezer containers of choice.
Greens	Wash leaves and remove the stems. Blanch for 2 minutes and cool. Drain and pack into containers of choice. If packing into jars, leave a ½-inch headspace before capping.
Herbs	Wash and dry herbs, but do not blanch. Herbs can be frozen on the stems, or you can remove the herbs from the stems and freeze just the leaves. If freezing whole, wrap small portions of herbs in waxed paper and place in freezer containers of choice. Otherwise, freeze in containers of your choice without wrapping first.
Mushrooms (Raw)	To freeze raw mushrooms, wash and remove the bases, then sort by size. Blanch small, whole mushrooms for 4 minutes. Larger mushrooms should be sliced and blanched for 4 minutes. Cool and drain before packing in desired portions.
Mushrooms (Sautéed)	No blanching is required for cooked mushrooms. Simply prepare as desired, cool, and pack in preferred portions.

Okra (for Frying)	Wash and slice okra into desired sizes. Batter as desired and place coated pieces on a wax paper–lined baking tray. Freeze in a single layer before placing in containers of your choice. Fry directly from frozen; do not thaw.
Okra (Plain)	Wash and remove stem ends. Blanch small pods for 3 minutes, medium pods for 4 minutes, and large pods for 5 minutes. Cool and portion before freezing.
Onions	Chop and cook (if desired) before freezing. Blanching is not recommended for chopped onions, including green onions. If onion bulbs are whole, blanch for 3-7 minutes, or until the center is heated, before cooling and draining the bulbs. Freeze whole bulbs or chopped onions in containers of choice.
Parsnips and Turnips	Remove leaves, wash, and peel. Slice or dice as desired and blanch for 4 minutes. Cool and drain before freezing.
Peas	Shell as needed and blanch for 2 minutes. Cool and drain before freezing. For easiest use, freeze in a single layer before adding to freezer containers of choice.
Peppers	For hot peppers, freeze whole after washing and draining. For sweet peppers, wash and remove stems and seeds. Chop if desired before freezing. Pimiento peppers should be washed and deseeded, then peeled by boiling or roasting. Cool and drain before freezing.
Potatoes (Sweet)	Wash, peel, and cut sweet potatoes as desired. Bring a pot of water to a boil and boil chunks for 3-5 minutes. Cool and drain before freezing in desired containers.
Potatoes (White)	Wash, peel, and rinse. Chop as desired and blanch for 4 minutes. Cool and drain before freezing in desired containers.
Pumpkin	Cut into sections and remove seeds. Steam or bake until flesh is soft, then scoop the pumpkin away from the peel. Puree, cool, and freeze in desired containers. If packing into jars, leave a $\frac{1}{2}$-inch headspace.
Squash (Summer)	Wash, slice, and blanch for 3 minutes. Cool and drain before packing into containers of your choice.
Squash (Winter)	Process the same as pumpkins.
Tomatoes (Whole)	Freeze tomatoes whole, without washing or peeling, if desired. To peel before use, place frozen tomatoes a few at a time into hot water. Leave the tomatoes in the hot water for 1-2 minutes, then pull the skin toward the stem end; it will remove easily. Once peeled, remove seeds if needed and process as normal.

CHAPTER 4

FOOD PRESERVATION, PART II
Dehydrating and Freeze-Drying

While canning and freezing provide a lot of options for preserving food, adding the ability to dehydrate or freeze-dry can give you even more flexibility to build a deep pantry. For example, while you can freeze casseroles, doing so in bulk requires a lot of freezer space and is dependent on electricity. However, freeze-drying those same casseroles creates a shelf-stable option that only requires water to rehydrate and enjoy.

For my family, having more options is always a good thing and allows us to choose the best preservation method based on the food type as well as the desired shelf life and our preferred final texture. Let's start by looking at some of the differences between preservation methods so that you can decide which is right for your family.

FOOD PRESERVATION METHODS

- *Freezing.* Most things can be frozen, but the longevity of those items can be as short as one month, while others can be good for up to a year. Additionally, freezer space can be limited and since the items are not shelf-stable, it's possible that a power outage could wipe out large parts of your food supply.

- *Canning.* This method allows you to create delicious jams, jellies, and pie fillings through the water bath process, as well as ready-to-heat soups and stews (among other things) with pressure canning. Home-canned goods can last up to five years and, in the case of meats and vegetables, have a texture as if the food had been boiled.

- *Dehydrating.* This process can be used to make fruit leather, raw crackers, and jerky, or to dehydrate fruits and vegetables. Since this method uses heat to remove the water from the food, the texture, size, and color of the food changes in the process. Dehydrated foods are shelf-stable for up to two years when stored properly.
- *Freeze-Drying.* This preservation method is great for leftovers, dairy products, both raw and cooked meats in their original form, fresh veggies and fruits, and more. The texture, shape, and color of the food often doesn't change at all, since a cold vacuum process is used to remove the water content. Additionally, 99.7 percent of the nutrients are retained through the freeze-drying process. Shelf-stable for up to twenty-five years, freeze-dried foods are a win for long-term food storage as well. While freeze-drying is the most expensive option, it has the most flexibility, and the foods preserved with this method have the best texture, taste, and shelf life.

All four of these methods have their place, and I plan on using each for the foreseeable future. For example, canning is by far my favorite method for preserving potatoes, while I love dehydrated grapes (raisins) instead of freeze-dried grapes. Likewise, butter can't be freeze-dried, but it can be stored in bulk in the freezer. It's important to understand how each preservation method fits in the food preservation system so that you can create the most efficient and enjoyable food supply based on your family's needs and tastes.

DEHYDRATING

Dehydrating food is something that has been done for thousands of years by using the power of the sun. Today, we can bring that process inside our homes and enjoy the bug-free benefits of electric dehydrators. While not everything can be

Bell peppers ready to dry in our dehydrator. I received this unit as a wedding present from my grandfather almost twenty years ago!

dehydrated for long-term storage—for instance, raw meat or dairy—it's a wonderful option for creating shelf-stable fruits and vegetables that don't require canning and take up less room due to the water content being removed from them.

Unlike canning, however, dehydrated food is not cooked during the process, so for most foods, heating or cooking is still required before consuming. The only exceptions are fruit items or pre-cooked foods such as jerky or sautéed onions. One more thing to note: If you do dehydrate a large portion of your food supply, you will also want to make sure that you have more water on hand than what you need for drinking and bathing, since water is required to rehydrate your food.

Best Machine Features

Fresh figs from our orchard ready to dehydrate whole.

There are many great dehydrators available on the market. Instead of giving you a list of brands to consider, I'm going to share a few features that I recommend having in the unit you purchase:

- *Solid trays.* Many units come with several round trays that have holes in the middle of them. While this is fine for cut fruits and vegetables, it creates issues when trying to make fruit leather or crackers. Look for a dehydrator that has solid trays that are not round.

- *Clear temperature settings.* Some units only have three temperature settings: high, medium, and low. Instead, look for a unit that has temperature settings marked at least to five-degree increments.

- *Airflow.* Proper circulation is essential in food dehydration because it ensures even drying by distributing heat uniformly across all surfaces. Without it, some parts of the food may dry faster than others, leading to uneven results, longer drying times, and an increased risk of spoilage from lingering moisture. Most units will have an explanation of their airflow systems.

- *Timer.* This isn't a must-have but having an automatic timer sure is nice. It can help your food not to become too dry, especially in the case of fruit. Having an automatic timer also ensures exact cooking time. Be aware that dehydrated items can start to rehydrate from the moisture in the air if they are left too long inside the dehydrator. If you purchase one with an automatic shut-off feature, be sure to set an alarm elsewhere to check and process the finished food quickly to avoid it rehydrating once the unit is off.

General Dehydrating Times and Temperatures

Though the following drying times may vary based on your machine and the size of the food being dried, these general guidelines will give you some level of expectation as you preserve with this method. Ultimately, the food needs to be as dry as possible, unless you are dehydrating for something like fruit leather, raisins, or halved tomatoes, which are best when a little moisture remains. Just note that the shelf life of items in which moisture remains may be less than items with the moisture fully removed.

We keep dried and powdered spinach on hand to sprinkle into sauces or over rice. One tablespoon of powdered spinach is the equivalent to a cup of fresh spinach!

Item	Temperature (°F)	Dehydrating Time (Hours)
Fruit		
Apples	135°F–140°F	6–12 hours
Bananas	135°F	6–12 hours
Blueberries	135°F–140°F	12–20 hours
Grapes (Raisins)	135°F	20–36 hours
Mangoes	135°F	8–12 hours
Peaches	135°F–140°F	8–16 hours
Pears	135°F	8–16 hours
Pineapple	135°F	8–16 hours
Strawberries	135°F	7–15 hours
Vegetables		
Carrots	125°F	6–10 hours
Green Beans	125°F	8–12 hours
Mushrooms	125°F	4–7 hours
Onions	125°F	6–10 hours
Peppers (Bell)	125°F	6–12 hours
Potatoes (Sweet)	125°F	7–11 hours
Tomatoes	125°F	10–18 hours
Zucchini	125°F	6–12 hours
Jerky	160°F	4–8 hours
Fruit Leather		
Apple	135°F	6–10 hours
Berry	135°F	4–8 hours
Mixed Fruit	135°F	4–10 hours
Herbs	95°F	2–4 hours

Uncle Sam's Beef Jerky

My brother, known as Uncle Sam, loves making homemade beef jerky. His recipe is tender, flavorful, and easy to make!

Ingredients

3 pounds beef round steak, cut into thin strips

½ cup pineapple juice (as a tenderizer)

¼ cup brown sugar*

¼ cup tamari or soy sauce*

3 tablespoons Worcestershire sauce

1 tablespoon liquid smoke

1 tablespoon smoked paprika

1 teaspoon freshly ground black pepper

1 teaspoon red pepper flakes (optional)

1 teaspoon onion powder

½ teaspoon garlic powder

* You can substitute your favorite barbecue sauce for the brown sugar and tamari, if desired.

Instructions

1. Combine all ingredients in a dish and toss to coat the meat well. Cover and marinate in the fridge for 8 hours or overnight.

2. Remove beef strips and place between two pieces of plastic wrap or parchment paper. Pound to $1/8$-inch thickness.

3. Place beef strips in a single layer on dehydrator trays and set the dehydrator to 160°F. Allow the dehydrator to run for at least 4 hours. Remove the jerky once it's to your desired level of dryness.

4. Cool completely before storing in an airtight container with a moisture absorber and oxygen absorber. Store for a few weeks at room temperature, for 3 months in the fridge, or up to 6 months in the freezer.

BEST STORAGE PRACTICES

It's important to note that once your food is dried, it's *not* fully ready to add to a jar and place on the shelf! You first need to condition the food to ensure there is no remaining moisture that can cause mold to grow.

Conditioning

Not all foods dry at the same rate when you're dehydrating them. You might check a few pieces and find them perfectly done but then discover that others are still a little damp and need more time. Because of this possible difference in moisture levels, it's important to process the dehydrated food to allow the moisture levels to even out.

Fruits, vegetables, and herbs need to be conditioned, as they will likely be stored for long periods of time. Jerky is typically stored in the fridge, even after drying, so it doesn't need to be conditioned. Snack mixes that will be eaten within a week can also forgo the conditioning process. Here are the steps for conditioning food:

1. *Fully dry.* First, fully dehydrate your food to what feels like the finished texture desired. This will vary by unit and even by time of year, but the table on page 169 is a good starting point.

2. *Place in a jar.* Add your dried food to a jar, making sure there is enough space around the food to allow some movement. This doesn't have to be the jar you will store the food in, but it should be clean with a lid. Make sure there isn't too much space, because the extra air could reintroduce moisture. Do not vacuum-seal the jar.

FOOD PRESERVATION, PART II 171

3. *Shake.* Once a day for five to seven days, shake the jar gently to allow the product to move freely. Examine the jar for moisture on the glass and food sticking together or to the glass. If food sticking to the glass is the only thing you see and it easily shakes loose (without effort), it's fine. If it doesn't move easily, or if you see moisture in the glass or clumps of food sticking together, immediately return your food to the dehydrator for more drying time.

4. *Discard.* If at any point mold appears on the food—even the smallest bit—it means that mold has taken root in the jar and the entire batch must be discarded.

A Note on Powdered Foods

If you are dehydrating food that will be powdered when it's fully dry, follow the conditioning process above and then grind the food to a powder. Once the powder is to your desired texture, set your oven to the lowest setting and spread the powder in a thick layer on a cookie sheet. Allow the powder to dry in the oven for about 20–30 minutes before removing. Let the powder fully cool before transferring it to an airtight container.

Storing Dehydrated Foods

Much like other dry goods, dehydrated foods need to be kept in a cool, dark place for the best shelf life. And while you technically don't *need* to use anything in your dried food storage container to keep the food from spoiling once it's properly conditioned, I tend to err on the side of caution. There's nothing like building up a huge food supply only to discover half of it went bad before you could use it!

At a minimum, I recommend an airtight container, a silica packet, and an oxygen absorber placed in the top of every bag or jar of food. Store your dehydrated foods in smaller portions so that you aren't constantly opening a large container and introducing moisture. Small jars and mylar bags work well. I like to use small mylar bags with zip-tops for easy access.

Three Ways to Rehydrate

In some cases, such as with dried fruit or jerky, rehydrating is not required. However, if you want to use fruit or vegetables in various dishes, you'll need to rehydrate them for easier use. There are three simple ways to do this, each with its own place depending on the desired use of the food once it's rehydrated:

1. *Boiling water.* Just like it sounds, boiling water can be poured over the dehydrated food and allowed to sit for about 20–45 minutes. Depending on the type of food and its density, the food may take more or less time to rehydrate. For fruit, you can use boiling juice instead to strengthen the flavor. Add more water or juice as needed as the food absorbs the liquid.

2. *Soaking.* This is the best way to rehydrate food that you want to use in the same way you would use fresh produce, though it will have a different texture from fresh. Simply add the amount of food you want to use to a large bowl and cover it with filtered water, about 1–2 inches above the food. The more water the better! Let it sit overnight so the pieces can rehydrate fully. Any water left over can be used in soups or smoothies (depending on the food you are rehydrating), as it will have some of the flavor and nutrients of the food that was soaked.

3. *Simmer.* Perfect for soups or stews where you will be heating the food anyway, simmering your dehydrated items just requires adding them to a pot of boiling water or broth and allowing them to cook until tender. Meal-in-a-jar recipes can be rehydrated this way and are then ready to eat in less than thirty minutes!

Place your silica and oxygen absorber packets at the top of the container, closest to the lid, for best results.

Fruit leather can be dehydrated on parchment paper, then cut into strips and rolled for easy storage.

DEHYDRATED MEAL-IN-A-JAR RECIPES

Here are four simple, shelf-stable meal-in-a-jar recipes using dehydrated or dried ingredients. Each recipe serves four and can be stored in mason jars with an oxygen absorber and silica pack for up to one year. These make great gifts when you add a tag with the instructions for cooking!

Taco pasta mix ready to be sealed and put on the shelf.

COOKING MEAL-IN-A-JAR RECIPES

To prepare, add contents to a pot with cups of boiling water. Cook for 20–30 minutes or until contents are tender and any meat is rehydrated, stirring occasionally. Garnish and serve as desired.

Hearty Vegetable Soup in a Jar

½ cup dried lentils

¼ cup dried split peas

¼ cup dehydrated carrots

¼ cup dehydrated celery

¼ cup dehydrated onions

2 tablespoons dehydrated tomato powder

2 teaspoons garlic powder

2 teaspoons dried parsley

1 teaspoon dried thyme

1 teaspoon salt

½ teaspoon black pepper

¼ teaspoon red pepper flakes for heat (optional)

Chicken and Rice Soup in a Jar

½ cup instant rice

½ cup freeze-dried chicken

¼ cup dehydrated onions

¼ cup dehydrated carrots

¼ cup dehydrated celery

1 tablespoon dried parsley

1 teaspoon garlic powder

1 teaspoon salt

½ teaspoon black pepper

½ teaspoon dried thyme

½ teaspoon dried rosemary

Taco Pasta in a Jar

1 cup pasta (small shapes like macaroni or fusilli work best)

½ cup freeze-dried ground beef (optional)

¼ cup dehydrated onions

¼ cup dehydrated bell peppers

2 tablespoons taco seasoning mix

1 tablespoon dehydrated tomato powder

½ teaspoon salt

Curry Lentil Stew in a Jar

1 cup dried lentils

¼ cup dehydrated onions

¼ cup dehydrated peas

½ cup instant rice

2 tablespoons coconut milk powder

2 tablespoons curry powder

1 tablespoon garlic powder

1 tablespoon dried cilantro

1 teaspoon turmeric

1 teaspoon salt

½ teaspoon black pepper

FREEZE-DRYING

To avoid overworking your freeze dryer, place it in an area of your house that never gets warmer than 85°F.

Known for years as "astronaut food," freeze-dried foods are nothing new. Hikers have long used them on the trail due to their light weight and long shelf life. In fact, when properly preserved and stored, most freeze-dried foods can last up to twenty-five years. But instead of having to buy freeze-dried foods in bulk from a supplier, you can make them yourself thanks to the invention of the home freeze dryer.

Freeze-drying works by freezing the food to a very cold temperature and then creating a vacuum in the chamber. This causes the water to go directly from ice to vapor and allows the food to retain its shape and texture since the water doesn't turn to liquid in the process.

Is Freeze-Drying Worth the Cost?

For years, I hesitated to invest in a freeze dryer due to its high cost. A medium-sized unit, for example, can cost several thousand dollars. I thought the technology was amazing, but I struggled to understand how it was going to truly help my family. I didn't regularly use freeze-dried foods, and the savings comparisons often highlighted benefits for preppers or campers, which didn't apply to my family. However, once I purchased a freeze dryer, the financial benefits quickly became clear!

For example, my family consumes around five pounds of apples each week. Prices can fluctuate significantly, but by buying apples in bulk at their lowest price and freeze-drying them, we save around $440 annually. We also consume two pounds of bananas and one pound of strawberries weekly and freeze-drying them at their lowest prices saves us an additional $161 per year.

Another significant area of savings is with raw milk, which we can only buy from an A2/A2 dairy several hours away from our homestead. Previously, we made monthly trips to purchase and freeze the milk, but by freeze-drying it, we can now make just two

176 CREATING A MODERN HOMESTEAD

trips per year. This change not only saves freezer space but also reduces travel costs, adding up to $450 in gas savings. In total, we saved more than $1,000 in our first year using the freeze dryer, from those few items alone!

Our freeze dryer has also been invaluable in preserving garden produce that we didn't want to can or freeze, such as pumpkin and butternut squash. My family does not like the texture of canned pumpkin and butternut squash, and they both take up too much room in the freezer. Instead, we can freeze-dry the cooked vegetables for an easy-to-rehydrate and shelf-stable option!

The bottom line is that having a freeze dryer has given me a versatile method to preserve our food, reduce waste, and save both time and money, which has proven to be a worthwhile investment for our homestead.

Freeze-drying strawberries is a great way to enjoy seasonal savings without canning with sugar.

A large variety of foods can be freeze-dried, from milk to fruit, candy to cookie dough, and almost everything in between!

FOOD PRESERVATION, PART II

What Foods to Freeze-Dry

When I first bought my freeze dryer, I had two goals: to freeze-dry honey as a powdered sugar alternative and to preserve butter as powder. Both failed miserably because I didn't know that home freeze dryers don't have enough power to freeze-dry high-fat or high-sugar items. That's not to say you can't freeze-dry cheese or cake, but items that are pure fat or pure sugar just don't dry at all. Other than that restriction, you can freeze-dry almost anything! You can preserve entire lasagnas, ice cream, fruit, vegetables, meat (both raw and cooked), dairy products, broth, and more. Each item maintains its color, shape, and texture when rehydrated.

Eggs can be scrambled or cracked whole onto the freeze-dryer trays. Whole eggs can be gently rehydrated and fried normally!

Best Practices

Because freeze dryers do 99 percent of the work for you, freeze-drying is one of the easiest ways to preserve food, in addition to giving you the longest shelf life. In general, all you have to do is place cold or room-temperature food into the machine and it will do the rest. However, there are a few things that you can do to help ease the process and ensure the best finished product.

- *Raw food.* When prepping raw fruits or vegetables, try to maintain a relatively even size to the pieces. Blueberries and grapes should be poked to allow the moisture to escape, or they will not dry fully.

- *Cooked food.* Dense items such as mashed potatoes should be kept in a thin layer so that the moisture can be fully pulled out by the vacuum. Casseroles or lasagna can be cut into pieces and placed on a tray once cooled after cooking.

- *Don't overpack.* Allow enough room around each item for proper air circulation. While it can be tempting to cram a lot of food onto every tray, limit each batch to about a pound of food per tray. This will prevent too much ice buildup in the machine as the water is pulled out, which can result in the batch failing to dry properly. For example, if your unit has four trays, your entire batch should only contain a total of 4 pounds of food. If one tray has 2 pounds of mashed potatoes, then you have 2 more pounds to allot to the other three trays. However, again, try to limit each tray to a total of 1 pound of food each, if possible.

- *Prefreeze.* If freezing will not alter the taste and texture of your food, prefreezing will help speed up the drying process. This is great for things like cookie dough, milk, broth, and so on. But for items where freezing will affect the texture, such as with fresh fruit, you can skip this step.

- *Mixed batches.* Don't be afraid to freeze-dry ice cream and onions in the same batch, on different trays! I have found that there is no crossover flavor in the finished product. To be safe, you can pack "smelly" things on the top of the machine, as the air is pulled in that direction when it processes. This will keep more delicate flavors safe on the bottom—though again, it's never been an issue for my family.

Storage Practices

Unlike dehydrated foods, once fully processed in the freeze dryer, freeze-dried foods are ready to store right away. Simply remove them from the trays and place them in mylar storage bags with an oxygen absorber and a silica packet. With freeze-dried foods, you can use a large mylar bag and remove what you want as needed. However, if you have opened the package often, say five to six times, add a new oxygen absorber and silica packet and reseal.

Glass jars are not recommended for long-term storage, but if you will be using an item fully within a few months, they're fine for the

You can mix various foods in batches, but I would recommend keeping like items on a single tray. For example, don't add sautéed onions to the same tray as sliced berries.

FOOD PRESERVATION, PART II

short term. Nutrient quality tends to go down after that point, but the food is still edible.

Powdering Foods

For foods such as eggs or milk, it's easier to store and measure them for use later if they are fully powdered before storing. You can simply process the food as normal and then add the finished product to a food processor or blender. Run on high for about 2 minutes, stopping to scrape down the sides as needed, then add to a jar with silica and oxygen packets for storage. One gallon of milk freeze-dries and powders down to store easily in a single quart jar.

Freeze-dried eggs being powdered in a blender before storing.

How to Rehydrate

This process is similar to rehydrating dehydrated foods; however, since you can also freeze-dry whole meals, there are a few differences to consider. Unlike dehydrated foods, raw foods that are freeze-dried are almost identical to their fresh state when rehydrated. For items that were freeze-dried raw, you should use cold water, whereas for items that were cooked when processed, hot water is generally best. Here are a few ways to introduce cold or hot water, depending on the item:

- *Spraying.* Finicky foods— items that you want to look perfect and fresh when they are rehydrated, such as fresh raspberries or herbs for garnish—can be sprayed with hot or cold water as needed. Simply fill a spray bottle with water at the desired temperature and spritz the food gently. Allow it to sit for a moment before spraying again. For large foods like whole berries, you may need to gently reposition the items before spraying again so that you can get every angle.

- *Cooking.* Just like with dehydrating, you can simply put freeze-dried items in hot water. This method is best for vegetables, broth, stew meat, cooked and freeze-dried soups, or anything else that would be added to a soup anyway.

- *Soaking.* For this method, you can use cold water, since you will soak it for a long time. Place your items in a bowl and cover with 1–2 inches of water. Allow items to soak for several hours at room temperature, or in the fridge for up to two days until you are ready to use them. Raw items will take much longer than cooked items.

- *Hot water pour-over.* From a kettle or a glass measuring cup, pour simmering water over your freeze-dried foods. Go slowly to avoid mushiness. Start with a few drops at a time, let the item soak up the water, and drip more as needed. Cover with aluminum foil and allow to sit for a few minutes once the water starts to stand. This method is best for items that are already cooked and assembled, such as cakes, casseroles, or lasagna. We also rehydrate meat and potato dishes this way but then pan-fry or oven-heat them to fully bring them back to that freshly cooked texture.

RECIPES FOR GIFTING FREEZE-DRIED FOODS

Though the uses for freeze-dried foods are nearly limitless, I wanted to share two of my favorite ways to mix and utilize them on a regular basis. Not only have these recipes been great for my own family, but they both make great gifts as well! Just fill a mason jar and seal it, then add a tag with the instructions!

Hot Chocolate Mix

We make a large batch of this hot chocolate mix every year and enjoy it all season long.

Ingredients

2 cups powdered sugar

1 cup Dutch-processed cocoa powder

2½ cups powdered freeze-dried milk

2 teaspoons arrowroot powder

1 teaspoon sea salt

Instructions

Add all ingredients to a large bowl and mix until well combined. Store in an airtight container with oxygen and silica packets for up to 1 year. Add a ¼–½ cup of this mix to 1 cup of almost boiling water and stir until fully dissolved.

Dry Pancake Mix

Keep this on the shelf for busy mornings or give it as a housewarming gift along with a new spatula and kitchen towel! All it requires is adding water!

Ingredients

3 cups (360g) all-purpose flour

3 tablespoons sugar

3 tablespoons baking powder

¾ teaspoon salt

6 tablespoons powdered freeze-dried milk

3 tablespoons powdered freeze-dried whole eggs

Instructions for Dry Mix

In a large bowl, whisk together all the dry ingredients until well combined. Store the pancake mix in an airtight container or jar with silica and oxygen packets. It should stay shelf-stable for several months if kept in a cool, dry place.

To Prepare Pancakes

1. In a medium bowl, combine 1 cup of the pancake mix with ¾ cup water.

2. Stir until just combined. If the batter is too thick, add a little more water (1 tablespoon at a time) until you reach the desired consistency.

3. Heat a nonstick pan or griddle over medium heat.

4. Pour about ¼ cup of batter per pancake onto the hot pan.

5. Cook for 2–3 minutes, or until bubbles form on the surface, then flip and cook for another 1–2 minutes until golden brown.

6. Serve with your favorite toppings, such as syrup, butter, or fruit.

CHAPTER 5

GROWING YOUR OWN FOOD

For most of you on the homesteading path, growing some, or all, of your food is the ultimate goal. We have been blessed to grow the vast majority of our own fruits and vegetables for the last nine years, and I can tell you with complete confidence that there is nothing like the feeling of popping a fresh tomato, bright red and still warm from the sun, into your mouth. It's almost like that homegrown tomato is a different food entirely from what's available in the grocery store. The taste, the crispness, and the nutritional value are all a world away from what most people experience on a daily basis.

Perhaps you, too, have been blessed with fresh fruits and vegetables from your own plants—whether a single tomato plant grown on an apartment balcony, or a variety of plants, vegetables, and fruit grown in a kitchen garden in your backyard. Or maybe you've only dreamed of harvesting food for your family. Either way, this chapter is going to help you solidify your methods to ensure that your gardens and food supply are secure for years to come.

UNDERSTANDING YOUR GARDENING GOALS AND NEEDS

Before we launch into the different types of gardening methods available and which one makes the most sense for your needs and climate, your goals for this garden and the food that it produces needs to be considered first. These goals may be predetermined for you based on your available growing area. However, in the event that you have the space to grow as much as you want, you need to decide how much food you want to grow for your family.

Often, new gardeners have no idea how much food they can grow in a small space, and they end up overplanting. I know, because we have done that many times!

185

Trellising green beans on twine allows them to freely move in the breeze and can help increase the yield.

One year my husband planted 40 feet worth of green bean plants and then trellised them up 6 feet. That's a lot of green beans! He ended up harvesting green beans for six to eight hours a day, every other day, for almost six straight months. I canned more than 1,500 quarts of green beans that year, gave away as much as we could, and fed the chickens the rest. That was almost four years ago, and we *still* have canned green beans left from that summer!

All that to say, overplanting by a little is fine, but creating a situation where you become a slave to the harvest is not.

WHY DO YOU WANT TO GROW FOOD?

One goal that is important to define is why you want to grow food in the first place, as this will help you in the next stages of planning. Let's stop for a second to consider what you realistically want to get out of your garden.

Growing Food for Fun

If you like the idea of growing some of your own food and want to have that experience, but you aren't compelled to start relying on your garden as a food supply, then the sky is the limit. You don't have to be practical with your plant choices, but can grow in whatever space you have, and with whatever varieties strike your fancy!

This might mean that you do in fact grow a large garden, but it might also mean that you simply grow food in containers on your back patio and enjoy whatever harvest comes from them.

If you don't want to rely on your garden for consistent food, then just having fun with interesting varieties would be perfect.

Growing Food to Supplement Your Budget

As grocery prices go up and nutritional values go down, having some strategic foods growing in a backyard garden will help stretch your food budget quite a long way.

With this goal you'll want to choose to grow only the foods that you most frequently buy and that you know your family will eat. To start filling out your dream team of plants to grow first, take a look at what you are normally buying on a weekly and monthly basis.

We grew sugar beets for fun one year because I wanted to try making my own sugar. It was a success, but the yield was too low for the amount of space it took up in our garden.

If you are limited on space, you'll want to choose small-space, high-yield plants first. We will talk about harvest yields later, but a good example is zucchini. One plant will yield dozens of fruit every week for months! It doesn't vine and only takes up a 4' × 4' area. This type of plant makes the perfect supplement to your budget as it yields a lot of food in a very small space.

Growing Food for a Year-Round Supply

Having a year-round food supply is obviously the most intense goal of all the options and will require a bit more logistical planning, but it is completely doable! Here are a few questions to consider before moving to the next phase of calculating your gardening needs:

- How many people are you growing for?
- How much land can you dedicate to growing food?

- How long is your growing season? (Don't worry too much about this because modifications such as hoop houses and row covers can extend your growing season. We will talk more about that later.)
- Which foods do you want to prioritize?
- Do you have space to can/freeze/store the food once it's harvested?

Once you have the answers to these questions, you can start to calculate your food needs for a whole year.

Calculating Your Family's Needs

It can seem like an overwhelming task to plan how much you need to grow in order to feed your family year-round, but all it takes is a little math! For example:

Corn dried after harvesting is perfect for long-term storage as a milling grain.

- My family likes to eat pizza once a week as well as pasta once a week.
- For my family this equals about 1 quart of tomato sauce per week, or approximately 52 quarts per year.
- My standard tomato sauce recipe needs approximately 4 pounds of tomatoes to make 1 finished quart.
- I then know that I need to grow about 208 pounds of tomatoes to meet my family's tomato sauce needs for a full year.
- Each plant yields about 10 pounds of tomatoes per month during the growing season, and our season is nine months long. In our climate, I need three tomato plants to meet the requirements for our family's tomato sauce consumption.

Note: I also need to calculate for other meals using tomatoes (like chili or homemade ketchup) to understand exactly how many tomatoes I need in total.

Here's another example:

- We enjoy eating potatoes about three times per week: mashed potatoes, french fries, or baked potatoes. To feed my family, each meal requires about 1.5 pounds of potatoes total.
- For a full year of potatoes at that rate of consumption, we will need around 234 pounds.
- Each potato plant yields about 3 pounds of potatoes, so I need about seventy potato plants since we only have one growing season (spring) for potatoes in my location (you may have two seasons).

Now it's your turn to create a solid plan for your own family. It won't take too long to complete. You can do it in one afternoon! Once complete, you'll know that you have all your needs accounted for as you start growing your garden. Here's what you need to get started:

1. Grab a sheet of paper and start writing down everything your family eats on a regular basis. Note any and all ingredients that could be replaced with homegrown produce or home-canned goods.
2. Calculate how many pounds of fresh produce are needed for any of the homemade or home-canned items you will require throughout the year.
3. Combine all like plants together into one number. For example, if you need tomatoes for eight different dishes, combine the numbers for each dish into one line item for "tomatoes."
4. Calculate your growing season length by finding your last and first frost dates. The days in between those two dates would be considered your growing season. Take the total number of days and subtract "days to maturity" for each plant (see pages 216–17).

Unlike other spinach varieties, Malabar spinach is a vining variety and is very heat tolerant. Just four plants can completely cover a six-foot-tall trellis and produce hundreds of pounds of dark leafy greens.

GROWING YOUR OWN FOOD 189

For example, if you have a growing season of 200 days and tomatoes have a "days to maturity" of 60 days, then you will only have 140 days of harvesting your fresh tomatoes. Again, your growing time can be extended by using a greenhouse (or hoop house) or by starting seeds indoors before the last frost date. We will talk more about those workarounds/tricks later.

5. Once you have all of your needs listed, make note of how much space each plant takes up and multiply to find how many square feet of gardening space you need for each plant variety.

6. Add all the numbers together to find your total garden square footage requirements.

You may be tempted to buy an extra plant to have just in case, but I don't recommend it (see green bean example above!). It's better to have a little less than you anticipated and then know you need to plant more the next year.

With this information in mind, let's move into the specifics of planning your garden space needs.

HOW MUCH SPACE DO YOU NEED TO GROW FOOD?

As with the previous section, determining how much garden space you need is going to depend on your goals. If you just want to grow food for fun, or to supplement your food budget, then you can use whatever space you have available to you. You can even grow nutrient-dense food in an apartment by growing sprouts in a mason jar, as long as you have a sunny windowsill or a small balcony!

However, if growing food for your family for an entire year is the goal, then based on my experience, you'll need at least 1,500 square feet of land with full sun in order to reach your goals for a family of four.

I bet that you're probably shocked by the idea that a 30' × 50' growing area is all you need! But it's true. We have been growing our own food and helping others do the same for almost a decade, so there is a lot of background knowledge that goes into that answer. Here are some of the experiences I'm using to base this number on:

- We've been growing 80 percent of our family's food for almost a decade. Things like rice and wheat are still outsourced.

Cut-and-come-again lettuce is a great option for growing in a small space. This type of lettuce allows you to harvest leaves from the outer edges without uprooting the entire head. It can grow like this for months, yielding a continual source of food from one plant.

- We've helped thousands of other families do the same.
- We feed seven people full-time and have enough left over to feed our chickens, give away to neighbors, as well as can/preserve for later in the year.
- We use the Back to Eden gardening method, which produces more vegetables in a smaller space. More about this later.
- We choose foods that store well and have long growing seasons.
- The foods that we grow are ones that we actually eat (not just ones that we thought would be fun to grow or experiment with in the kitchen), which means all of the food is eaten and nothing is wasted.

While the conventional "wisdom" is that you can grow about 1 pound of food per square foot, we have found that number to be closer to 6.5 pounds per square foot of garden space. But even if you only harvested 1 pound of food per square feet, 1,500 square feet of garden will still provide a pound of fresh produce per person, per day, for a family of four for a whole year!

With the average person consuming about 3–4 pounds of food per day—and accounting for meats and grains—then you can assume 2–3 pounds of produce per day per person in your family. Let's calculate for a family of four:

- 3 pounds per day times 4 people equals 12 pounds per day
- 12 pounds per day times 365 days equals 4,380 pounds of food per year
- 4,380 pounds of food needed divided by an average of 3 pounds of food per square foot equals 1,460 square feet of garden space needed

Now it's your turn. Simply adjust the calculations for your own family to see how much space you will need.

But remember, you don't need enough space to grow *all your food* to make gardening worthwhile. Even with a small space—say 200 square feet, which is a 10' × 20' area—you can grow up to 1,300 pounds of food each year. And with balcony gardening, you could grow dozens of pounds of fresh food a month!

These three tomato plants, grown with the Back to Eden method, took up a total of 48 square feet but yielded more than 900 pounds of tomatoes during the growing season. That's more than 18 pounds of food per square foot!

WHICH GARDENING METHOD IS RIGHT FOR YOU?

Depending on where you live, and where you are on your path to food security, you may already have some idea of how you want to grow your food. Or maybe you've had issues with pests, waterlogging, or low yield and you're ready to try something else.

In this section, I'm going to break down some of the most popular gardening methods, who they are right for, and when they should be avoided. Let's start with a quick overview of each method, and I'll talk more about setup and maintenance a little later.

Traditional In-Ground Till-and-Plant Method

When you think of backyard gardening, this is likely the method that pops into your mind. Till the soil, plant the seeds, add water and fertilizer, then harvest. While this can be a very effective method for growing food, there are also times when a traditional in-ground till-and-plant garden will not serve you well. Let's look at when you should and should not use this method.

When to use this method:

- *If you have hard, compacted soil.* In this case, tilling can help new gardens become established faster by breaking up the soil to allow new materials such as compost to integrate faster.

- *If you have little to no microorganism activity.* When there are no or hardly any bugs present in your soil, it can mean that the soil is relatively "dead" and needs a lot of work to bring it back to life. In this case, tilling will not harm the ecosystem, as there isn't one present.

When to avoid this method:

- *If you have been working on creating better soil.* Have you done any sort of modifications to the soil in question? If so, it would be best to leave it alone. Disturbing the topsoil by turning it under in any way when you have been working to increase its quality would see much of your hard work vanish as the soil below is brought to the top.

- *If you have active and alive soil.* Do you see lots of bugs thriving in your soil? Don't till it! These bugs are crucial to building high-quality soil, and by tilling it you are likely to destroy this system.

Back to Eden Gardening

Pioneered by Paul Gautschi, the Back to Eden gardening method was born out of his observations of how nature cultivates plants in the wild. There are no tillers or soaker hose watering systems in nature, no daily weeding or pest control. So how do wild berries thrive? How do peaches grow year after year? By striving to understand the answers to those questions, Paul Gautschi created the Back to Eden method for growing food.

This is the method that my family has used in Texas for almost a decade now, and even in the brutal heat, the no-weeding, no-watering promises of the Back to Eden method have proven very true. Yes, even in the 110°F heat of July through September, our garden thrives and continues to produce food! Consider the following to see if Back to Eden is right for you.

When to use this method:

- *If you have poor soil quality.* One of the functions of the Back to Eden method is that it works to improve the soil quality below the surface of the garden as well. It creates an environment where beneficial bugs thrive, and as a result the soil is improved.

- *If you have limited space.* Since the Back to Eden method results in high yields per square foot, you can grow much more food in a small space than with other methods.

- *If you want a more hands-off approach.* Another fabulous point in favor of this method is that you can prep the beds, plant the seeds, and then wait for the harvest. There is little to no work required

The Back to Eden gardening method yields giant plants! This is my hand next to the leaf of a three-month-old zucchini plant.

in between those processes. No daily weeding or watering required!

- *If you need to conserve water.* We like to try to use collected rainwater for our gardens. Because of this, we wanted to make sure we were using the most effective method for conserving water. The Back to Eden method uses a heavy mulch covering that swells during rainfall and then releases the moisture/water into the soil over time. As a result, little to no extra watering is needed.

When to avoid this method:

- *If you need a raised gardening area.* While I adore the Back to Eden method, it is an in-ground gardening method meant to restore the soil quality of your garden. If you have physical limitations and can't bend over to harvest food or check the soil moisture, then this method wouldn't be a great choice for you. However, it is possible to combine raised beds with some of the Back to Eden principles!

Our okra plants thrive even in 115°F weather without water thanks to the deep mulch of the Back to Eden method.

Raised-Bed Gardening

There are many different ways to create a raised bed garden. Whether you want to use cinder blocks or limestone, cedar fence posts, or pallets—all you need is a raised enclosure to keep your soil in place.

We have a few raised beds and are transitioning to more as we have fewer mouths to feed and are reducing the amount of food we are growing. At first, we created beds out of wood, which lasted several years. But as we moved to fewer beds, we started investing in limestone from a local stone supplier (much cheaper than getting it from

the hardware store). The resulting beds will last much longer than the wood beds, and they are very pretty to look at too! Here's a look at who this method may be right for.

When to use this method:

- *If you don't want to bend down.* Physical limitations are of course the most common reason for wanting raised-bed gardens; it's much easier to harvest and maintain the beds if they are a bit higher!

- *If you want aesthetically pleasing gardens.* There is great beauty in a row garden, but if you also want to create a statement piece with where you grow your food, raised bed gardens are a great way to do that.

- *If you are low on space.* Raised beds are a good way to maintain the boundaries of your gardening efforts. Unlike in-ground gardens, where a pumpkin plant might take over a 30-square-foot area, raised-bed gardens will make sure that plants stay where they are planted (provided you trim them as they spill over).

When to avoid this method:

- *If you aren't sure where you want your gardens to be placed.* Building raised beds only to have to move them later can be a costly endeavor, both in time and money. Make sure you know where you want your raised beds before you build.

- *If you need to grow a lot of food.* Growing food in bulk is not conducive to raised-bed gardening, as there is limited space. You could certainly build enough beds to grow large amounts of food, but it would likely be very expensive!

Container Gardening

I firmly believe that everyone, no matter where they live, can grow food for themselves and their families. No matter what your living space, you deserve to grow and eat fresh food! Container gardening is a wonderful way to add homegrown produce to your life in a limited quantity. And while everyone can container garden in some way, there are some reasons why you may not want to attempt it!

When to use this method:

- *If in-ground gardening isn't an option.* Whether you rent a house or an apartment, sometimes in-ground or raised beds just aren't an option. In those cases, growing individual plants in containers is a great alternative.

- *If you want to start small.* Even when you can grow food in the ground, sometimes starting small is a better way to start. By growing a tomato plant and some fresh herbs, you can build your confidence before going big!

- *If you want to get started for very little money.* Just like the last point, starting out by spending a few dollars can be much more manageable than investing a large sum into a set of raised beds.

When to avoid this method:

- *If you are prone to forgetting about plants.* I'll raise my hand here, because I am terrible about remembering to water and care for my indoor plants! Container gardening does require a bit more hands-on effort than an in-ground garden that will benefit from rain and natural care from the elements.

- *If you have animals.* While in-ground and raised-bed gardens can certainly be affected by animals (whether livestock or wild), container gardening is more susceptible to ruin when animals knock over or dig out the plants. If you take care to keep your containers safe from animals, then you should be fine. If you don't have a place to keep them away from animals, this method may not be the best for you.

Now that we've talked about the pros and cons of the various gardening methods, let's take a closer look at how to create each type.

GROWING YOUR OWN FOOD 197

CREATING A TRADITIONAL IN-GROUND GARDEN

If you've decided that an in-ground till-and-plant garden is for you, let's talk about how to set it up in the best way possible.

Choosing the Best Spot

Selecting the right location for your till-and-plant garden is crucial for a successful harvest. Here are some things to look for as you choose your garden setting:

- *Sunlight hours.* You'll want to choose a spot that gets plenty of sun, as most vegetables need at least six to eight hours of direct sunlight each day.
- *Water.* Be sure to consider how close the location is to a water source. In order to make watering easier, make sure that there is easy access to a faucet for hand-watering with a hose or to attach soaker hoses.

Soil Testing and Amendments

Before you start tilling, it's a good idea to test your soil. Soil testing kits are available at most garden centers, or you can send a sample to your local extension office for a detailed analysis. Little electronic meters are sold online that will give you an instant read of your pH level.

Most vegetables prefer a pH between 6.0 and 7.0. Based on your soil test results, you may need to add lime to raise the pH or sulfur to lower it.

While soil testing is optional, it will help your garden performance and yields if you are able to adjust pH levels.

The amount of lime or sulfur you need to add to your garden soil to adjust the pH depends on the soil type and how many points (units) you need to raise or lower the pH level.

Since it's unlikely that you will be gardening in much more than 1,000 square feet, I have included calculations in the table on page 200 based on that size. You can divide or multiply that amount as needed for the space in which you will be gardening!

If you aren't sure of your soil type, here is a quick breakdown to help you determine the soil you have as a base:

When it comes to selecting the right location, each garden method will have different needs, but there are four parts of the process that will always be the same: seed quality, proximity to harvest, timing of planting, and spacing of your plants.

1. **Seed quality.** Make sure you have good seeds from the start. We like to use seeds that are heirloom, non-GMO because we want to be sure we can harvest seeds from our crops and use them again the next year, without worrying whether or not they will produce food (versus just plants without produce!).

2. **Proximity to harvest.** This will always be the same, no matter which method you choose! Make sure the spot you pick for your garden isn't so far away that you won't see it daily. Life can get busy and you may forget to harvest your garden for days or weeks! Having a spot close to the house also makes it easier to bring in the harvest for processing. It's frustrating to have to lug 50-100 pounds of food back to the house when you have to carry it across multiple acres to get there!

3. **Timing.** Depending on when you prepped your beds, you may need to wait to plant until the weather is right. Obviously, you don't want to plant tomatoes in the dead of winter, or they will die. Instead, find the last frost date for your gardening zone and plant based on that date. (I will break this down in more detail in the plant-specific growing guide section of this chapter, but for now know that you will need to take frost date into account when planting.)

4. **Spacing.** This part is simple! Just follow the instructions on the seed packets or plant tags for the correct planting depth and spacing. Each plant is different and may require more or less space, so you'll need to take a plant-specific look at spacing. Proper spacing ensures that plants have enough access to sunlight and nutrients in order to thrive.

- *Sandy soil.* Typically, very coarse and gritty, sandy soil is just what it sounds like: sandy! While this type of soil has great drainage, nutrients are usually very low as they are washed away with the water as it rushes through.

- *Loam.* Often considered the perfect soil for gardening, loam is a mix of dirt, sand, and clay. Loam is crumbly and holds moisture well without becoming waterlogged, and also typically has a nice nutrient level.

> Every county in the United States has an extension office staffed with agents who collaborate with university-based specialists to provide answers to questions about animal husbandry, gardening, agriculture, and pest control. These agents are a great resource to utilize, and the service is free!

- *Clay.* This soil is usually very easy to spot because it's dense and hard to dig into! If you've ever tried to dig a post hole in your yard, only to get stuck after a few inches, you likely have clay! Having clay soil is a great reason to choose the till-and-plant method since it needs to be broken up and amended before growing is possible.

Adjusting Soil pH with Lime (Raising pH)	Adjusting Soil pH with Sulfur (Lowering pH)
Lime (calcium carbonate) is commonly used to reduce acidity and raise soil pH levels. This list provides a general idea of how much lime to add per 1,000 square feet to raise the pH by one point: • Sandy soil: 20–50 pounds • Loam: 50–75 pounds • Clay: 75–100 pounds	Sulfur can be used to increase acidity and lower soil pH. This list provides a general idea of how much sulfur to add per 1,000 square feet to lower the pH by one point: • Sandy soil: 10–15 pounds • Loam: 20–25 pounds • Clay: 30–40 pounds

Adding Compost and Other Organic Matter

If your soil is clay or sandy in nature, it's likely that you'll need to add nutrients to it before planting. Loam without bug activity could also benefit from augmentation as well. These additions help not only with nutrients but also with soil structure and drainage. Here are a few of my favorite things to add to soil, with tips on how to do it safely:

- *Compost.* This can be homemade or store bought, but if the compost contains animal manure, make sure that it is well aged before using it on the garden. When "hot manure" from cows, horses, pigs, turkeys, or chickens is fresh, it will burn the plants as the nitrogen breaks down. If livestock manure is mixed into compost, it should be turned and processed for six months before using.

- *Manure.* If you have manure that you want to use on its own, that's great! Just like compost, you'll need to make sure that it is broken down before you use it. "Hot manure" needs to be completely dry and broken down into a soil-like appearance when used on its own. "Cold manure" from rabbits, llamas, alpacas, sheep, or goats can be used immediately on a garden without issues.

- *Organic fertilizers.* There are many organic and natural fertilizers that you could add to your garden soil, from fish emulsions to bone meal, kelp powder to worm castings. I'm not going to cover them all here but know that you can amend your soil even further with organic options and you don't need to use chemical fertilizers to grow your food.

Setting up Your Garden for Planting

With the in-ground plant-and-till method, tilling the soil is a critical step in preparing your garden. It helps break up compacted soil, incorporate organic matter, and create a loose, crumbly texture that roots can easily navigate as they grow. Here are the steps you need to follow for preparing your garden:

1. *Timing.* Make sure that the soil is not too wet. Wet soil will become compacted as the tiller goes over it. Even if you are using a hand tiller or hand tools, simply working the soil while it's wet will remove the air and lead to very hard soil when the moisture evaporates.

GROWING YOUR OWN FOOD 201

Depending on the length of your growing season, you may need two separate spaces for melons and winter squash; the melons may still be yielding when it's time to plant the squash.

2. *Prep.* Sprinkle any soil amendments, such as lime or fertilizer, based on your needs over the top of the untilled land. This will allow you to incorporate them during the tilling step with ease.

3. *Depth.* If you want to till once, till your soil at a depth of 8–12 inches, working in rows about 2 feet apart. While this doesn't create the best soil or work the additions in as fully as possible, it will still work well enough. Depending on your time and/or physical capacity, one pass may be all you can do. If you can till twice, till the first time in a diagonal pattern to the desired finished rows at a depth of 6–8 inches. Then go back again and till the final rows in the desired direction.

Be careful not to over-till, as this can destroy soil structure and compact it. One or two passes with the tiller should be sufficient.

Planting in Your In-Ground Garden Space

With your soil prepped and ready to go, it's time to start planting! Here are the steps that you'll need to follow:

1. *Planting.* When the timing is right for your area, you'll plant your seeds or seedlings directly into the freshly tilled soil. Traditional gardens like this are often set up using the row planting method, but block planting can maximize space and reduce weeds. Choose the method that suits your garden size and layout.

2. *Watering.* Most vegetables need about 1 inch of water per week, either from rainfall or irrigation. While you can water by hand (depending on the size of your garden), setting up a soaker hose system or a simple arch sprinkler that you move throughout the day will help ensure that your plants are getting enough water.

Adding a soaker hose to our limestone strawberry beds has been very helpful for keeping them thriving through the Texas heat.

3. *Fertilizers.* You may need to apply additional fertilizers according to the needs of your plants. For example, leafy greens benefit from nitrogen-rich fertilizers, while fruiting plants like tomatoes need more phosphorus. Even if you fertilized the soil during the tilling process, you may want to fertilize again during the growing season as needed.

Best Tips for Traditional Gardening

Once you've tilled your garden and planted your seeds or seedlings, there are a few additional things you need to be aware of that will help protect your plants and increase your harvest volume:

1. *Water consistently.* Most vegetables need about 1 inch of water per week, and without a mulch top, your garden will be susceptible to moisture evaporation. Water deeply and less frequently to encourage deep root growth and consider using soaker hoses or drip irrigation to deliver water directly to the soil. Not only does this relieve you of the need to remember to water, but it also helps reduce evaporation.

GROWING YOUR OWN FOOD

2. *Control weeds regularly.* Weeds compete with your plants for nutrients, water, and sunlight, so it's important to keep them to a minimum! Regularly check your garden for weeds and remove them by hoeing or hand-pulling anything that you see.

3. *Monitor for pests and diseases.* Keep a close eye on your plants for signs of pests and diseases. Early detection and intervention are key! I'll talk more about this specifically in a bit, but it is especially important to be aware of potential issues for success around this aspect of gardening.

4. *Rotate crops annually.* Avoid planting the same family of vegetables in the same spot year after year. This practice will help prevent nutrient deficiencies and reduce pest and disease problems. Rotate crops with different nutrient needs and pest resistances each season.

CREATING A BACK TO EDEN GARDEN

If you've chosen the Back to Eden gardening method for your new growing efforts, I'm so excited to help you get started. This has been the primary way we've grown food for nearly a decade! Back to Eden gardening produces low-effort, high-yield results that allow you to enjoy your fresh produce without it ruling your life.

Choosing the Best Spot

There are only a few things to consider when choosing a spot for your new Back to Eden garden, but they are very important! Sometimes they may go against where you want to have your garden space, but they will play a huge part in the success of your gardening efforts, so don't discount them easily. Here are things to think about when planning on the best spot for your garden:

- *Sunlight hours.* Most vegetables need at least six to eight hours of direct sunlight each day, so pick a sunny spot. If you are planting herbs or other plants that don't require much sunlight, you will need a partially shady spot in your garden as well.

- *Water.* Since the Back to Eden method is set up to be relatively low effort in the watering department, you can be farther from a water source than other gardening methods. However, don't forget about it completely. There may be times of extended drought when you will still need to water your garden a few times.

Soil Amendments

Unlike the traditional till-and-plant method, Back to Eden gardening builds soil on top of what is already there. You don't need to know what your soil type is, you don't need to test for pH, and you don't need to augment the soil. Instead, we will create the garden bed directly on top of the existing soil and plant in the manufactured soil.

Setting up Your Garden for Planting

One of my favorite things about the Back to Eden method is that you can create the beds and plant in them right away. The process is very simple, and depending on the size of your garden, you can set everything up in an afternoon! Here are the steps for setting up your garden:

1. *Weed barrier.* First, create a weed barrier. We like to use entire newspaper sections, not single sheets, for creating weed barriers. Depending on your preferences or needs, you can use cardboard, weed cloth, or nothing (if you're brave!). The goal here is to create a weed barrier that will eventually break down but will give your garden a head start against the weeds.

2. *Compost layer.* Next, add 5–6 inches of well-aged compost over the entire garden area (this is the soil that your plants will actually grow in and will attract beneficial bugs to enhance the soil below as well). Just like I mentioned before, your compost needs to be well-aged (at least six months old) and well turned if it contains "hot manure" from cows, horses, pigs, turkeys, or chickens. If you have llamas, alpacas, rabbits, sheep, or goats, their "cold manure" can be mixed into compost and used right away. Using hot manure before it is fully processed will burn your plants as the nitrogen processes out. You want that process to be complete before adding it to your garden.

3. *Mulch layer.* Ah, the magic ingredient in the Back to Eden gardening method! Wood mulch creates a barrier for the topsoil (compost layer) that not only protects it from heat but also holds and releases moisture from rainfall and watering efforts. You will add 3–5 inches of aged wood mulch to the top of your compost layer. "Aged mulch" has been chipped and sitting for at least six months and should have darkened and broken down some during that time. Just like hot manure, fresh tree

mulch will cause the same issues if it's processing on your garden. Depth of mulch can vary depending on your climate. For hotter growing zones, I recommend at least 5 inches (up to 6 inches) as a protection against the heat and to retain maximum moisture. Here in South Texas, we always strive for a full six inches of mulch top on our Back to Eden garden spaces.

Planting in Your Back to Eden Garden Space

With your soil prepped and ready to go, it's time to start planting! Let's talk about timing, spacing, and care for your new garden space:

While most seed packets will tell you to plant heavy and thin back, I have found that due to the dense nutrient nature of the Back to Eden method, you can leave any seed that sprouts to grow to harvest. These plants are very close together, but still produced beets that were much larger than the average size.

1. *Planting.* When the timing is right for what you are planting, you'll plant your seeds or seedlings directly into the compost layer. To do this, simply use a hoe to create trenches about 4 inches deep in the mulch. If planting from seeds, wait until the seedlings are about 4–5 inches tall and then pull the previously moved mulch around them. For seedlings, you can bring the mulch back around them right away, as long as they have leaves above the mulch level.

2. *Watering.* Due to the mulch top, you can just give your garden a good soaking after you plant and then leave it alone. If you have planted seeds and the mulch is not pulled around them yet, water them well (about 1 inch of water) at planting and then water again with a good soaking once the mulch is in place after the seedlings have grown enough. Additionally, you'll want to periodically test your soil by sticking your finger into it. If the soil is dry no more than 2 inches from the top, you can leave it! If it's dry farther down, you will want to water. If you are getting regular rainfall, no watering should be needed. In periods of prolonged drought, occasional watering may be required.

3. *Fertilizers.* You should not need any additional fertilizers for your Back to Eden garden, so long as you used high-quality compost. However, if your plants start to look sickly, read the soil testing and amendment section of this chapter for more information on adjusting your soil.

Best Tips for Back to Eden Gardening

While this method is very hands-off, there are a few things we've learned over the last decade that have helped make our gardens even more successful:

1. *Be quick.* Don't take more than a few days to finish the beds. Start small and make sure you can finish the area in no more than a day or two. You don't want your weed barrier material to fly away or the compost to dry out. Finish your beds about two days before a good rain if you can, as this will help solidify the bed and will get everything prepped for planting. If you can't time your bed prep with a rain, just give the bed a good soaking as mentioned above.

2. *Perfection isn't the goal.* Don't agonize over perfection. Likely you will not have the perfect 4–6 inches of mulch coverage over the whole bed. That's okay. If it's 4 inches here and 6 inches there, it really is fine! Just get it done and move on.

3. *Mow and edge with care.* Be careful as you mow around the beds. Make sure that the mower isn't throwing grass seeds into the beds by positioning the chute away from the garden. While the Back to Eden method keeps weeds and grass from growing up through the compost and mulch, it is a great environment for plants to grow, so those grass seeds will take root, and you will have to weed. Do your best to avoid that!

GROWING YOUR OWN FOOD 207

CREATING A RAISED BED GARDEN

Over the years, and as we've gotten older, we have started transitioning our Back to Eden garden into raised bed versions of that method. However, re-creating the Back to Eden method in raised beds is not the only option, so let's take a look at building materials, best sizes to consider, and the various methods for filling your raised beds.

Choosing the Best Spot

Just like with the other methods, you will want to consider a few factors when choosing where to build your raised beds:

- *Sunlight.* A major factor that doesn't change from gardening method to gardening method is that most vegetable plants will need six to eight hours of full sunlight each day. Be sure you take into account any shadow cast by your house if you are planning to place beds near it.

- *Harvesting ease.* Unique to raised beds, you will need to make sure you can get all the way around each bed and that you can reach into the middle of each bed easily. You don't want to create a bed that is 6 feet across and then realize later that you can't harvest the produce growing in the middle. Aim for 36–48 inches wide at most, depending on your arm length. Having a raised bed won't do much to help your back if you have to bend and stretch drastically to reach the middle. The beds can be any length you want, as long as you can access both sides. If only one side is accessible, then consider 18–24 inches as a max width.

- *Access to water.* Depending on your filling method, your raised beds will likely need

Vining plants still need to be planted at ground level, otherwise they not only create more work as you strive to keep them trimmed, but also can become a tripping hazard.

to be watered frequently, so make sure your water source is close enough to access easily on a regular basis.

- *Longevity.* Raised beds are not easy to move, especially when built out of stone! Make sure that you are certain of where you want your beds for the long term before you place them. This will save you a lot of headaches in the future.

Choosing the Best Material

This section is wildly subjective, as what is "best" for me and my family may be completely different for you. However, I'm going to give you a few points to consider as you decide what is best for you:

- *Durability.* The most important factor to consider when choosing a building material for your raised beds, in my opinion, should be durability. While it might be great to build with free pallet wood, you will likely need to rebuild your beds again in just a few years. This may not be a deal-breaker for you, but it's something to keep in mind. It will entail removing all the soil, breaking down and rebuilding the beds as well as refilling them before planting again. We did that for several seasons before moving to something more permanent, so if that's where you are, great! But if you can avoid the hassle, your growing experience is going to be much more enjoyable.

- *Cost.* Cost is a huge consideration when building raised beds, especially if you are looking to build more than one or two of them! Trying to build several beds is a likely reason why you might choose to go with something less expensive that would need to be replaced sooner rather than later. However, keep in mind that low costs repeated over time still add up to a lot of money. If you can start with a few permanent beds and add more over time, you will reduce your costs in the long run.

- *Size.* As you consider cost, be sure you calculate the size and height of the beds in question. An 18-inch-high bed is going to cost half the price of a 36-inch-high bed. If you find a material that you like, be sure to run the numbers on different heights before you make your final decision.

GROWING YOUR OWN FOOD   209

- *Ease of use.* More simply put, can you lug the material into place? My father-in-law used to work for the telephone company, and at one point we discussed using old telephone poles as our garden edging. While it would have been free material and a great way to recycle, the practicality of transporting, moving, and positioning the poles was going to be too much for us at that time. The same may be true for you as you consider large slabs of limestone, or even 5-pound limestone blocks. Make sure that you can actually use the material with the strength and resources you have available to you.

- *Availability.* I love limestone, and thankfully it is readily available at a low cost in my area, but that's not the case everywhere. Contact material suppliers in your area to find out what your local options are for rock and wood at lower prices. Be sure to include any necessary delivery costs into the calculations! Additionally, for visual cohesion you'll want to make sure that if you add more beds later on you can match the material easily.

- *Appearance.* Finally, consider the actual appearance of the material you choose. I love the look of wood or limestone for my beds, but I knew that a dark orange stone material (also available in my area) was not something I would love long term. Ultimately, these beds will likely be around for a long time, and you will be looking at them daily! Make sure that the material matches your aesthetic for your gardening space if possible.

This cedar bed came together in about thirty minutes and was filled with sticks in the Hügelkultur method before being topped with compost and mulch.

Filling Your Raised Beds

As I mentioned before, we are transitioning our Back to Eden beds into fewer raised beds using the same method. But that's not the only option you have for filling your beds. While this is not an extensive list, here are some of the most popular ways to fill your raised beds using readily available materials:

- *Traditional soil mix.* This is a straightforward approach that will provide a balanced growing material with good drainage and nutrients. Simply create a mix of 60 percent topsoil, 30 percent compost, and 10 percent perlite or vermiculite (both of which are tiny rocks). You can use whatever topsoil you have on your property for this mix. After mixing, fill your beds and plant!

- *Compost only.* This method is as simple as it sounds. Just fill your beds with 100 percent well-aged compost and plant! This gives your plants a wonderful soil filled with nutrients that promotes easy growing. It's perfect for anyone who has been composting and needs something to use it for!

- *Back to Eden.* Because raised beds are much deeper than a ground-level Back to Eden bed, the layer depth is a bit different. However, the process is the same! In a raised bed, you will fill it with compost, leaving the top 3–6 inches for mulch. Once you top it with wood mulch, you're done! You can employ Hügelkultur if desired to make filling the bed less expensive and faster to finish.

- *Ruth Stout method.* Much like the Back to Eden method, the Ruth Stout method uses a deep layer of mulch to retain moisture and protect the topsoil. However, unlike the wood mulch used in the Back to Eden method, straw or hay is used instead.

- *Hügelkultur.* This Eastern European practice includes adding twigs and branches into the gardening area (in this case, raised beds) to promote easy drainage and increased nutrients over time. To employ this method, add small twigs and branches, no more than about 2 inches in diameter, to the bottom 30 percent of the bed space. From there, you can fill with whatever additional material you'd like. We use Hügelkultur in the bottom of our Back to Eden beds and fill up to 5 inches from the top of the bed with compost and then mulch for the rest. However, you can also just add compost or a topsoil mix to the top, if desired.

- *Wicking beds.* Similar to Hügelkultur, wicking beds use gravel or rocks to create drainage in the bottom of the raised beds. To use this method, fill the bottom 30 percent of the bed with gravel or other coarse material to create a reservoir, cover with landscape fabric, and then add your chosen soil mix on top.

GROWING YOUR OWN FOOD 211

Mixed beds work well if you have the space. Our garden utilizes both in-ground Back to Eden beds and raised beds.

Best Tips for Gardening in Raised Beds

While you're setting up your raised beds, there are a few things to consider during the process. These tips will not only help you create the best possible setup for your own ease of use but also prevent issues in the future for your plant growth and health:

- *Protect against weeds.* If you are building beds on top of grass, it's important to protect against weeds. You might be surprised that some weeds and grasses can grow through the soil and have roots up to 20 feet deep! Use weed cloth, cardboard, paper, or other materials under your beds to serve as a weed barrier.

- *Mulch layer.* No matter which method you choose for filling, if you add 3–5 inches of mulch on top, you'll be protecting your topsoil and adding a moisture protection layer as well!

- *Don't seal it too tight.* You want a good amount of drainage in the beds, otherwise the soil can become waterlogged. This can in turn lead to disease and pest issues.

Instead, make sure that there are many, many holes in the bottom and sides of your beds (especially if you are using metal tubs or something fully closed) and don't seal the material as you build. For example, our limestone beds are simply stacked without any mortar between the stones.

CREATING A CONTAINER GARDEN

When you're short on space, having a container garden can be just the thing you need to start growing your own food. It also allows you the opportunity to start small and expand as you have time, space, and money to do so.

Choosing the Best Spot

Often, deciding where to put your container garden is made by virtue of your available space, whether that be a backyard patio, a windowsill in your kitchen, or an apartment balcony. You may not be able to position your container garden for optimal sunlight hours or to benefit from rainfall. However, there are two things you can consider that will help as you work within the options you have available to you:

- *Sunlight.* Most vegetable plants need six to eight hours of full sunlight each day. If you don't have a spot that offers that, you may need to consider shade-tolerant vegetables, herbs, or even sprouts. I'll talk more about specific plant needs a little bit later, but for now just know that you may need to carefully choose which foods you grow.

- *Water.* Container gardening makes this consideration easy! You can water with a hose if you have one, or with a watering can. Make sure that containers that are indoors have dishes under them to catch any water that drains out.

Container gardening doesn't have to be limited to small pots. You can also create larger containers out of sturdy wire and burlap cloth to help contain the soil.

GROWING YOUR OWN FOOD 213

Setting up Your Container Garden

This process is the same no matter the size of the container you use. You can repeat these steps for as many containers as you would like to have, either all at once or over time:

1. *Select your containers.* Depending on the size and type of plant, and your available space, choose the containers in which you want to plant. Consider how large the plant will grow and save time and money by buying the largest container, instead of starting small and needing to transplant.

2. *Fill.* For container gardening I recommend a traditional potting mix. You can make your own by mixing 60 percent topsoil, 30 percent compost, and 10 percent perlite or vermiculite (both of which are tiny rocks). However, depending on how many containers you will be using, buying a bag of potting mix may be easier. Start with some rocks or sticks in the bottom of the pot to allow for drainage; be sure not to block the hole in the bottom of the pot! Fill the rest of the pot with loose potting mix in preparation for planting.

3. *Plant.* Add your plants or seeds according to the recommended depth indicated on their packaging. Gently pat the dirt around the top of the plant to compress the soil, but not too hard. You want the soil to be compressed enough to not blow away in the wind, but loose enough to allow water to soak through.

4. *Water.* Water your plants well, about 1-inch worth, which will give them a good start. You will need to water them at least once a week since they will likely not have the benefit of rainwater naturally watering their soil.

5. *Placement.* Finally, place your containers in a sunny spot and enjoy!

Best Tips for Container Gardening

Container gardening is straightforward, but there are a few things I want to mention that can help you with its practical aspects, as well as with the mindset of growing in small spaces:

1. *Mobility.* As you're choosing containers, remember that some plants may need to come indoors during colder seasons. This may result in your needing to move the

214   CREATING A MODERN HOMESTEAD

plants in and out periodically. If you are growing something like a dwarf lemon tree, for example, you want to make sure that the pot, soil, and tree combination are not too heavy for you to move! A large ceramic pot may be beautiful, but if you can't move it during a freeze and your tree dies as a result, it won't be so desirable! Instead, choose a lighter pot or make sure it has a base with wheels.

2. *Maintenance.* Water once a week, or as indicated on the seed/plant packaging. Look for signs of distress or pests and treat accordingly. I'll talk more about troubleshooting your plant health later.

3. *Be content.* You might feel frustrated that your container garden isn't row crops . . . and I completely understand that feeling. However, growing tomatoes on your apartment balcony or enjoying a mason jar full of broccoli sprouts on your kitchen windowsill is still something to be celebrated! Enjoy what you are able to do in this season of life and know that you are making a difference for your family.

PLANT-SPECIFIC PLANTING TIMES AND CONDITIONS

Now we can get into the nitty-gritty of planting your seeds or seedlings! On pages 216–17 you will find a table with an overview of each plant variety, when to plant them based on your last frost date, how long it will take them to go from seed to harvest, and whether it is best to plant them as seeds or seedlings.

I've also included the optimal soil temperature for planting, as sometimes the soil hasn't warmed up even though the last frost date has long passed. The "When to Plant" column should be viewed as an *approximate* earliest plant-by date, but again, you will need to check the soil temperature to confirm your garden is ready to receive the plants.

By planting corn a few weeks late you can avoid potential cross-pollination with GMO varieties.

GROWING YOUR OWN FOOD 215

Variety	When to Plant	Days to Maturity	Seeds or Seedlings	Optimal Soil Temp (°F)
Beans (all)	1–2 weeks after last frost	50–60	Seeds	60–85
Beets	2–4 weeks before last frost	50–70	Seeds	50–85
Broccoli	2–3 weeks before last frost	60–100	Seedlings	55–75
Brussels Sprouts	4–6 weeks before last frost	90–100	Seedlings	55–75
Cabbage	4–6 weeks before last frost	60–100	Seedlings	55–75
Carrots	2–3 weeks before last frost	70–80	Seeds	55–75
Cauliflower	2–3 weeks before last frost	55–100	Seedlings	55–75
Corn	1–2 weeks after last frost	60–100	Seeds	60–95
Cucumbers	1–2 weeks after last frost	50–70	Seeds or Seedlings	60–95
Eggplant	1–2 weeks after last frost	70–90	Seedlings	75–90
Kale	4–6 weeks before last frost	55–75	Seeds or Seedlings	45–85
Lettuce	4 weeks before last frost	45–55	Seeds	40–75
Melons (all)	1–2 weeks after last frost	70–90	Seedlings	70–90
Onions	4–6 weeks before last frost	100–120	Seedlings or Sets	50–85
Peas	4–6 weeks before last frost	60–70	Seeds	40–75

Variety	When to Plant	Days to Maturity	Seeds or Seedlings	Optimal Soil Temp (°F)
Peppers	1-2 weeks after last frost	70-90	Seedlings	65-85
Potatoes (nonsweet)	2-4 weeks before last frost	90-120	Seed Potatoes	45-75
Pumpkins	1-2 weeks after last frost	90-120	Seeds or Seedlings	70-90
Radishes	4-6 weeks before last frost	25-30	Seeds	45-85
Spinach	4-6 weeks before last frost	40-50	Seeds	45-75
Squash (winter and summer)	1-2 weeks after last frost	60-90	Seeds or Seedlings	70-95
Tomatoes (all)	1-2 weeks after last frost	60-85	Seedlings	60-85
Turnips	2-3 weeks before last frost	50-60	Seeds	60-105

Harvest Yields by Specific Plant Varieties

Let's take a look at each plant variety to better understand how many you will need for the yields your family requires. As you are glancing over this list, you may not see a specific plant that you are looking for. Be sure to look for the family, not the specific variety of plant. For example, watermelon, cantaloupe, and honeydew are all covered by the melon family, not listed individually.

The following numbers are given for a single plant harvest over the course of a single month of growing conditions. For example, if you have a single green bean plant, over the course of one month

GROWING YOUR OWN FOOD 217

Trellising cucumber plants not only increases yield but also saves you a lot of garden area that can then be used for other plants.

you will see an average yield of 1–2 pounds. You can then multiply that by the number of plants and the number of months in your growing season.

Keep in mind, these numbers are averages! In our area, with the Back to Eden method, our yields have been much higher than those given here. However, depending on your growing method, soil quality, local climate conditions, and specific variety of each plant, your numbers might be higher or lower:

- *Beans:* 1–2 pounds
- *Beets:* 1–2 pounds, including leaves
- *Broccoli:* 1 large head (additional smaller side shoots may follow). This is a total, not per month.
- *Brussels Sprouts:* 1–2 pounds
- *Cabbage:* 1 large head. This is a total, not per month.

- *Carrots:* 1–2 pounds

- *Cauliflower:* 1 large head. This is a total, not per month.

- *Corn:* 1–3 ears

- *Cucumbers:* 5–10 pounds

- *Eggplant:* 5–10 fruits (approximately ½–1 pound each)

- *Kale:* 1–2 pounds (continual harvesting of leaves)

- *Lettuce:* 1–2 heads or 1–2 pounds of loose leaves

- *Melons:* 3–5 fruits

- *Onions:* 1–2 pounds

- *Peas:* 1–2 pounds

- *Peppers:* 4–6 fruits (approximately 1–2 pounds)

- *Potatoes:* 2–4 pounds

- *Pumpkins:* 1 fruit (approximately 5–10 pounds, varies widely by variety)

- *Radishes:* ½–1 pound, including leaves

- *Spinach:* 1–2 pounds (continual harvesting of leaves)

- *Squash:* 3–5 pounds (summer squash) or 1–2 fruits (winter squash)

- *Tomatoes:* 4–6 pounds, depending on variety

- *Turnips:* 1–2 pounds, including leaves

Again, these yields are averages and can fluctuate based on a variety of factors. Regular watering, proper fertilization, and pest control will help maximize the yield of each plant!

PREVENTING PESTS AND DEALING WITH DISEASE

We have found that healthy soil equals healthy plants. As a result, pest issues tend to be minimized on their own because they don't like healthy plants! However, problems can arise. So, if you're trying to keep your garden as organic and natural as possible, here are some strategies that can be used to mitigate pest and disease issues.

Planting in the Correct Season

When planting in an off season, in an attempt to yield a larger harvest, we have found that more pest problems appear. When planting in the right season, this doesn't happen as much!

Planting when the soil temperature is right for the plant in question also reduces the likelihood of disease, as the plants will grow and thrive quickly instead of being stunted and susceptible to various issues.

Scent Confusion

When you plant large swaths of the same plant, their scent will attract pests. However, if you can companion-plant with strong-smelling herbs or flowers, then it will lessen the overall individual scents and keep the pests away. Additionally, companion planting can strengthen the plants themselves and typically attract more pollinators for a larger yield! For a guide, see the companion planting table on pages 226–27.

If you look closely, you can see many bugs on this pepper plant. Slip on a pair of gardening gloves and simply remove the bugs and squish them. If you have chickens, you can collect the bugs to feed to your flock instead.

Barn Cats

For dealing with small rodents and snakes, cats have been our biggest asset! We had a terrible mole problem that resulted in many lost plants until our barn cats came onto the scene. Thankfully, they made short work of the issue and are living their best life as very loved and doted-upon farm cats.

Additionally, the smell of cat urine is very strong and will help to keep snakes and rodents naturally at bay. This is useful if you are keeping chickens as well, since snakes are drawn to their eggs.

Diatomaceous Earth

When you are dealing with tiny pests, diatomaceous earth is a great way to treat your plants that is also natural and beneficial overall. Diatomaceous earth is the fossilized remains of tiny aquatic organisms called diatoms that are ground into a tiny white powder. This powder is very sharp and coarse and destroys tiny pests naturally. It's also a fabulous source of calcium, so your plants will benefit from the application.

Note: Diatomaceous earth can be harmful to bees as well, so be sure to treat around the base of the plants, rather than dusting the tops where a bee might come in contact with it accidentally.

Since diatomaceous earth is a very fine powder, it's advisable to wear a face covering when you apply it, especially in large quantities, as it can be harmful to your lungs if inhaled.

Powdery Mildew

You may start to see the leaves on your plants turning white or having some kind of dust on them. This is a common fungal disease known as powdery mildew that can affect many different types of plants. Fortunately, there are some simple ways you can prevent or minimize its occurrence! Just follow these steps:

- Ensure adequate spacing between plants to allow air circulation.

- Water at the base of the plant, avoiding overhead watering that can promote moisture on the leaves.

- Apply a thin layer of organic mulch (if not already present) around the plants to reduce moisture evaporation and splashing of spores.

GROWING YOUR OWN FOOD 221

Blossom End Rot

Have you ever seen a beautiful fruit growing on your plants, only to notice its end is rotting? This is blossom end rot! It is common in zucchini, as well as other fruits such as tomatoes and peppers, and is primarily caused by calcium deficiency.

There are several ways to deal with blossom end rot, but the fastest method we've found is to just pour milk around the base of the plant. Usually about a quart of animal milk per plant is enough. You can also use powdered calcium around the plants to save them. Just sprinkle the powdered calcium around the base of the affected plants and then add about half an inch of water around the same place. However, the calcium in the milk is much more readily available for the plants to utilize than it is from other sources, since the milk doesn't need to be broken down from a solid form. We usually see the fruit setting and growing again within two to three days when treated with milk!

While it's normal to see the flower rot off of the fruit, if the rot extends up to the produce, you are dealing with blossom end rot.

> Here are some options for adding calcium naturally to your soil to avoid blossom end rot:
>
> • Crushed eggshells
>
> • Limestone dust
>
> • Oyster shells

Poor Pollination

Depending on the bee population in your area, you may start to notice that while you have flowers on your plants, you do not see any fruit forming. This is due to a lack of pollinators! Thankfully, it's a simple process to hand-pollinate your plants:

- To improve pollination, you can gently transfer pollen from the male flowers to the female flowers (if applicable) using a small brush or cotton swab.
- Additionally, attracting pollinators like bees and butterflies to your garden by planting pollinator-friendly flowers nearby can greatly enhance the chances of successful pollination.

Squash Bugs

Squash bugs are common pests that can damage any variety of squash plants, usually by eating through the base of the plant, causing it to die. Creating physical barriers such as row covers can also prevent squash bugs from reaching the plants, but this isn't always practical. You can also use scent confusion to help prevent them from even knowing the plant is there!

To control squash bugs once they are present, start by regularly inspecting the plants and removing any eggs or nymphs you find on the underside of leaves.

Thankfully, the plants you might add to attract pollinators can do double duty and distract any squash bugs from feasting on your plants. Ultimately, if you're not able to prevent squash bugs from getting into the garden, you'll need to manually remove them and their eggs to prevent them from eating your plants.

Tomato Hornworms

While mostly found on tomatoes, these giant worms can technically eat other things as well. However, I've only ever seen them on tomatoes. Thankfully, we've only had a few in our decade of growing food, and even more thankfully, they are easy to deal with! If you see one, handpick it off your plants and feed it to your chickens—or squish it and throw it away. Be sure to look under the leaves of your plants to find and remove any eggs as well.

To avoid hornworms altogether, scent confusion via companion planting works really well.

Caterpillars

Just like hornworms, caterpillars can be dealt with and avoided relatively easily! You can handpick them off your plants and look for and remove any eggs from the underside of your plant leaves.

To prevent them, companion planting is the best practice. I have found that caterpillars are the worst when large amounts of cruciferous vegetables are planted together. However, strong-smelling companion plants like oregano or chives will cause scent confusion and help prevent the caterpillars from discovering the plants in the first place.

Caterpillar eggs can be found on and around leaves. Remove them fully when you find them.

Pill Bugs

Also known as roly-poly bugs or doodle bugs, these little black bugs can be a menace, but they are also very beneficial. One amazing function of these bugs is removing heavy metals from your soil. They are also crucial in breaking down organic materials and aerating the soil! But if you have an abundance of them, they can eat your small sprouts and keep your garden from ever producing anything. If you are dealing with the latter case, there are a few things you can do to reduce the excess numbers:

- *Keep your soil healthy.* Planting in dirt without soil modifications can lead to an abundance of pill bugs. Make sure your soil is healthy and vibrant, as pill bugs tend to be drawn to low-quality soil.

- *Keep your garden clean.* Remove any fallen fruit, weeds, or clumps of old plants. Pill bugs are drawn to damp areas and getting rid of those areas can eliminate any enticement to take up residence in your garden.

- *Set a beer trap.* Put beer in a used can or plastic cup and push it into the soil, deep enough that the lip of the container is at soil level. Pill bugs will drown themselves in the beer. Check the trap daily and replace the beer at least every two days.

- *Diatomaceous earth.* As mentioned earlier, diatomaceous earth is a great way to get rid of many unwanted bugs, though it can also destroy many helpful bugs. Use it only as needed.

COMPANION PLANTING

Companion planting is the act of grouping beneficial plant varieties near each other in order to boost the health of the plants, increase produce yield, reduce disease, and prevent pests. We interplant our herbs with our fruits and vegetables in order to benefit both plants. For example, onions or garlic planted with strawberries deepen the flavor of the fruit, and marigolds (neither a crop nor an herb) are crucial in maintaining a healthy potato crop in our area. Not all plants are beneficial to one another, so it's important to know which plants to group and which to keep separated. See the table on pages 226–27 for more information.

GROWING YOUR OWN FOOD 225

Plant	Grows Well With	Helps Control Pests	Does Not Grow Well With
Basil	Oregano, Peppers, Sage, Thyme, Tomatoes		
Beans	Broccoli, Carrots, Corn, Cucumber, Peas, Rosemary, Strawberry, Tomatoes		Chives, Garlic, Leeks, Onion, Peppers
Broccoli	Beans, Carrots, Chives, Cucumber, Dill, Garlic, Onion, Rosemary, Sage, Spinach, Thyme	Oregano	Peppers, Squash, Strawberry, Tomatoes
Carrots	Beans, Broccoli, Chives, Leeks, Lettuce, Onion, Parsley, Peas, Peppers, Rosemary, Sage, Thyme		Dill, Potatoes, Tomatoes
Cauliflower	Beans, Carrots, Chives, Cucumber, Dill, Garlic, Onion, Rosemary, Sage, Spinach, Thyme	Oregano	Peppers, Squash, Strawberry, Tomatoes
Chives	Broccoli, Carrots, Parsley, Sage, Thyme, Tomatoes		Beans, Peas
Cilantro	Sage, Thyme	Spinach	
Corn	Beans, Cucumbers, Dill, Melon, Parsley, Peas, Sage, Squash, Sunflower, Thyme		Tomatoes
Cucumber	Beans, Broccoli, Corn, Dill, Lettuce, Onion, Peas, Peppers, Sage, Thyme, Tomatoes		Potatoes, Sage
Dill	Broccoli, Corn, Cucumber, Lettuce, Onion, Sage, Thyme		Carrots, Tomatoes
Garlic	Broccoli, Cauliflower, Lettuce, Strawberry, Sage, Thyme, Tomatoes		Beans, Peas
Leeks	Carrots, Onion, Spinach, Sage, Thyme		Beans, Peas
Lettuce	Carrots, Cucumber, Dill, Garlic, Onion, Sage, Spinach, Squash, Strawberry, Thyme, Tomatoes		Broccoli
Melon	Corn, Marigold, Sage, Squash, Sunflower, Thyme		
Onion	Broccoli, Carrots, Cucumber, Dill, Leeks, Lettuce, Parsley, Sage, Strawberry, Swiss Chard, Thyme, Tomatoes		Beans, Peas, Potatoes

226 CREATING A MODERN HOMESTEAD

Plant	Grows Well With	Helps Control Pests	Does Not Grow Well With
Oregano	Basil, Peppers, Sage, Thyme	Broccoli, Cauliflower	
Parsley	Carrots, Chives, Corn, Onion, Peas, Peppers, Sage, Thyme, Tomatoes		
Peas	Beans, Carrots, Corn, Cucumber, Parsley, Peppers, Sage, Spinach, Squash, Strawberry, Thyme		Chives, Garlic, Leeks, Onion
Peppers	Basil, Carrots, Cucumber, Oregano, Parsley, Peas, Rosemary, Sage, Squash, Swiss Chard, Thyme, Tomatoes		Beans, Broccoli, Cauliflower, Potatoes
Potatoes	Broccoli, Cauliflower, Chives, Corn, Leeks	Marigolds	Carrots, Cucumbers, Onions, Peppers, Squash, Tomatoes
Rosemary	Beans, Broccoli, Carrots, Cauliflower, Peppers, Sage, Thyme		
Sage	A beneficial plant to most things in your garden—too many to list!		Cucumber
Spinach	Broccoli, Cauliflower, Leeks, Lettuce, Peas, Sage, Strawberry, Thyme	Cilantro	
Squash	Corn, Lettuce, Marigold, Melon, Peas, Peppers, Sage, Thyme		Broccoli, Cauliflower, Potatoes
Strawberry	Beans, Garlic, Lettuce, Onions, Peas, Sage, Spinach, Thyme		Broccoli, Cauliflower
Swiss Chard	Beans, Broccoli, Cauliflower, Onions, Peppers, Sage, Thyme		
Thyme	A beneficial garden herb that can be planted widely!		
Tomatoes	Basil, Beans, Chiles, Cucumber, Garlic, Lettuce, Marigold, Onion, Parsley, Peppers, Sage, Thyme		Broccoli, Carrots, Cauliflower, Corn, Dill, Potatoes

GROWING YOUR OWN FOOD 227

EXTENDING YOUR GROWING SEASON

If you have calculated your growing season and realized that you might need a bit more time to harvest the amount of food you need for your family, worry not! You can do several things to extend your growing season, depending on where you live:

- *Start indoors.* The easiest thing you can do to extend your growing season is to start your seeds indoors when possible. Not all plants are suitable for transplanting, but many are. Look back at the planting table on pages 216–17; if "seedlings" is listed in the "Seeds or Seedlings" column, that plant family can be started early and transplanted for a faster yield. Typically, you will start your seeds inside six to ten weeks before you want to transplant them into your garden. This allows them to grow large enough to transplant safely and will then cut the time from planting to harvest dramatically.

Cucumbers started indoors can be planted as soon as the soil warms up and be yielding cucumbers within weeks. These small cucumbers are perfect for sweet gherkins.

- *Greenhouses.* If you have enough space to start your seedlings outside in a greenhouse or hoop house (which is just another form of a greenhouse, made with thin rods or plastic pipes bent into a hoop and covered with plastic sheeting), this can serve the same function as starting your seeds indoors, but on a larger scale. You can even start growing lettuce and other cold-weather crops for harvest right in the greenhouse over the winter.

- *Ground coverings.* Another method for extending your season is to lay a covering over your garden beds to raise the soil temperature. Typically, you start with a black plastic covering that does not allow light through it. Once the soil temperature is in the ideal range for your desired plants, you can transplant or plant seeds and water well. Once planted, the seeds and seedlings still need to be protected from the cold and the soil kept warm. However, now you want light to penetrate the covering, so you can switch to using a transparent "frost cloth." Check the protection rating for any frost cloth you consider and make sure it will protect against the average lows in your area. Using these ground coverings can drastically increase your growing season and allow you to get started months before your climate would naturally allow.

Even in deep snow, the ground in the hoop house is still warm, which helps raise the temperature of the air inside.

While this list is certainly not exhaustive, the general principles can be applied in many different ways and natural climates.

GROWING YOUR OWN FOOD

FINAL THOUGHTS

My hope for this chapter is that it has served as a guide as you work through the process of beginning to grow some or all of your fresh produce. There are many other options for gardening out there, so feel free to experiment, but remember to keep an eye on yields if self-sufficiency is your goal.

The best way I've found to really judge how my gardening efforts are working is to keep a gardening journal. It doesn't have to be anything fancy—it could be a $0.99 school notebook that you got on sale during back-to-school season, or even a blank piece of typing paper tucked into this book. But no matter what method you choose to employ, keeping track of a few stats will help you understand what's working and what needs to change. Write down the following information each season so you can keep track of what is working best for you and make adjustments accordingly:

- Varieties planted.

- When you planted each variety.

- If you planted seeds or seedlings into the garden.

- How many plants of each variety you planted.

- Total yield for each plant type (we weigh each harvest by variety and make a note daily).

- How long your growing season was for each variety.

- Any pest or disease issues you encountered and how you dealt with them.

- Also note if you ran out of a certain food earlier than anticipated. This means you need to plant more the next year!

During the down seasons, you can add up your yields per variety and make the decision on whether to plant more or fewer next year. Ultimately, it's very unlikely you'll be able to achieve your gardening goals right out of the gate and never have to do any tinkering with plant varieties or quantities. Play the part of a scientist when it comes to your garden and really examine the numbers as you go. Then make adjustments and take steps to improve during the next season.

CHAPTER 6

KEEPING BACKYARD CHICKENS

Raising backyard chickens is a dream for many homesteaders. From the idyllic scene of looking out over your hens free-ranging on bugs, to collecting and enjoying fresh eggs daily, chickens have a lot to offer and can be a really fun addition to your modern homestead. Perhaps you will actually be keeping chickens in your backyard, or maybe you have several acres on which they can roam. No matter where you are, this chapter will help you understand exactly how to keep them in the healthiest (and least time-consuming) way possible.

THINGS TO CONSIDER BEFORE YOU BUY CHICKENS

Ten years ago, we left the big city and moved to the country with dreams of starting a homestead. Though we started and established a garden first, buying chickens was the very next thing we did to grow our homestead. While keeping chickens has been wonderful for us, there are a few things I wish I had known before we started our chicken efforts! Knowing these things earlier would have allowed me to mentally prepare for having chickens, and it wouldn't have been such an adjustment period. Now I want to offer you the chance to be prepared! Here are some things to consider when thinking about having chickens:

- *They can be messy.* If you have free-range chickens, it's important to know that they will leave their droppings everywhere. Porches, walkways, swings and play structures, outdoor chairs, and benches will all be covered in chicken poop. Most things are easy to spray down with a hose, but that continual need is something to be aware of.

- *The rooster must be gentled.* I'll get more into the details of this process later, but for now, just understand that roosters (male chickens) can be very aggressive and will attack you and your children if you do not train them well. This is a good thing for your flock, as a diligent rooster will keep them safe from hawks and other predators. However, you want to make sure they learn to be gentle with you and your family.

- *Eggs must be gathered daily.* I know, this is somewhat of a "duh" thought, but the constant nature of gathering eggs is something that many people overlook as they are getting started. If you like to travel or you have days where you don't get home until after dark, gathering eggs every day can start to feel like a burden. Have a plan in place for dealing with those situations before they arise, such as asking a neighbor or family member to come gather the eggs; in return, they can take them home to enjoy!

- *Snakes are inevitable.* Snakes are a reality of homestead living in most areas, but chickens will attract even more snakes than you might have had before. They tend to curl up in the nesting boxes and devour the fresh eggs. One easy way to cut down on the snake population is to have outdoor cats around your flock. Snakes consider cats to be predators, so they tend to stay away. Additionally, cats will eat or kill the small vermin that snakes are also attracted to, making your homestead and chickens less appealing to the slithering intruders.

- *The chickens will die.* Whether a hawk manages to outsmart the rooster, or a racoon gets into the coop at night, eventually some or many of your chickens will die. The grief that came when we lost our first hen surprised us. But when you bring an animal into your life and commit to taking care

The first time we lost chickens to a hawk, we found out by discovering a huge pile of feathers by the coop.

234 CREATING A MODERN HOMESTEAD

of it, any situation that causes you to fail at that job can be difficult to cope with. Chickens can also fall prey to diseases. There are all sorts of ways to protect your chickens from predators and diseases, which we will talk about later. But even with a well-protected flock, you will still experience a loss at some point.

FLOCK SIZE AND SPACE

As you decide if you want to keep chickens, and how many, there are several things to consider. Even if you have multiple acres available to you, thinking through these points will help you start off on the right foot with your new flock:

- *HOA restrictions.* In many areas, HOA (homeowner association) restrictions do not prevent you from having hens, though they may restrict the size of your flock. If the restrictions say you can't have birds larger than a macaw, chickens are likely still allowed, as their weights are similar. Be sure to check your local regulations before getting started.

- *Noise consideration.* Noise requirements in the city may mean that you can only have hens (female chickens), since a rooster will crow very loudly. Even if you don't have any specific language in your HOA or city ordinances that would prohibit having a rooster, if you will be keeping the chickens in a location that is closer than 150 feet from your neighbor's house, it would be considerate to not keep a rooster. Even in the country, we keep our flock in the middle of the fields so that they are as far away from our neighbors as possible.

- *Flock size.* While the conventional free-range "wisdom" is that each bird should have at least 8 square feet of pasture, this can vary wildly depending on your area and the weather. In cold months, when bug availability is low, chickens need more space to truly free-range. You can feed them more, but that will drive up your feed costs. Instead, plan to have 20–30 square feet per chicken to ensure easy access to bugs and fresh grass. Ideally, you want to move your flock every week or two. This not only gives them fresh grass and bugs but also helps keep them healthy (which I will talk more about later). Rotational grazing helps ensure one area doesn't get overgrazed while another area is overlooked. Having four to six spaces that you can rotate your chickens through is enough. Calculate how much space you have

KEEPING BACKYARD CHICKENS   235

in your yard to devote to chickens, divide it by 4 or 6, and then again by 25 to determine how many chickens you can have.

- *Static coop.* If you don't have enough space in your yard to rotationally graze your chickens, that doesn't mean you can't have chickens! Instead, build a coop large enough for each chicken to have at least 5–10 square feet of space and know that you will have to fully supply feed for them. There will be no free-ranging for these chickens. You can let them out of the coop for short periods of time, if desired. However, it is easy for chickens to fly over residential fencing, so be sure you keep a close eye on them.

COOP TYPES

Even if you free-range your chickens, if you want to collect eggs you will need a coop of some sort. Additionally, having a way to fully lock your flock up at night will help protect against predators. No matter which type of coop you choose to build, be sure to fully seal it up, plug any holes, and keep any mesh to a maximum size of two inches

This static coop runs along our garden space, which provides a heavy bug supply for the chickens. We use this coop for turkeys once a year, and for our hens when we go on vacation for long periods of time.

wide to prevent rodent or racoon access. You'll also want to check your coop frequently to ensure that no breaches develop unbeknownst to you. Fix any issues that arise that same day before dark, or you will likely lose some or all of your flock. It doesn't have to be a pretty fix, and you can make it better the next day if time is short but get some sort of fix in place immediately. Here are some examples of coops and other helpful ways to care for your chickens:

Meat birds do really well in chicken tractors and love the fresh grass every day.

- *Chicken tractor.* If you are raising meat birds and will not need nesting boxes, a chicken tractor is a great way to move your chickens and keep them on fresh grass. Low to the ground, these units don't need roosting bars and allow about 2–5 square feet per chicken. Since they can be easily moved, rotating the chickens daily to fresh ground only requires a few minutes and gives them fresh grass and bugs each day. A water source is still needed but can be attached to the side of the tractor so it moves with the unit.

- *Static coop.* As mentioned above, this coop is perfect for small spaces, is built in place, and never moved. It will need to be cleaned frequently, as detailed on page 249 in the Caring for Your Flock section. For a static coop, allow at least 5–10 square feet per bird, with nesting boxes and roosting bars. If possible, make the coop at least 6 feet tall so that it's easy to get into it to clean.

- *Mobile coop.* Ideal for rotational grazing, a mobile coop can be very small, as the chickens will only use it for sleeping and laying eggs. When chickens sleep, they bunch together tightly, so even forty fully grown chickens can fit in a 6' × 6' mobile coop. The rest of their waking time should be spent on pasture.

- *Netting.* Free-ranging chickens can range up to a football field length away from their coop and still come back at night. That may sound great, especially if you have the land to let them range. However, if you want to collect eggs, it's not ideal. They will eventually find a place to lay their eggs that is more appealing to them

than the nesting boxes. If you have many chickens and acres of land, finding the eggs becomes a full-time job. Instead, consider using electric chicken netting to keep them in a dedicated space that can easily be changed as needed. Even in a small space or yard, netting can help define your rotational grazing space.

CHOOSING A BREED

Just as some cow breeds are best for milk and others for meat, chickens, too, have breeds that are considered best for one use or another. Once you know how large your flock will be, it's time to determine what type(s) of chickens you want to raise. Here are things to consider:

- *Use.* If you want to raise chickens for both meat and eggs, there are many dual-purpose breeds that will work well. However, if you just want eggs, choosing a dual-purpose breed will require more feed than a dedicated egg-layer breed would. Likewise, if you just want the chickens for meat, you don't need to worry about nesting boxes since the chickens would only be kept for a short period of time and would never reach the point of laying eggs.

- *Egg color.* Traditionally, eggs from the store are either light brown or white. However, when you raise chickens, you can create a beautiful bouquet of egg colors ranging from light pink to olive green, depending on the breeds you choose. Mixed flocks will allow you to enjoy a variety of egg colors.

- *Natural camouflage.* One factor that's often overlooked when choosing breeds is the color of the terrain in your area. When we purchased pullets (female chicks) to grow our original flock, we purchased a bright-white variety of Ameraucana chickens. They were beautiful and stood out nicely against the backdrop of our homestead. For several months we enjoyed having them on our land, until a hawk came in and killed all of them over the course of a few days. The thing that we loved so much turned into the very reason they were noticed by the hawk—they stood out. Meanwhile, the black speckled Plymouth Rock flock was completely left alone because they blended in very easily with the surrounding area. Chickens come in all different colors, so choose ones that blend in well with your homestead or yard.

MIXING FLOCKS

Don't worry too much about picking a single breed or getting everything just right on the first try. Over time, you may want more of one type of chicken, or you may want to try a new breed. In those cases, you will need to mix new chicks with an existing flock. The process is simple but can take a little bit of time. Here are a few things to think about when growing your flock:

- *Strength in numbers.* When a single new chicken enters a flock, she will likely be singled out and bullied by the existing hens. Instead, try to give the new hens a chance by introducing them in equal or greater numbers to those in the current flock. For example, if you have ten hens, incubate or purchase at least six or eight new female chicks. You will not want to introduce more male chickens (roosters), so make sure you have all female chicks before proceeding. More roosters will only cause increased fighting among the two flocks!

Our Barred Plymouth Rock chickens at twelve weeks old being moved to pasture for the first time.

- *Visual before physical.* Once your new chicks are ready to move to grass, place them near the old flock but far enough away so the old flock can't interact with the new hens.

- *Separate feed and water.* Bring the new chicks' feed and water units into the pen when you combine the flocks. This will prevent fighting over food and hopefully allow for a smooth transition.

- *Be patient.* Finally, you'll have to give the chickens time to adjust. The old flock will likely peck at or attack the new flock, and many feathers will be lost. This is normal, but you can mitigate it to some extent if you are out with the flock regularly and gently distract the birds when a fight starts.

The table on pages 241–42 highlights some of the most common and widely available chicken breeds, including their coloring, egg color as well as egg size, and primary use. Use it as a jumping-off point to quickly see the differences between the breeds and to determine which you might like to include in your own flock. Once you pick the breed you are most interested in, I encourage you to do further research to make sure it's the best fit for you.

Breed	Bird Coloring	Egg Color	Egg Size	Characteristics	Primary Usage
Ameraucana	Black, Blue, Blue Wheaten, Brown Red, Buff, Silver, Wheaten, White	Blue/ Green	Large	Known for their colorful blue/green eggs and excellent egg-laying capacity	Eggs
Ancona	Mottled White and Black	White	Extra-Large	Exceptional white egg layers; prolific producers of large eggs	Eggs
Australorp	Black	Brown	Large	Popular breed for light-brown eggs; heavy bird used for meat as well	Dual
Brahma	Light, Dark, Buff	Brown	Large	Large, heavy breed, known for good egg production and gentle nature	Eggs
Buckeye	Mahogany with Black Tail Feathers	Brown	Large	Dual-purpose breed with excellent meat and egg production	Dual
Cornish	Dark, White, White Laced, Blue, Brown	N/A	N/A	A meat breed; known for fast growth and high-quality meat	Meat
Delaware	White with Black Neck and Tail Feathers	Brown	Large	Excellent dual-purpose breed with good egg production and suitable for meat	Dual
Easter Egger	Many, as they are a mixed breed	Blue/ Green	Large	This hybrid chicken breed is known for laying eggs in various shades of blue and green	Eggs
Jersey Giant	Black, Blue, White	Brown	Large	Large, heavy breed used for egg production and meat	Dual
Leghorn	Light Brown, Dark Brown, White, Buff, Black, Silver, Red, Black Tailed Red, Columbian	White	Extra-Large	Prolific and efficient egg-layer	Eggs

KEEPING BACKYARD CHICKENS 241

Breed	Bird Coloring	Egg Color	Egg Size	Characteristics	Primary Usage
Maran	Black Copper, Wheaten	Dark Brown	Extra-Large	Known for their very dark-brown eggs and dual-purpose use for meat	Dual
New Hampshire Red	Red	Brown	Extra-Large	Dual-purpose with a focus on meat production, though still a good egg-layer	Dual
Olive Egger	Many, as they are a mixed breed	Olive Green	Large	A mixed breed of a brown egg-layer and a blue egg-layer, their eggs are a beautiful shade of olive	Eggs
Orpington	Black, Blue, Buff, White	Brown	Large	Heavy dual-purpose breed and an excellent egg-layer; known to lay well in the winter months too	Dual
Plymouth Rock	Barred, White, Buff, Partridge, Silver Penciled, Blue, Columbian	Brown	Large	Dual-purpose broody chickens that make good mothers and do not mind the cold	Dual
Polish-Bearded and Non-Bearded	Golden Silver, White, Buff Laced, White Crested Blue, Black, Crested White	White	Medium	Prolific egg-layers, similar to Leghorns though their eggs are smaller; unique appearance due to their crests	Eggs
Rhode Island Red	Dark Red with Black Tail Feathers	Brown	Large	Known for being the best egg-layer as a dual-purpose breed	Dual
Sussex	Speckled, Red, Light, Brown, Silver, Buff	Brown	Large	Hardy and docile, excellent for both meat and eggs	Dual
Welsummer	Orange-Red with Dark Tail Feathers	Very Dark Brown	Large	Good egg-production breed; cold weather hardy with a docile temperament	Eggs

ACQUIRING CHICKS

Once you've determined which types of chickens you'd like to have, it's time to set about acquiring them. The easiest way to do that is to purchase pullets and raise them. However, you may have the opportunity to incubate and hatch your own chicks from eggs, so let's talk about both options:

- *Purchasing pullets.* If you are just starting out with chickens, this is the route I would recommend because someone else will incubate the chickens and also check the sex of each chicken before sending them to you. This ensures that you get mostly hens, though sometimes a rooster will slip through. You can purchase pullets online or in person at your local farm and feed store. Be sure to overorder by a few chickens, as

KEEPING BACKYARD CHICKENS 243

some may die during transportation or in the first few weeks on the homestead. If your only goal is harvesting eggs, then purchasing pullets makes sense, as a single flock will serve you well for years.

- *Incubation.* We have incubated many chickens, and it's always such a fun and interesting experience for the whole family. Getting to watch the chicks hatch and go from wet to fluffy in a few hours is incredible. The process is fairly simple, but you need to keep the eggs at a consistent temperature and humidity level. For that reason, I recommend an automated incubator that measures and adjusts those levels appropriately and also rotates the eggs on a timer. You can purchase a decent incubator online for a few hundred dollars. If you have roosters in your flock and thus have fertilized eggs, buying an incubator and hatching your own eggs will pay for itself very quickly, especially if you are raising meat birds. If you are incubating eggs, be aware that the hen-to-rooster ratio may be drastically skewed, meaning you may need to incubate several batches of eggs before you can build up enough hens for your desired flock size. In our last batch of eggs, we hatched seventeen roosters and eleven hens.

Brooding Chicks

Raising chicks is a rewarding process. I love to watch them "skate" around the brooder as they grow. I never knew what people meant when they said chicks "skate," but it really does look like they are ice skating as they happily run around. But beyond just getting to watch them grow up, there are a few important things to remember while brooding chicks, which are the same whether you purchase pullets or incubate them yourself:

- *The brooder.* This is simply a protected place that keeps the chicks

For fewer than five chicks, a small brooder like this one can be built to easily hold them until they can be moved onto grass.

contained. It can be a wooden pen that you build or even a large cardboard box. Fill the brooder with at least 4 inches of mulch as you would for a garden bed or use wood shavings (which you can purchase from a farm supply store). Mulch absorbs more than wood shavings and doesn't need to be changed at all during the few weeks that the chicks will be in the brooder; it also can then be used in the garden after the manure ages. Wood shavings do have to be changed frequently, as they will become soiled and can cause health issues if not replaced. The depth of the brooder should be at least 2 feet to allow for the deep mulch bedding while still leaving enough wall height to keep the chicks from easily jumping out or being cramped when the lid is added at night (if needed).

- *Keep the chicks warm.* Chicks need consistent warmth, especially during their first few weeks. Use a heat lamp or brooder heating plate to keep the temperature around 95°F. Keep enough heat sources in the brooder so that all of the chicks can fit under them but leave enough space so they can also move away if they want. They will naturally adjust their position to the heat sources if they become too hot or too cold.

- *Protection.* Make sure the brooding area is secure from drafts and predators. Even indoor spaces can attract small predators or curious pets, so ensure the enclosure is sturdy and closed off. We keep our brooder in the barn so that it can be sealed off at night, but if you are brooding in an outdoor space, you can simply put a piece of plywood over the top and weigh it down with enough heavy items that a raccoon will not be able to easily move the lid. If the brooder is on grass or dirt, you will need to protect the coop from being accessed by a predator digging under the edges. To prevent this, take chicken wire that is larger than the coop by one foot and place it on all sides, then set the brooder on top, and finally fill the brooder with mulch.

- *Space.* Chicks grow quickly, and they need room to explore. Make sure the brooder is large enough for them to move around comfortably, as overcrowding can lead to stress or injury. For a pullet batch of thirty chicks or less, we use a 6' × 6' bed, which is plenty of room for them, without taking up too much space. Try to allow at least 1 square foot of space per chick.

- *Look for pasty butt.* This is a common issue where droppings stick to the chick's vent in a white, sticky paste, potentially blocking elimination. If not taken care of, it can be fatal. To check for pasty butt, simply pick the chickens up and look at their tail end; you will easily be able to see if their vent is blocked. If you identify any chicks with this condition, simply bring them to a warm water source and gently clean the area until the blockage is clear. Dry them off—again, gently—with a towel and blow dry on low heat before taking them back outside. We typically only have to do this once per flock, and only with a few birds. Having ample space in the brooder helps avoid it happening too often.

This brooder has hinged top sides that are mostly a tight mesh. This allows for air circulation but can be weighed down at night to protect the flock from predators.

- *Feed crumbles only.* Starter crumbles are the only food chicks should be offered until they are out on pasture. Not only are crumbles specially formulated to meet chicks' nutritional needs, but they are also small enough for the chicks to eat easily. Once you move the chicks out into the field, they can forage for bugs and grass as desired. However, you don't want to switch to layer feed—feed formulated for laying-age hens—until they are sixteen weeks old.

- *Transitioning to grass.* Once the chicks reach the age where they have feathers instead of fluff, it's time to move them outdoors. This is the best time to do so, as their feathers will keep them warm, and they will not need a heat source provided for them. When transitioning your chicks, make sure their enclosure has mesh small enough that predators like raccoons can't reach in. This will allow the growing chicks the best protection at night. Even when they are in a locked coop, though, some rodents can still get into the coop to harm or even kill chicks while they are small.

CARING FOR YOUR FLOCK

It's easy to worry that you're not doing enough to keep your flock healthy, happy, and safe. But in reality, chickens are one of the easiest farm animals to care for. With just a few fundamentals to be aware of, you can maintain a healthy flock in just a few hours a week of total effort.

KEEPING BACKYARD CHICKENS

Feed Requirements

More than water and bugs, there are a few nutritional requirements to be aware of that will help ensure a healthy flock, while optimizing egg production and meat growth.

- *Water.* Providing fresh water daily is important, but more important is how the chickens are able to access it. If they can fully access the water—for instance in a large bowl or trough—they will get into the water and muddy it with dirt or feces. This can easily and quickly lead to health issues among the flock. Instead, buy a waterer that only allows beak access to the water and place it on a brick or two to elevate it. This will keep the chickens from scratching dirt and muck into the water. Be sure to buy a waterer that is rated for the number of chickens you have or buy several if needed. Check the water every few days during temperate weather, daily during the summer and winter, and refill or adjust as needed. A heated source of water in the winter may be needed in very cold areas, or you can place the waterer in a protected area and add a heat lamp to keep the water thawed.

- *Free range.* While this may not always be possible, fresh grass is where chickens thrive the most. Free access to bugs and grass also produces dark-yellow yolks, which are very good to consume. Ideally, chickens should have about 20–30 square feet of fresh grass available to them each week, with a new paddock being marked off the following week. As I mentioned before, having four to six of these areas would be best, but if you can only provide two to three on a rotational basis, that's still better than nothing! Using a mesh netting made specifically for poultry is the easiest way to do this, as the netting can be moved quickly by just one person.

- *Supplied feed.* Once your hens are over the age of sixteen weeks, it's time to decide if they will be on layer feed or just pasture. If you want to fully pasture your chickens and allow them to only eat bugs and grass, that's perfectly fine, especially for meat birds. But for egg-layers that may mean you get few to no eggs, depending on the bug population and types available to your flock. Instead, you can supplement with purchased feed at a ratio of about one cup per chicken, per day. You may need to adjust that amount depending on how many eggs it yields. Start with a cup per chicken per day and continue that for about a week. If your egg production goes up, stay there; if your egg production stays the same or goes down, you'll need to raise the rations. We opt for a soy-free, organic feed purchased through a co-op, as the quality of food we give our chickens directly translates into the quality of the eggs we receive.

- *Grit.* Chickens don't have teeth, so they need grit in order to grind their food properly. Grit is stored in their gizzard, and their bodies naturally pull from that source as they eat. If they are free-range chickens, they can find rocks and gravel to use as grit, but often you need to supply some to the flock. You can find grit at your local farm supply store; the amount per bird for the grit variety is listed on the bag.

Additional Tips for Keeping Your Chickens Healthy

Simply doing these things will be enough 90 percent of the time to maintain a healthy flock; however, there are a few additional things you can do to raise that percentage. In our nearly ten years of keeping chickens, we have only lost one flock to disease, and it was when we thought we could ignore the advice I'm about to share with you! Here are some helpful tips for a healthy flock:

- *Coop maintenance.* If you have a static coop, it is important to clean it at least once a month, though twice a month would be better. This involves scraping the mulch and manure out of the bed of the coop and adding fresh, clean mulch. The old mulch can then be set aside to age and be used in your garden once it's not "hot mulch" anymore. (See more about "hot mulch" in the gardening chapter on page 205.) By cleaning the coop out frequently, you will be able to prevent most, if not all, diseases from affecting your flock. A mobile coop does not need to be cleaned, since it can just be moved to a new location along with the flock.

- *Probiotic water.* While this might seem ridiculous for chickens, adding a few tablespoons of apple cider vinegar to their water supply each time you change it can help balance their pH levels and reduce the chance of disease.

- *Fermented grains.* This process is so simple and can make your feed last longer as well. Simply add about three days' worth of feed to a bucket and add water to cover the grains. Let it sit at least overnight, but up to three days, before using. This fermentation process unlocks additional nutrients and makes it easier for your flock to digest, so they will be able to get the same nutritional value or more from the feed with less feed given. This stretches your feed, reduces your cost, and is

KEEPING BACKYARD CHICKENS 249

healthier for the chickens. Start another bucket before the first runs out so that you always have grains ready to give.

- *Dust bath.* Chickens like to clean themselves in a dust bath and will create one for themselves within a few days of being introduced to a new space. If you see a bald patch in your grass, this isn't a sign to move the flock—instead, it is normal and healthy behavior.

Weather Protection

Chickens can adjust their behavior based on the weather to keep themselves safe and healthy. However, they need a place to get into the shade, such as under a tree or even under the coop itself, a place to get out of the wind in cold weather, and a place to stay dry in the rain. In most cases, the coop itself will provide this protection. However, in extreme wind and depending on your coop design, you may need to add a plastic tarp for a season to create a wind barrier.

We do this by stapling onto the coop a plastic painting tarp that has been folded several times for an easy and cost-effective way to protect the flock from the elements. They will free-range during the day as needed and take breaks to warm up in the coop before going back out again. In the summer, they will take breaks in the shade during the heat of the day, foraging in the morning and afternoon.

Note: The tarp should be removed during the summer to avoid overheating the space.

How to Raise Friendly Chickens

If you have kids around or you want to be able to easily collect eggs, it's very important to gentle your hens and roosters. If you are raising meat birds that you will interact with little to never, it's not as much of an issue, but it's still useful to have friendly chickens. Thankfully, the process for doing so is very easy!

When the chicks are brand-new to your homestead, establish a routine for handling each one every single day: pick them up, stroke their feathers, speak sweetly to them, and so on. Have everyone in the family do this if they want to be able to walk freely around the flock. Repeat this process daily and continue to go out to the flock and pet them once they are on pasture as well. This will create a bond, so they understand you are not a threat.

Have your children help handle the chicks each day to get the chicks used to human contact. Be sure to systematically go through the flock so you don't miss any chicks.

As I mentioned earlier, a rooster will generally only attack if it perceives you as a threat to the flock. Actions such as walking in a slow circle around the coop are sometimes necessary as you check for breaches or hunt for missing eggs, but a rooster can view these motions as aggression from a predator and attack you. This can happen even if the rooster is typically gentle and has been handled a lot while growing.

If you experience this more than two times where it's easy to identify why it happened (i.e., you were circling the coop), it's time to re-gentle your rooster. All you need to do is pick the rooster up and secure him in your arms, and then you cuddle him. I know, it sounds so silly! But hold him and stroke his feathers while speaking calmly. Once you can tell he is calm, continue for a few more minutes before letting him down. Repeat this for a few days before returning to your normal routine.

BEST EGG PRACTICES

How to Keep Eggs Clean

Naturally clean eggs straight from the coop are crucial for their shelf life. They can last at room temperature for weeks, whereas eggs that have to be cleaned may only last for a few days at room temperature because their natural protective coating is removed during cleaning. Pulling a poop-covered egg out of the nesting boxes is hardly appetizing, and it's actually quite easy to avoid the issue altogether. Whether you want to water glass them for storage, sell them for profit, or just enjoy eggs without muck on them, here is what you need to do to ensure naturally clean eggs:

- *Limit the number of boxes.* For a flock of thirty-six hens, we only have six nesting boxes. This means that the hens can't camp out in the boxes and poop, since other hens are waiting and squawking to get in. As a result, they lay their eggs and get out quickly.

- *Keep the boxes clean.* If you can close the nesting boxes at night, that's the easiest way to keep them clean. Otherwise, the chickens will roost there and poop in the boxes overnight. This means dirty eggs and more cleaning for you because you'll have to change the shavings (if you use them).

- *Time the harvest.* While collecting eggs once a day in the morning is common, it's also the best way to ensure that any eggs laid after that point will be dirty. Collect eggs in the late morning and again in the afternoon before the sun starts to dip.

A week of eggs from our flock, clean and ready to use.

- *Find missing eggs quickly.* If you find that your egg production suddenly drops without a change in feed or weather, you may need to hunt for eggs around the yard or enclosure. Often, chickens will find a clump of grass that they love and they will lay their eggs there instead. If you find a cache of eggs, it's fine to take them in and float-test them for freshness.

FLOAT-TESTING EGGS

The float test is an easy way to determine if an egg is fresh and safe to eat. Simply place the egg in cold water and observe how it sits. All you need to do is:

- Fill a large cup or bowl halfway with cool water and gently place the egg in the water. Test only one egg at a time.

- Wait for the egg to settle before reading its placement.

- If it sinks or stands on end, it's fine. If any part of it floats above the water, that's a sign too much oxygen has gotten into the egg and it's no longer safe for use.

Cleaning Dirty Eggs

If you aren't able to keep the nesting boxes clean or harvest multiple times a day, you may need to clean your eggs. To do so, gently rub the muck off with a soft, dry towel and store the eggs at room temperature for about a week. If the eggs are dirty enough that you need to wash them under water, do so with cold water and dry them right away. Store the washed eggs in the fridge, not at room temperature. The "bloom" on an egg refers to the natural protective coating on an eggshell. Washing or scrubbing an egg damages the bloom and can allow bacteria to enter through the porous shell, so they need to be refrigerated.

KEEPING BACKYARD CHICKENS   253

WATER GLASSING EGGS FOR LONG-TERM STORAGE

There is no right or wrong way to preserve the extra eggs your family has on hand. You can use them when making pasta or homemade quiches, freeze them, or even freeze-dry them. For us, water glassing our eggs allows us to keep them at room temperature (no electricity needed) and gives us full control over what they'll be used for when we are ready to eat them.

While this method isn't currently recommended by the FDA, water glassing eggs is a centuries-old technique that allows the preservation of eggs at room temperature.

If the bloom on an egg is damaged by washing or scrubbing, it can allow bacteria to enter through its porous shell.

You'll want to do your own research on the subject, but for us and thousands of other homesteaders, it's a trusted method of storing eggs long term. Traditionally, water glassing was done with water and sodium silicate; however, this method yields egg whites that won't whip, and there's never really been any testing done on the long-term impacts of regular consumption of sodium silicate for breakfast. Instead, the modern version of water glassing eggs uses a substance that is used often in pickling recipes: pickling lime, which is just ground limestone with nothing else added.

When the limestone is mixed with water, it effectively seals the porous eggshells, keeping them safe from oxygen and bacteria. This means the eggs stay fresh in the limewater solution for up to eighteen months and can be used as needed. Whatever eggs you have on hand—whether they are chicken, duck, or quail eggs—*as long as they are fresh, clean, and unwashed* so that the bloom on the eggs is still intact, they can be water glassed using this same method.

The Water Glassing Process

Ingredients

1 ounce pickling lime

1 quart filtered water

16 eggs (fresh and clean with bloom still intact)

Instructions

1. Measure 1 ounce of pickling lime using a scale. This is about 3 tablespoons if you don't have a scale.

2. Add the clean eggs to a clean half-gallon jar.

3. In a large measuring cup, whisk the lime into the water until it is fully incorporated.

4. Pour the water and lime mixture over the eggs. If the eggs are not fully covered, add a bit more water or remove some of the eggs.

5. Rinse the mixing jar as quickly as possible. If the lime mixture dries on your items, it is very difficult to remove. Soaking it in vinegar helps, but the lime is still hard to remove.

6. Secure an airtight lid to the jar, mark the date on the lid (or on a piece of tape), and store your eggs in a cool, dark place for up to eighteen months.

7. Open and enjoy the eggs as you need them, no need to use them all at once. Just close the jar after each egg removal.

Best Tips for Water Glassing Eggs

We've been enjoying water glassed eggs for several years now. Here are my top tips for making sure your eggs are in perfect condition when you use them later. While these tips are all simple, they make a huge difference in the life and quality of your preserved eggs:

- *Use large jars.* You can use small jars for this process, but if you have hens you likely need to store large quantities of eggs. Instead, opt for a large jar and simply add more eggs as they come in. When in doubt about how large of a jar you will need for your eggs, go larger than you think you'll need. A half-gallon jar is a great size for storing a lot of eggs and is a better use of shelf space than a small jar but isn't too heavy to carry around. Be sure to get a jar with a wide enough mouth that you can fit your hand in it.

- *Act quickly.* Instead of leaving your eggs at room temperature until you have enough to fill a jar, water glass them as they come in. This helps keep the bloom intact and will yield the best results when you go to use them later. Eggs that have been left out for more than a day or two before being water glassed tend to have broken yolks when you crack them later, which makes them impossible to separate.

- *Not all eggs qualify.* You must use eggs that are fresh, clean, and unwashed so that the bloom on the eggs is still intact. The bloom protects the eggs from anything getting through the shell, which is why fresh eggs can sit on the counter for weeks and still be completely fine. Once the eggs have been washed or sanitized (like those in the store), the bloom is broken down. Depending on state and local regulations, local farmers may be required to wash their eggs before selling them. As a result, it's best to only

Water glassed eggs ready to be placed in the pantry for long-term storage.

water glass the eggs that you have collected yourself, when you can verify the state of the shell and bloom.

- *Consider the storage area.* Just as with general food storage, eggs do best when protected from harsh conditions. Be sure to store your eggs in a cool, dark place for best results. Eggs that are water glassed but then exposed to sunlight may crack in the heat and rot in the jar. You will know they are spoiled because they will turn black, the water will be cloudy, and the smell will be overpowering when you open the jar.

PROCESSING MEAT BIRDS

I'm not going to cover the process for butchering chickens here, but I will make some recommendations. First of all, if you do find that you want to butcher your own flock, I would recommend asking a local chicken owner with experience to mentor you. Ask them if you can help the next time they process a flock. Most people will jump at having help and are glad to share their experience. In many cases, they will also be available to take your flock and process the birds for you for a fee if you do not want to do it yourself.

Another option is to find a local processing facility that will process and pack your birds for you. This is usually fairly inexpensive, around $5–$6 per bird. Be sure to confirm with the facility that they have measures in place to ensure you get *your* processed birds back. You don't want to spend the time and energy raising grass-fed chickens only to get a different set of birds back instead. This doesn't happen all the time, but it's important to understand how the processing facility protects against mix-ups.

No matter what you choose to do with your meat birds, know that you are in for the best meat you've ever had! Homegrown chickens are tender and full of flavor and are perfect for canning or just enjoying as a simple oven-roasted dinner. It is such a rewarding feeling to know that you gave your flock the best life they could have, filled with love, and now they are nourishing your family.

CHAPTER 7

BAKING WITH SOURDOUGH

Sourdough products feature a delicious, tangy quality and natural rise that is created through a fermentation process using wild-caught yeast found in the air instead of dry yeast from a packet. The process of catching the wild yeast in your home establishes what is called the "sourdough starter." The starter is then "fed" with fresh flour and water on a regular basis to keep it alive until you're ready to bake with it.

Creating your own sourdough starter is often where the journey into homesteading and self-reliance starts. Perhaps you were inspired by a friend, or maybe by a video on social media, but finding yourself elbow deep in sourdough products is a wonderful place to begin your homesteading efforts. Or maybe you haven't been hit by the sourdough craze and you are just discovering it now.

Either way, this chapter will help you start and care for a sourdough starter, understand how to enjoy the rhythm of sourdough without allowing it to be all-consuming, and enjoy a solid collection of tried-and-true recipes that your family will love.

WHAT IS SOURDOUGH?

Sourdough stems from the process of mixing flour and water and allowing the wild yeast in the air to feed on the mixture. It can be traced to many civilizations and as far back as five thousand years ago. The resulting yeast-fed mixture—the starter—can be kept alive for hundreds of years because you bake with a portion of it while keeping a portion held back to feed for the next loaf of bread.

A sourdough starter has two stages: active and discard. Active starter has been fed 6–12 hours before the time of use and has reached the peak of its growth. Discard starter has peaked and begun to fall; it can be used in any recipe that calls

259

The characteristic holes found in sourdough bread are easy to spot when the loaf is sliced.

for "discard," or it can be fed to make active starter so that it reaches its peak once again.

Unlike modern recipes that call for dry yeast and a 1–2-hour rising process, sourdough fermentation can take up to 36 hours, depending on the recipe. During the fermentation process, the starter feeds on the flour, breaking down the gluten for easier digestion, unlocking nutrients in the wheat, and creating a natural rise that doesn't require store-bought yeast. The fermentation process is also responsible for that characteristic tang that accompanies sourdough products.

ENJOYING SOURDOUGH WITHOUT LETTING IT TAKE OVER YOUR LIFE

You may have heard people joking about their sourdough recipes dominating their time. "I can't make it on Thursday, I've got to do stretch-and-folds every hour from 8 a.m. until 2 p.m.!" And while it's said jokingly, there's some truth to the idea that sourdough can become a bit overwhelming if you don't understand how to make it fit *your* life, instead of the other way around. In the spirit of finding your flow and only keeping things on your homestead journey that serve you, I want to share a few tips that will help as you get started with sourdough:

1. *Simplify your feeding schedule.* Instead of letting your sourdough starter dictate your day, set up a feeding schedule that works with your daily routine. You don't have to feed it every morning; you can feed it right before bed, if that works better for you. In fact, you don't have to feed it daily at all! You can simply feed it and store it in a sealed container in the fridge if you're not baking regularly. If you do this, you will want to feed it weekly, if possible, though I have gone as long as a month between fridge feedings. Then, when you know you'll be baking soon, you can take your starter out to feed it at room temperature for a few days before your baking day.

2. *Don't waste the discard.* Instead of letting sourdough discard pile up, plan a weekly "discard day" where you use it to make simple recipes like pancakes, crackers, or pizza dough. This keeps waste down and baking efforts to a minimum. Any recipe that calls for "ripe or discarded starter" will work with both active starter and that which has been removed from the bulk starter and not fed. For example, if you had a cup of starter that needed to be fed, but you only chose to measure and feed two tablespoons of it, the remaining starter would be considered discard and could be used in any appropriate recipe. Set your discard aside in the fridge for up to a week and then use it all at once.

3. *Plan bulk baking days.* Set aside one day a week—or at the very least every two weeks—for bulk sourdough baking. Preparing in advance means you won't feel like you're constantly tending to dough and will allow you to be present and enjoy the process, instead of dreading it. I use both ripe and discard starter on my bulk baking days. Usually, I like to make several loaves, a few pizzas, a quadruple batch of waffles, and some crackers on my bake days. Yes, that's a full day of baking, but it's also a great way to fill up my freezers with high-quality food while still allowing me freedom from the constraints of daily sourdough tending.

A NOTE ABOUT FLOUR

Just as in the From Scratch Cooking chapter, all-purpose einkorn flour is used in these recipes. However, no modification is needed if you are using another variety of all-purpose wheat flour. I have found that sourdough tends to be the great equalizer between einkorn and non-einkorn flour types. Freshly milled flour, regardless of variety, does need some modification, which I have specified in each recipe. Additionally, salted butter and whole, raw, A2/A2 milk are our preferences in these recipes, but use what you have on hand!

Depending on the climate, humidity, and temperature of your kitchen, the flour may not absorb liquid at a standard rate and adjustments may be needed. If you notice that your dough is *very* sticky after fermenting for a while, adjust it by adding more flour right before shaping. Add a few tablespoons at a time, as needed. However, understand that einkorn dough produces a better product if it has more liquid, so it should be somewhat sticky! Likewise, if the dough is too dry before shaping, work a little more water into it to achieve a soft, smooth texture.

STARTING AND MAINTAINING A SOURDOUGH STARTER

If you don't already have a starter, this method for making your own is very simple and will leave you ready to start baking with sourdough in just a few weeks, at most. If you find that you just can't seem to get a starter going, that's okay!

Ask around in your local groups, and you will likely be able to fairly quickly find someone willing to share some of theirs. If you do get a starter from someone else, feed it with the following ratios for at least three days to turn it into a 100% hydration starter, which is the type of starter used in the recipes shared in this chapter.

If you read other sourdough recipes, you may see starter hydration levels at 35% or 55%. These percentages simply refer to the ratio of water to flour in the starter. I have found that a 100% hydration starter is the most common type used and it also tends to be the most forgiving.

Be sure to allow enough room for your starter to double or even triple. Here's an example of what might happen if you miscalculate, as I did!

Sourdough Starter

Ingredients

Flour   Water

Instructions

Depending on whether you have had sourdough in your house before, the process of capturing the wild yeast in your air may take between 3 and 15 days. It will take less time to see bubbles in your starter if you have previously had sourdough starter in your house than if you haven't. If you don't see bubbles at the 14-day mark, your kitchen may be too cold, or you may have the airflow in the container too restricted. Try to find a warm place to store the starter—even in a cabinet will work! The mix needs to breathe in order to ferment, so do not seal the jar. Make those two adjustments and continue feeding for another week. And see more tips in the Sluggish Starter section on page 264.

1. **Day 1.** Mix ¼ cup flour (29g) and ¼ cup water. Place in a glass container and cover loosely with plastic wrap. Store in a warm, dark place for 48 hours.

2. **Day 3.** Mix 2 tablespoons starter with 2 tablespoons water and ¼ cup of flour. *Or equal parts starter, water, and flour by weight.* Cover again, but do not seal, and leave at room temperature.

3. **Day 4 and beyond.** After day 3, continue to feed your starter at least once every 24 hours, or up to 3 times per day, if desired. Follow the feeding ratios given in Day 3.

Notice the loose covering on this jar; it's not clamped shut with a lid, but rather draped across and formed around the jar to secure.

When Is the Starter Ready to Use?

Once your starter shows significant rise and bubbles through within 6–10 hours of feeding, it is ready to use in sourdough recipes.

Keeping Your Starter Happy

Once you get your starter going, it's a fairly simply process to keep it happy and healthy. Sourdough starter really only needs two things to thrive: cozy temperatures and a consistent food supply. Be sure to keep your active starter between 70°F and 85°F for use. Feed it at least once every 24 hours, or as many as 2–3 times per day.

Hibernating Your Starter

If you don't use your starter often or just want to take a break but don't want to start over later, you can store your starter in the fridge and feed it once a week. Please note,

You can also dehydrate your starter at about 115°F and crumble it into a powder once it's fully dried and cooled. This will allow you to restart your starter later on with ease. Just mix one teaspoon of powdered starter in with the flour on day one of the feeding instructions.

I don't recommend hibernating your starter until it is well established, for example, it is active and bubbling within 6 hours of feeding. After that, you can safely hibernate your starter.

To feed a starter in hibernation, simply remove it from the fridge, feed it with one-part starter, 1-part water, and 2-parts flour ratio (by volume) *or equal parts starter, water, and flour by weight*, cover, and immediately put it back in the fridge. Of course, if you want to take it out of hibernation for use, you will feed it and leave it at room temperature to expand.

Troubleshooting Your Starter

Here are a few common problems that may occur on your way to a healthy and stable starter:

- *A sluggish starter.* You may notice that your starter just isn't taking off. This is considered a sluggish starter and can usually be jumpstarted pretty quickly. In addition to making sure that your starter is in a warm place, with a loose covering, you can also feed the starter more often. Instead of feeding your starter once every 24 hours, start feeding every 6–12 hours for a few days until it becomes more active.

If you are using freshly ground flour and finding that your starter is sluggish, it's likely that your flour needs to age a bit before being used to feed the starter. To do this, place your freshly milled flour in a bowl at room temperature and cover it lightly with a dish towel for one or more weeks before using it to feed your starter. Once the starter is established and you're ready to bake with it, you can use freshly ground flour as the flour ingredient in the recipe; it does not need to be aged.

- *Alcohol or nail polish odor.* If you smell a strong alcohol or nail polish aroma coming from your starter, it can be a sign it isn't being fed enough, but not always. If the starter looks good, has bubbles, and there is no liquid on the top, it's likely this is just the natural by-product of the fermentation spike after being fed. However, if there is liquid on the top of the starter along with the smell, you may need to increase feedings to twice a day for a period of time (usually a few days). If increased feedings don't fix the problem, take 2 tablespoons of starter, add ¼ cup of water, and ¼–½ cup of flour. Just do this once and then resume normal feeding ratios.

- *Moldy starter.* If you see that your sourdough starter has developed mold, it's okay. Your hard work is probably fine! The first thing you need to do is assess your starter. If the mold is only on the surface, scrape it away, gather some of the fresh starter underneath, and refresh as normal. If the mold reaches the interior and there is no clean, fresh starter available, then unfortunately it's time to start over. But the good news is that you'll probably have less time to wait for your new starter to be active since you previously had an active starter in your home.

SOURDOUGH RECIPES

These tried-and-true sourdough recipes are perfect to help you get started the right way. While this is not an exhaustive collection, I want you to have a few staples that will serve your family well.

Classic Sandwich Bread or Artisan Bread

Use this recipe to make a sturdy sandwich bread that holds up to any filling, from peanut butter and jelly to a BLT! Or, with some extra steps, you can create a traditional crusty bread that pairs well with stew, pasta, or just with a thick layer of butter. Either way, this recipe yields 1 loaf of einkorn bread, or 2 loaves if non-einkorn flour is used.

Ingredients

5¼ cups (627g) all-purpose flour

1 cup (175g) sourdough starter, active and stirred before measuring

1¼ cups water (1½ cups if using freshly milled flour)

1 tablespoon salt

Instructions

1. Combine flour, water, and starter by hand into a shaggy dough. Let sit at room temperature for 1 hour. Sprinkle with salt and using a pinching motion, work salt into dough.

2. Using wet hands, grab half the dough and stretch as far as it will go without breaking away from the ball. Fold over ball.

3. Rotate the bowl ¼ turn, stretch, and fold. Repeat two more times until the ball has been stretched and folded four times total.

4. Cover and let sit for 30 minutes. Repeat steps 3 and 4. At no point should you punch down the dough. You want the air bubbles!

5. Cover and let sit for 30 minutes. Repeat steps 3–5 until the dough has been stretched a total of four times. Cover and let ferment for 2 hours at room temperature. Place in the fridge for 12–18 hours.

6. Remove from the fridge and let the dough come to room temperature for 1 hour. Scrape dough onto a NON-FLOURED surface. Use a scraper to form dough edges into a ball. Let sit for 20 minutes. If you are not using einkorn, divide dough into 2 balls and repeat the following process for both portions.

For Sandwich Bread

1. Flour the top of the dough and use your scraper and wet hands to flip the dough over. Stretch ⅓ of the dough out and fold over. Repeat with the other third. Place dough seam side down into an 8" × 4" loaf pan. Let rise for 2 hours, covered, in the fridge.

2. Preheat oven to 450°F and remove dough from the fridge. Slash top of dough with a sharp knife in your desired pattern. Bake for 35 minutes.

3. Thump top of bread. If it sounds hollow, it's ready! If not, bake for another 5 minutes, then thump again. Allow to cool for at least 2 hours on a rack or cutting board before cutting.

For Artisan Bread Loaf

1. Flour the top of the dough and use your scraper and wet hands to flip the dough over. Stretch ⅓ of the dough out and fold over. Repeat with the other ⅓. Fold the ends up and pinch to form a ball. Place dough seam side up into a cloth-lined and floured bowl to proof. Let rise for 2 hours, covered, in the fridge.

2. Place your Dutch oven into a cold oven and preheat to 450°F for the last 30 minutes of the rise time.

3. Remove dough from the fridge and flip onto a piece of parchment paper. Gently remove any parts of the cloth that stuck to the dough. Slash top of the dough with a sharp knife in your desired pattern.

4. Remove lid of the Dutch oven and place parchment paper and bread inside. Replace the lid and bake for 30 minutes. Remove lid and bake for another 10 minutes to brown top of bread.

5. Thump top of bread. If it sounds hollow, it's ready. Allow to cool for at least an hour on a rack or cutting board before cutting.

Notes: If baking two loaves, place your empty Dutch oven back in the hot oven once the first loaf is out. Let the Dutch oven heat up for 15 minutes, then bake the second loaf in the same manner as the first.

If you don't have a Dutch oven, simply preheat an empty oven to 450°F, place cold dough (after step 1) onto a parchment-lined baking sheet and bake for 40 minutes, or until loaf sounds hollow when thumped.

Pizza Dough

An old world–style crust, this pizza dough is delicious with any combination of toppings. Yields two 14-inch pizza crusts.

Ingredients

- 3½–4 cups (~400g) all-purpose flour
- 1 teaspoon salt
- 1 teaspoon honey
- 1⅓ cups water (1½ cups if using freshly milled flour)
- 1½ tablespoons (25g) starter (ripe or discarded)

Instructions

1. Combine dry ingredients and honey in the bowl of an electric mixer.
2. Add starter and water. Mix until ball forms.
3. Adjust with more flour if dough is too sticky, or with more water if dough is too dry.
4. Cover and let sit overnight at room temperature.
5. The next day, deflate dough and divide in two. Roll out on parchment paper to the size of your pizza pan. Add desired toppings.
6. Bake at 450°F for 15–17 minutes or until dough is golden brown.

If using a pizza stone: Put your pizza stone into a cold oven and preheat to 450°F. Transfer pizza dough on parchment paper to the stone and set a timer for 3 minutes. When the timer goes off, remove pizza from the parchment paper (it should slide easily out from under pizza). Cook for another 10–13 minutes, or until dough is golden brown.

BAKING WITH SOURDOUGH

Soft and Sturdy Tortillas

These tortillas are perfect for breakfast burritos, fajitas, and more! Yields eight 8-inch tortillas; the batch can be doubled or tripled as desired.

Ingredients

1½ cups (180g) all-purpose flour

¼ teaspoon salt

¼ teaspoon baking powder

2 tablespoons lard, tallow, or other fat

¼ cup (66g) sourdough starter

½ cup water, almost boiling (¾ cup if using freshly milled flour)

Instructions

1. In a food processor or by hand, combine flour, salt, and baking powder.

2. Add fat and pulse or cut in until mix forms coarse crumbs. Add starter and pulse again until combined.

3. Turn on the food processor and drizzle in warm water, just until dough ball forms. (You may not need all the water.) If the dough is too sticky, add a teaspoon of flour and mix again until the right consistency is achieved.

4. Remove the dough from the food processor, form a smooth ball, and cover in plastic wrap. Let rest at room temperature for at least 4 hours but up to 24 hours.

5. Divide the dough into 8 pieces, roll into balls, and flatten each ball to ¼"-thin tortillas.

6. Place in a hot, dry skillet or griddle over medium heat. Cook for 1–2 minutes until large bubbles form. Flip and cook other side for 30 seconds.

7. Let finished tortillas rest on a plate under a towel.

Flaky Pie Crust

Sturdy and sweet, this flaky pie crust is perfect for dinner or dessert! Our favorite use for this crust is to make homemade cottage pies, as the tartness of the sourdough pairs wonderfully with the savory fillings. Though it is delicious as a fruit pie crust as well.

Ingredients

3 cups (360g) all-purpose flour (315g if using freshly milled flour)

⅔ cup (176g) sourdough starter

1 cup butter, melted and cooled

¼ cup honey

1 teaspoon salt

270   CREATING A MODERN HOMESTEAD

Instructions

1. Combine all ingredients in a bowl and mix until just combined. You should still see streaks of flour; you don't want to overwork the dough. Cover bowl and let dough sit at room temperature for 4–5 hours.
2. Split the dough into two and form into round disks. Wrap each disk and place in the fridge for 12–48 hours. Dough will sour more the longer it ferments.
3. After refrigerator ferment, use the dough right away or freeze until later. Follow the pie recipe's instructions for baking the dough, as it will vary based on the filling.

Pancakes or Waffles

A wonderful breakfast, or meal any time, these pancakes and waffles are a delight. Serve with butter and maple syrup, or top with fresh fruit. You can also make them in bulk to freeze for an easy breakfast on busy days. A single batch makes about 8 pancakes or waffles, and you can increase the batch as many times as you'd like.

Ingredients

- ½ cup (132g) sourdough starter (ripe or discarded)
- 1 cup milk (1¼ cups if using freshly milled flour)
- 1¼ cups (150g) all-purpose flour
- 2 tablespoons honey
- 2 tablespoons butter, melted
- 2 eggs
- 1 teaspoon baking powder
- ½ teaspoon salt

Instructions

1. Mix starter, milk, and flour in a large bowl. Cover with plastic wrap or a dish towel and let sit at room temperature for at least 8 hours.

2. Mix in remaining ingredients. Batter will be thicker than normal pancakes. Heat a pan over medium heat and add a teaspoon of butter, grease, or coconut oil.

3. Using a ¼ or ⅓ cup measuring cup, pour batter into pan, making two pancakes at a time (or more if you can). Cook until bubbles appear, then flip.

4. **For waffles:** If you are making waffles, you'll want to thin the batter with a bit more milk. It should still be thick but flow easily from a measuring cup when poured.

5. Serve with butter, maple syrup, or any topping you would like!

Chocolate Cake with Buttercream Frosting

This chocolate cake is delicious with a light maple-sweetened buttercream frosting, but you can pair it with any frosting you'd like! Make this recipe as two 8-inch round layers or in a single 9" × 13" inch pan.

Ingredients

Chocolate Cake

1 cup (265g) sourdough starter (ripe or discarded)

1 cup milk (1¼ cups if using freshly milled flour)

2 cups (240g) all-purpose flour

1½ cups sugar

1 cup butter, melted and cooled

2 teaspoons vanilla extract

1 teaspoon salt

1½ teaspoons baking soda

¾ cup cocoa or cacao

2 large eggs

Maple-Sweetened Buttercream

1 teaspoon gelatin

1 cup butter, room temperature

½ cup water, room temperature

¼ cup maple syrup (or to taste)

Instructions

1. Combine the starter, milk, and flour in a large mixing bowl. Cover and let rest at room temperature for 2–3 hours.

2. Preheat oven to 350°F. Grease and flour two 8" round pans or a 9" × 13" pan.

3. In a separate bowl, combine sugar, butter, vanilla, salt, baking soda, and cocoa. Mix will be grainy.
4. Add eggs one at a time to sugar/butter mixture. Then combine with the flour mixture, gently stirring until smooth.
5. Pour into the prepared pans. Bake for 25–35 minutes or until toothpick comes out clean.
6. Let cakes cool before removing from pan while you make the icing.

Frosting

1. Gently heat water just enough to dissolve gelatin. Stir well, remove from heat, and allow to come to room temperature.
2. Beat butter until creamy and smooth, then add maple syrup. Slowly add the water/gelatin mix and beat until light and fluffy. Scrape down the sides often. I have found that if I turn up the mixer to high and shield the edges with a towel (to avoid splashing), it takes about 5 minutes to incorporate the water.
3. Add icing to the cooled cakes as desired.

FINAL THOUGHTS

It's time to take your dreams of a simpler life and start making them a reality. If you haven't already, now is the time to pick your first new skill and start practicing. You may choose to start cooking from scratch as your first endeavor, as I did. Or you may decide to go full tilt and purchase a flock of chickens. No matter what, these first steps are a big deal!

Don't allow yourself to get overwhelmed with the idea that you're doing something wrong or that you're doing things out of order. There is no wrong order! Instead, know that simply working toward your own version of modern homesteading is enough, as long as you are satisfied with what your efforts provide for your family. If you're not, then as we've discussed before, it's time to reevaluate and decide what to add or cut.

Our family sitting down to enjoy a pot roast, fresh from the oven, with a side of homegrown and canned green beans! JESSIE WATTS (IG: @JESSIEWATTS)

You will undoubtedly come to a point where you feel like you can't actually call yourself a homesteader. Maybe you feel like you haven't mastered your chosen skills yet, or perhaps you don't feel like you have chosen to adopt enough aspects of homesteading in general. Banish these thoughts! No one can tell you what is or is not allowed to be considered homesteading. I have homesteading friends who have only ever raised animals and have done nothing else considered a "homesteading" task. Because they eat a carnivore (meat only) diet, just raising animals for meat makes the most sense for their family. They have no need of a vegetable garden or fruit trees. Instead, they have cultivated a version of homesteading that fits their life perfectly. The same will be true for you. There is no perfect combination of homesteading skills—only the combination that is best for you, your family, and your goals.

FINDING COMMUNITY

The easiest way to combat these thoughts of imposter syndrome, or not feeling good enough, is to find a group of like-minded people who are also working toward creating a modern homestead. Often there are groups on Facebook with names like "Crunchy Moms of XYZ Town" where you can find people with the same goals and values as you and your family. Additionally, your local health food store or farmers market are both great places to check for a local community.

When you have someone in your area who understands what it means to lose a beloved chicken, to cry when you accidently kill your sourdough starter (it happens!), or to whoop with joy when you harvest your first fresh strawberry, it suddenly becomes a lot easier to manage the bad times and fully enjoy the good.

SHARING YOUR KNOWLEDGE

As a final thought, I want to encourage you to share what you learn with those around you. If you try your hand at sourdough and work to understand the process until you have success, share that information! After your first few batches of pressure-canned vegetables, call a few friends to come over and learn the process too. Even if they never end up using the skill, helping others learn will not only help you solidify the knowledge but also help expand their own horizons in a way they may never have expected to enjoy.

You may be thinking that you have to master a skill before you can teach others, but that is really not the case. While you may not be an expert of all things canning-related, you can still help someone understand the basics even as you yourself are still learning. Just this week I was able to teach a very capable friend how to make bread from scratch. Though she does many other amazing homestead-minded things, baking fresh bread was a skill she had never learned. The joy and fellowship we shared during our two-hour lesson was as much a blessing to me as it was to her!

EMBRACING THE DREAM

My mission for the last decade has been to help people overcome the idea that homesteading was out of reach. To move past the thought that canning food for your family while also working a full-time job or living in the city can't somehow coexist. They can, easily! Even if your life never looks like *Little House on the Prairie*, or you never have chickens happily laying eggs in your backyard, that doesn't mean that a life involving simple joy and traditional skills can't be found. You can bake fresh bread during the week and take your kids to their sports games on the weekend, if that's what you choose. But no matter how you decide to embrace the idea of homesteading, there is so much soul-satisfaction to be had. Enjoy the journey and know that I am rooting for you every step of the way!

James and I waited as long as we could to slice our fresh loaf of bread! Fresh butter and homemade blackberry jelly are ready to enjoy!

INDEX

apples:
Apple Butter, 133
Apple Juice, 133
Applesauce, 134
Apples for Baking/Pie Filling, 132
dehydrating, *169*
freeze-drying, 176
asparagus, 56, *162*

backyard chickens, 9
acquiring chicks, 243–44
breed chart, *241–42*
breed choices, 238–39
brooding chicks, 244–47
bugs, collecting for, *220*, 223
chicken coop types, 236–38
clean eggs, keeping, 252–53
feed requirements, 248–49
flock size and space, 235–36
friendly chickens, how to raise, 251
healthy chickens, tips for, 249–50
hot chicken manure, 201, 205
meat birds, *237*, 238, *241–42*, 244, 248,
251, 257
mixing flocks, 239–40
preliminary considerations, 6, 233–35
roosters, 234, 235, 240, 243, 244, 251
water glassing eggs for storage, 254–57
weather protection measures, 250
bananas, 88, *89*, *169*
barn cats, 220–21, 234
basil, *226*, *227*
beans:
black beans, *67*, 117
companion planting for, *226*
Cowboy Beans, 69

Dried Beans, pressure canning, 147
harvest yield estimates, 218
Lima/Butter Beans, pressure canning, 148
Maple Baked Beans, 62
planting times and conditions, 216
beef jerky, 171, 172
dehydrating, 45, 166, 167, *169*
Uncle Sam's Beef Jerky, 170
beets, *206*
canning, 153
freezing, *162*
harvest yield estimates, 218
planting times and conditions, *216*
sugar beets, *187*
berries:
Berry Juice, 134–35
dehydrating, 169
freezing, 179
rehydrating, 181.
See also individual berries
blackberries, 135
blanching:
figs, blanching before canning, 139
freezing, blanching items prior to, 156, 158,
159
vegetables, blanching requirements of, 161,
162–63
blenders/food processors, 15
blueberries:
Blueberry Muffins, 46–47
Blueberry Pie Filling, 136
dehydrating, *169*
freeze-drying, 178
bread, 22, 279
Biscuits, 26
bread hook use, 15, 24, 36, 40, 49

Dark Rye Bread, 33
einkorn flour, baking with, 23
freezing, 160
Fresh-Milled Honey Wheat Bread, 42
Hoagie Rolls, 40
New York–Style Bagels, 34
Sandwich Bread, 24, 36
storage length, 158
Sweet Cornbread, 43.
See also sourdough
breakfast, 43
Blueberry Muffins, 46–47
Chocolate Oat Granola, 37
Cinnamon Rolls, 47–48
Classic White Gravy with biscuits, 22
Crispy Breakfast Potatoes, 52
Easy Quiche Base, 54–55
Loaded Cheesy Eggs, 51
New York–Style Bagels, 34
Pancakes/Waffles, 183, 272–73
Soft and Sturdy Tortillas for breakfast
burritos, 270
Thick and Creamy Yogurt, 44–45
Waffles and Pancakes, 53–54
Yeast Donuts, 49
broccoli:
blanching before freezing, *162*
companion planting for, *226*
harvest yield estimates, 218
planting times and conditions, *216*
Brussels sprouts, *162*, *216*, 218
bulk buying, 2, 102, 115, 176
caution when buying in bulk, 116
for extended food supply plan, 109
of foods to freeze, 108, *159*
properly storing bulk purchases, 113
seasonal shopping and, 116
for thirty-day meal plan, 103
butter, 13, 111, 158, 166
buttermilk, 18, 26, 43, 68

cabbage:
in Coleslaw, 60
freezing, *162*
in Harvest Vegetable Soup, 64
harvest yield estimates, 218
planting times and conditions, *216*
cake:
Chocolate Cake with Buttercream
Frosting, 273–74
Classic Pound Cake, 91
Classic Vanilla Cake, 84–85
einkorn flour, baking with, 23
Ultimate Chocolate Cake, 82–83
canning:
air bubbles, removing, 126
boiling water canner, 124
canning salt, 142, 144, 146
canning terminology, 128
canning tools, 124
cooling after canning, 126
high-altitude canning, 127
for jams/jellies, 123, 129, 165
jar selection, 125
lid and ring selection, 125
lids, applying, 126
meat, pressure canning, 110
reprocessing, 127
seal testing, 127
stovetop recommendations, 125
Strawberry Jam canning example, 130–32
syrups for canning fruit, 111, 129–30
taste and texture changed by, 155
water, canning of, 118, 119–20.
See also pressure canning recipes; water
bath canning recipes
carrots:
Carrot Raisin Salad, 57
companion planting for, *226–27*
dehydrating, *169*
freezing, 162

harvest yield estimates, 219

planting, *216*

pressure canning, 149

cauliflower:

companion planting for, *226–27*

freezing, *162*

harvest yield estimates, 219

planting times and conditions, 216

Celiac disease, 12

chard, 153, *226, 227*

cherries:

Brandied Cherries, 136

Cherry Pie Filling, 137

freezing, 159

chicken:

canning, 111, 257

Chicken and Rice Soup in a Jar, 175

Chicken Broth, 149

Chicken Fried Steak, 22, 68

Chicken Salad, 74

Chicken Soup, 150

Roasted Chicken, 66

chives, 224, *226, 227*

cilantro, 144, 175, *226, 227*

coconut oil, 13

Coleslaw, 60

condiments:

Barbecue Sauce, 20

Chocolate Syrup, 19

Classic White Gravy, 22

Ketchup, 21

Marinara Sauce, 145

Mayonnaise, 17

Ranch Dressing, 18

Salsa, 144–45

cookies and crackers, 99

Butter Crackers, 30–31

Chocolate Chip Cookies, 81–82

einkorn flour, baking with, 23

freeze-dried cookie dough, *177*

Graham Crackers, 97–98

Molasses Cookies, 94

in Old-Fashioned Banana Pudding, 88

pre-freezing cookie dough, 160, 179

corn, *188*

companion planting for, *226*

cornmeal, 43, 58, 93

Corn Tortillas, 16, 29, 39

Creamed Corn, pressure canning, 151

freezing, 155, *162*

harvest yield estimates, 219

planting times and conditions, *215, 216*

Sweet Cornbread, 43, 69

Whole Kernel Corn, pressure canning, 151

crackers. *See* cookies and crackers

cranberries:

Cranberry Juice, 137

Jellied Cranberry Sauce, 138

Whole Berry Cranberry Sauce with Port
Wine and Cinnamon, 138

cucumber:

companion planting for, *226–27*

harvest yield estimates, 219

for pickles, 142–43, *228*

planting times and conditions, *216*

trellising cucumber plants, *218*

dairy:

freeze-drying, 166, 176–77, 178

freezing, 155, 158–59

length of storage, *158*

raw dairy, 12–13

dairy cows, 2, 7-8

deep pantry-keeping, 2

bulk buying, taking caution with, 116

dry goods, properly storing, 113

extended food-supply creation, 108–10

functional food-supply creation, 102–3

money management and, 114–17

non-food supplies, 120

rotation of food supplies, 117

seeds, storing, 121

shelf-life order, purchasing supplies in, 110–14

storage limitations, 106–8

supply chain interruptions, keeping in mind, 101–2

thirty-day meal planning, 103–6

water supply, 118–20

dehydrated foods:

best dehydrator machine features, 167–68

conditioning foods, 171–72

dehydrated meal-in-a-jar recipes, 174–75

rehydrating, 172–73, 180, 181

shelf stability provided by, 166–67

sourdough starter, dehydrating, 264

storing dehydrated foods, 172

times and temperatures for general dehydrating, 168, *169*

Uncle Sam's Beef Jerky, 170

yogurt, using dehydrator for fermentation, 45

desserts:

Chocolate Cake with Buttercream Frosting, 273–74

Classic Pound Cake, 91

Classic Vanilla Cake, 84–85

Frosting, Buttercream, 82–83, 84–85, 273–74

Fudgy Brownies, 92

Ice Cream Base, 98–99

Old-Fashioned Banana Pudding, 88, *89*

Ultimate Chocolate Cake, 82–83.

See also cookies and crackers; pastries

digital kitchen scales, 15

dill, *226*, *227*

dry goods:

bulk-buying, 2, 115

shelf life, 110

storage options, 107

ways to properly store, 113

eggplant, *216*, 219

eggs:

best backyard egg practices, 252–53

chicks, hatching from eggs, 243–44

collecting eggs, 234, 236, 237–38, 251, 252

crushed eggs, adding to soil, 222

dirty eggs, cleaning, 253

egg color, 239, 240, *241*

egg production, optimizing, 248–49

float-testing eggs, 253

freezing eggs, 159, 178

Loaded Cheesy Eggs, 51

powdering eggs, 180

snakes as drawn to, 221, 234

storage length, 158

water-glassed eggs, 110, 254–57

einkorn, 12, 23, 116, 261–62, 266

figs:

dehydrating, *67*

freezing, 159

Whole Figs, canning, 139

food preservation:

best storage practices, 171–73

dehydrating for preservation, 166–69

food preservation methods, 165–66

freeze-drying for preservation, 176–81.

See also dehydrated foods; freeze-dried foods freezing food

freeze-dried foods:

best practices, 178–79

chicken, 175

Dry Pancake Mix, 182

foods used in freeze-drying, 178

freeze dryer benefits, 176–77

fruits, 111

ground beef, 175

Hot Chocolate Mix, 182

for long-term food storage, 166

mixed batches, 179
powdering after freeze-drying, 180
rehydrating methods, 180–81
as space-saving, 165
freezing food:
blanching before freezing, 156, *162–63*
bread and baked goods, 34, 160
dairy items, 158–59
fruit and fruit-products, 159–60
general guidelines for freezing, 156–57
ice cream, *99*
as money-saving practice, 123
pastries, 160–61
prepared meals, 161–62
for short-term storage, 155
storage life of frozen items, 157, *158*, 165
vegetables, 161, *162–63*
fruit:
canning, 110, 111, 129–30
companion planting for, 225
conditioning, 171–72
dehydrating, 45, 166, 167, 168, *169*
freeze-drying, 166, *177*, 178, 179
freezing, 155, 158
Fruit Cobbler, 90
fruit leather, 45, 166, 167, 168, *169*, *173*
Fruit Pie, 87
fruit pie crust, 270
hot-packing, 128
organic fruit, 14
rehydrating, 172, 173.
See also individual fruit

gardens and gardening:
Back to Eden method, 191, *192*, 194–95,
204–7, 211, 218
blossom end rot concerns, 222
companion planting, 220, 224, 225, *226–27*
compost use, 193, 201, 205, 206, 207, *210*,
211, 214
container gardens, 197, 213–15

crop rotation, 204
diatomaceous earth use, 221, 225
family needs, calculating, 188–90, 192
fertilizer use, 201, 202, 203, 207
frost dates, 189, 190, 199, 215, *216–17*
garden journal-keeping, 230
greenhouse gardening, 190, 229
growing season, extending, 190, 228–30
hand-watering, 198, 203, 207, 213, 214
harvest yields, 187, 217–19
hoop house use, 188, 190, 229
Hügelkultur method, *210*, 211
over-planting, 185–86
pest problems, 204, 219–21, 223–25
planting times and conditions, 215, *216–17*
pollination of plants, 223
potting mix use, 214
powdery mildew, minimizing, 221
raised-bed gardens, 195–97, 208–13
row cover use, 188, 223
Ruth Stout method, 211
soaker hose use, 198, 203
soil testing and amendments, 198, 200, 205
space considerations, 190–93
sunlight hours, 198, 199, 204, 208, 213
till-and-plant method, 193, 201–2, 203
traditional in-ground gardens, 193, 197,
198–204
weeds, 203, 204, 205, 207, 212, 225
wicking beds, 211.
See also mulch; seeds and seedlings
garlic, 225, *226–27*
Gautschi, Paul, 194
glass jars:
barbecue sauce, storing in, 20
freezing, using for, 157
for short-term storage, 179–80
water, canning in, 118
gluten sensitivity, 12
grain mills, 15
grapes, 166

INDEX 283

dehydrating, *169*
freeze-drying, 178
Grape Jelly, 139
Grape Juice, 140
green beans, 64, *227*
   harvest yield estimates, 217–18
   hydrating, *169*
   pressure canning, 152
   trellising green beans, *186*

herbs:
   in Back to Eden Garden, 204
   companion planting for, 220, 225
   conditioning, 171–72
   in container gardens, 197, 213
   dehydrating, *169*
   freezing, *162*
   spraying herbs, 180–81

jams and jellies:
   Apricot Preserves, 134
   Blackberry Jam, 135
   Blackberry Jelly, 135
   freezing, 159–60
   gelling point, 128
   Grape Jelly, 139
   Jellied Cranberry Sauce, 138
   Red Plum Jam, 143
   water bath canning, 123, 129, 165
juice:
   Apple Juice, 133
   Berry Juice, 134–35
   Grape Juice, 140

kale, 153, *216*, 219

leeks, *226*, *227*
lemons:
   dwarf lemon trees, growing, 215
   Lemon Chess Pie, 93
lentils, 175

lettuce, *191*, *216*, 219, *226*, 229
lima beans, 148, 153, *162*

marigold, 225, *226*, *227*
meat:
   Beef Broth, 148
   Beef Stew, 149
   canned meat, 104, 110–11, 124, 146, 165
   Chili, 150
   Classic Meatloaf, 66–67
   dehydrating, 167
   freeze-drying, 166, 178
   freezing, *157*, *158*, 161
   ground meat, 153
   Melt-in-Your-Mouth Meatballs, 78–79
   pastured meat, 14
   Perfect Pot Roast, 76
   rehydrating, *174*, 181
   Sloppy Joe Sandwiches, 70
   stew meat, 155
   Uncle Sam's Beef Jerky, 170
melon, 129, *202*
   companion planting for, 226, 227
   harvest yield estimates, 217, 219
   planting times and conditions, *216*
mulch, *4*
   in Back to Eden gardening, 195, 205, 206–7
   chicken brooders, used in, 245
   hot mulch, 249
   powdery mildew, organic mulch used to
      combat, 221
   in raised beds, *210*, 211, 212
   in traditional gardening, 203
mushrooms, *162*, *169*

okra, 129
   in Back to Eden gardening, 195
   freezing, 155, *163*
   Fried Okra, 58
onions:
   companion planting for, 225, *227*

dehydrating, 167, *169*
freezing, *163*, 179
harvest yield estimates, 219
planting times and conditions, *216*
storage length, *158*
oregano, 224, *226*, *227*
oxygen absorbers, 173, 179, 180, 182, 183
   beef jerky, storing with, 170
   for dehydrated foods, 172, 174
   proper storage, used for, 113

parsley, *226–27*
parsnips, *163*
pasta:
   Classic Lasagna, 71–72
   Easy No-Egg Pasta, 32
   Macaroni and Cheese, 61
   pasta roller use, 16, 32
   pasta sauce, 78, 79
   Spinach Ravioli, 75
   Taco Pasta in a Jar, *174*, 175
pastries:
   einkorn, baking with, 12
   Flaky Pie Crust, 80
   freezing pastries, *158*, 160–61
   Fruit Cobbler, 90
   Fruit Pie, 87
   Lemon Chess Pie, 93
   Soft and Fluffy Churros, 95–96
peaches:
   blanching before freezing, 156, 159
   Brandied Peaches, 140–41
   dehydrating, *169*
   Peach Pie Filling, 141
   raw-pack canning, 128
pears, 141, *169*
peas:
   Black-eyed Peas, 154
   blanching before freezing, *163*
   companion planting for, *226–27*
   Green Peas, 154

harvest yield estimates, 219
planting times and conditions, *216*
pectin, 128, 129, 130
peppers, *220*
   blossom end rot in, 222
   companion planting for, 226–27
   dehydrating, *166*, 169
   freezing, *163*
   harvest yield estimates, 219
   planting times and conditions, *217*
pickles and pickling:
   Dill Pickles, 142
   pickling lime, 255
   Sweet Pickles, 74, 142–43, 228
   water bath canning, 123, 129
pies:
   Apple Pie Filling, 132
   Blueberry Pie Filling, 136
   canning pie fillings, 165
   Cherry Pie Filling, 137
   cottage pies, 161, 270
   Flaky Pie Crust, 80, 270–71
   freezing pie fillings, 159–60
   Fruit Pie, 87
   Lemon Chess Pie, 93
   Peach Pie Filling, 141
   quiche, pie crust for, 54–55
   water bath canning for pie fillings, 123, 129
pineapple, 143, *169*
pizza:
   Easy Homemade Pizza, 78–79
   pizza cutter, uses for, 31, 39, 75
   Pizza Dough, 269
potatoes:
   blanching white potatoes, *163*
   calculating family need, 189
   companion planting for, 225, *226*, *227*
   Crispy Breakfast Potatoes, 52
   freezing, 161, 178–79
   French Fries, 63
   harvest yield estimates, 219

INDEX   285

Mashed Potatoes, 59
planting times and conditions, *217*
Potato Chips, 38
Potato Soup, 73
pressure canning white potatoes, 146, 155
rehydrating potato dishes, 181
powdering foods, 172, 180
prepared meals, *158*, 161
pressure canning recipes:
Beef Broth, 148
Beef Stew, 149
Black-eyed Peas, 154
Carrots, 149
Chicken Broth, 149
Chicken Soup, 150
Chili, 150
Creamed Corn, 151
Dried Beans, 147
Green Beans, 152
Green Peas, 154
Greens, 153
Ground Meat, 153
Lima/Butter Beans, 148
Mixed Vegetables, 153
Stew Meat, 155
Sweet Potatoes, 154
White Potatoes, 146–47, 155
Whole Kernel Corn, 151
pumpkin, *163*, 177, 196, *217*, 219

raccoons, 234, 237, 245, 247
radishes, *217*, 219
raisins, 57, 166, 168, *169*
raspberries, 144, 180–81
raw milk, 12–13, *159*, 176
rice, 109, *168*, 175
rodents, 107, 113, 220, 221, 237, 247
rosemary, 52, 175, *226*, *227*

sage, *226–27*
seasonality, 109–10, 116

seed oils, 13, 17, 38
seeds and seedlings:
in Back to Eden garden space, 194, 206, 207
in container gardens, 214
for deep-pantry storage, 121
GMO seeds, 199, *215*
greenhouse growing, 229
in-ground garden space, planting in, 203
plant-specific planting times, 215, *216–17*
record-keeping for future seasons, 230
seed quality, 199
spacing, following instructions on, 199
starting seeds indoors, 190, 228
in traditional in-ground till-and-plant method, 193
silica packets, 98, 173, 180, 182, 183
for dehydrated foods, 172, 174
mylar bags, placing in, 38, 39, 179
proper storage, used for, 113
snakes, 220–21, 234
soups:
Chicken and Rice Soup in a Jar, 175
Chicken Broth, 149
Chicken Soup, 150
Harvest Vegetable Soup, 64
Hearty Vegetable Soup in a Jar, 175
Potato Soup, 73
sourdough:
describing and defining, 259–60
einkorn flour, baking with, 261
getting started, tips for, 260–61
hibernating a starter, 263–64
sourdough starter, how to make, 262–63
troubleshooting the starter, 264–65
sourdough recipes:
Artisan Bread Loaf, 267–68
Chocolate Cake with Buttercream Frosting, 273–47
Flaky Pie Crust, 270–71
Pancakes/Waffles, 272–73

Pizza Dough, 269
Sandwich Bread Loaf, 266
Soft and Sturdy Tortillas, 270
spinach:
canning, 153
companion planting for, *226–27*
harvest yield estimates, 219
Malabar spinach, *189*
planting times and conditions, *217*
powdered spinach, *168*
Spinach Ravioli, 75
sprouts, 121, 190
squash, *163, 177, 202*:
companion planting for, *226*
harvest yield estimates, 219
planting times and conditions, *217*
squash bugs, 223
stand mixers, 15
stew:
Beef Stew, 149
Curry Lentil Stew in a Jar, 175
pressure canning, 165
rehydrating, 173, 181
Stew Meat, 155
storage bags and containers:
freezer bag tips, 156, 157
gallon bags, 47, 58, 113
mylar bag tips, 107, 113, 116, 172, 179
plastic containers, 107, 156
vacuum-sealed bags, 157
strawberries:
companion planting for, 225, *226–27*
dehydrating, *169*
freeze-drying, 176, *177*
seasonal shopping for, 116, 123
soaker hose, adding to strawberry beds, *203*
strawberry jam, canning, 130–32, 145
sweet potatoes, 153, 154, *169*

thyme, *226–27*
tomatoes, 185

blossom end rot in, 222
calculating family need, 188, 189, 190
companion planting for, *226–27*
in container gardening, 197
dehydrating, 168, *169, 169*
fertilizer for tomato plants, 203
freezing, *163*
harvest yields, *192*, 219
planting times for, 199, *217*
tomato hornworms, 223–24
water bath canning for, 123, 129
tortillas:
Corn Tortillas, 29
Flour Tortillas, 16, 28, 51
Soft and Sturdy Tortillas, 270
Tortilla Chips, 39
tortilla press, 16, 29
turnips, 153, *163, 217*, 219

vegetables, 109
in Back to Eden gardening, 191, 204
blanching, 156, 158, 161
canning, 129, 165
caterpillars, threats from, 224
companion planting for, 225, *226–27*
conditioning, 171
in container gardens, 213
dehydrating, 166, 167, *169*
freeze-drying, 166, 177, 178
freezing, *158*, 161, *162–63*
greens, 153, *162*
organic vegetables, 14
pressure-canning, 111, 123, 124, 146, 153, 278
in raised bed gardens, 208
rehydrating, 172–73, 181
Roasted Vegetables, 56
rotating crops, 204
storing seeds for, 121
in traditional in-ground gardens, 198
vegetable soups, 64, 175

INDEX 287

watering vegetables, 203.
See also individual vegetables

water bath canning recipes:
Apple Butter, 133
Apple Juice, 133
Applesauce, 134
Apples for Baking/Pie Filling, 132
Apricot Preserves, 134
Berry Juice, 134–35
Blackberry Jam, 135
Blackberry Jelly, 135
Blueberry Pie Filling, 136
Brandied Cherries, 136
Brandied Peaches, 140–41
Cherry Pie Filling, 137
Cranberry Juice, 137
Dill Pickles, 142
Grape Jelly, 139
Grape Juice, 140
Jellied Cranberry Sauce, 138
Marinara Sauce, 145
Peach Pie Filling, 141
Pears, 141
Pineapple, 143
Raspberry Jam, 144
Red Plum Jam, 143
Salsa, 144–45
Strawberry Jam, 145
Sweet Pickles, 142–43
Whole Berry Cranberry Sauce with Port
   Wine and Cinnamon, 138
Whole Figs, 139
water supply storage, 118–20

yogurt, 12, 44–45

zucchini, 153, *169*, 187, *194*, 222